D1458441

The Knowledge Economy, Language
and Culture

Full details of all our publications can be found on http://www.multilingual-matters.com, or by writing to Multilingual Matters, St Nicholas House, 31–34 High Street, Bristol BS1 2AW, UK.

The Knowledge Economy, Language and Culture

Glyn Williams

MULTILINGUAL MATTERS
Bristol • Buffalo • Toronto

Library of Congress Cataloging in Publication Data
Williams, Glyn
The Knowledge Economy, Language and Culture / Glyn Williams.
Includes bibliographical references and index.
1. Knowledge management. 2. Information technology. 3. Language and culture.
4. Sociolinguistics.
I. Title.
HD30.2.W535 2010
303.48'33-dc22 2010005053

British Library Cataloguing in Publication Data
A catalogue entry for this book is available from the British Library.

ISBN-13: 978-1-84769-251-1 (hbk)
ISBN-13: 978-1-84769-250-4 (pbk)

Multilingual Matters
UK: St Nicholas House, 31–34 High Street, Bristol BS1 2AW, UK.
USA: UTP, 2250 Military Road, Tonawanda, NY 14150, USA.
Canada: UTP, 5201 Dufferin Street, North York, Ontario M3H 5T8, Canada.

The policy of Multilingual Matters is to use papers that are natural, renewable and recyclable products, made from wood grown in sustainable forests. In the manufacturing process of our books, and to further support our policy, preference is given to printers that have FSC and PEFC Chain of Custody certification. The FSC and/or PEFC logos will appear on those books where full certification has been granted to the printer concerned.

Typeset by Integra Software Services Pvt. Ltd, Pondicherry, India.
Printed and bound in Great Britain by Short Run Press Ltd

Contents

List of Figures

List of Tables

Preface

Our lives are embroiled in a range of profound changes that are not easy to understand. The impact of globalisation is far-reaching, while the new technology is altering how we live. Such developments are often treated as being of benefit to humankind, as the benefits that derive from progress. Historically we have relied on science in striving to realise such progress, science being regarded as the means of the mastery of humankind over nature. On the other hand, there is an increasing awareness that the world is confronting a range of problems, from a clash of civilisations to the effects of global warming. Some of these problems are blamed on how we have used science with little concern for any unintended consequences.

Society itself changes in response to the challenges presented, part of these changes involving new perspectives, and how they are expressed in the social sciences. There are two predominant thrusts to the theoretical developments in the social sciences. On the one hand, there is the claim that what we are living through involves a change from industrial to post-industrial society, from modernity to what is referred to as late or reflexive modernity. While it is not clear how these changes derive from globalisation and the new technology, some form of relationship is implied. On the other hand, the reappearance of a line of analysis and critique in the form of the work of French philosophers and social sciences during the 1960s that was labelled as post-structuralism has had an equally profound effect. It is linked with postmodernism and how the analysis associated with it undermines the orthodox understanding of Cartesian humanism, and the role of social actors in engendering change.

Language is not remote from such changes. As a feature of social life it is a feature of both the changes that we experience and how we choose to understand them. Yet the analysis of the role of language in these changes has been piecemeal and selective. Perhaps this is inevitable given how many social scientists systematically ignore language in their analyses, while many sociolinguists struggle to come to terms with the theoretical principles of the social sciences, consequently placing an exaggerated emphasis on language as an object rather than as an inherent form of social process and practice.

It is these changes that this book strives to come to terms with. In so doing it engages with a range of disciplines including sociology, linguistics, economics and political science. This is necessary if we are to understand the social nature of language. The implication is that all of these disciplines engage with society, even if they do so by reference to different foci and different perspectives. This has implications for the distinction between sociolinguistics and the sociology of language.

The main focus of this book is on language, culture and the economy. There has been a long-standing awareness that economies are embedded and determined in both social and political terms. Yet the role of language and culture in economic activity has not received much attention. Most of the work that has been undertaken has derived from among economists, sociologists or anthropologists interested in language. This is rapidly changing as a consequence of our understanding of the nature of work in the knowledge economy.

Whereas in the industrial economy most of the labour process involved individual workers operating separately from one another, in the knowledge economy the essence of work revolves around interaction and its relationship to the generation of knowledge. This is not to imply that knowledge has been missing from earlier understanding of the nature of the economy, but that there has been a change in emphasis. Teamwork comes to the fore, and it is this that stimulates a focus on language in work. It involves a recognition that effective interaction relies on language and culture, and that good teamwork insists on a shared meaning across all of its members. Presumably, it is this awareness that lies behind the repeated claim that one of the advantages that accrues to Europe in confronting the knowledge economy lies in its linguistic diversity.

The book is organised around an elaboration of several themes that contribute to our understanding of the role of language in society and, especially, its relevance for new forms of employment. Chapter 1 sets out the main features of change and the arguments associated with our understanding of them. It includes the shift from industrial economy to the knowledge economy and an account of the nature of the knowledge economy. It allows me to develop the main thrust of the subsequent chapters.

Among the most obvious influences of globalisation is how it changes the structure of the economy and, in so doing, how it undermines the role of the nation-state in the economy. This is the theme of Chapter 2. Given how the nation-state has played such a pre-eminent role in the construction of languages as objects, and how this has involved the role of language in the economy, it is understandable that these changes also have an influence on the relationship between languages or, more specifically, between language groups. This has been the predominant emphasis of most of the work undertaken by applied linguists on language and globalisation. However, this chapter tries to take the analysis further by integrating the issue of how language objects change with a deeper understanding of the economic process.

One of the more salient arguments about the operation of the economy is the emphasis that is placed on trust. An analysis of the relationship between language, culture and trust is the focus of Chapter 3. One of the problems of early studies in the sociology of language involved how they were based on a perspective wherein human agency was understood as a consequence of the position of the actors in the social structure. Similar arguments were made about the relationship between institutional organisation, trust and democracy. Once this was replaced by an emphasis on human agency as a feature of social practice, it was possible to confront the relationship between language and culture and their role in engendering trust.

If, as is argued, the role of the nation-state in the economy is changing, and if we are confronting the emergence of a multi-layered governance within which regional governance plays an increasingly important role, it begs the question of the role of regional language and culture in the economy. Chapter 4 addresses this issue by an analysis of the notion of regional innovation systems. It raises the potential of regional languages losing their minority status.

The level of analysis changes in Chapter 5 which seeks to address the operational framework for the knowledge economy. The focus is on team working and how it relates to developing a shared meaning across the membership of the team. It is here that the concept of communities of practice comes to the fore. The reader is led through a discussion of the concept with its various merits and problems. It is a concept that has had a profound influence in recent years.

Where Chapter 5 concludes with the criticism that a major problem with the concept of communities of practice is in its failure to address how shared meaning is operationalised, Chapter 6 confronts this issue. A major issue in such a confrontation is an awareness that much of our behaviour does not involve rationalisation, but rests on social practice and tacit knowledge. We cannot think about and reflect upon every word that we *enonce*, which means that language use is itself a form of social practice within which rationalism plays a relatively minor role. It is this that leads to a discussion of the relevance of working multilingually for creativity, arguing that the reflexivity involved in social practice is heightened when it confronts more than one language.

Chapter 7 confronts the issue of how the new technology changes the organisational structure of the economy. In developing this argument it focuses on the cultural economy, and how the new technology commodifies materials which hitherto had a limited commercial value. Museum materials are digitised and circulate within an entirely new context, one that could provide a material advantage to regional media companies confronting the transition from media to multimedia activities. Yet such developments insist on new organisational structures and new attitudes towards a range of institutions.

Chapter 8 provides the opportunity to draw together the various arguments presented in the preceding chapters. It highlights the nature of the changes in languages that derive from our understanding of social and economic change. It also addresses how new forms of governance such as those being touted by reference to the European Community (EC) will have implications for the goal of sustaining linguistic diversity. While those interested in the analysis of language as a social phenomenon should have much to say about such developments, they are slow in taking up the challenge.

Chapter 1

Change and the Knowledge Economy

Introduction

As the title states, the focus of the following discussion is on the relationship between language, culture and the knowledge economy. This involves an engagement with a range of disciplines including sociology, economics, linguistics, education and business. These areas of knowledge have tended to be treated as discrete entities and the relationship between them has not been widely explored. Yet there is an increasing awareness of two relevant thrusts. Firstly, that there is a degree of similarity in how the relevant disciplines have been subject to ontological reorientation in recent years. Secondly, that there is a relationship between theory and the socio-political circumstances within which it is developed.

Let me begin with the second point. The social sciences emerged at the same time as the modern state and were very much a product of Cartesian thinking. Furthermore, there is a direct relationship between the state and the concepts of the social sciences. Thus, each state had a single society, a single economy and a single state language and culture. This is largely a consequence of the role played by the state in regulating social institutions. The state regulated most aspects of social, cultural and economic life in striving to develop a uniform citizenry. While each state espoused their uniqueness, they also conformed with a universalism dictated by Enlightenment discourse.

This orthodoxy is giving way to new orientations, partly as a consequence of how globalisation undermines the salience of the state, its sovereignty and its authority. Recent theoretical perspectives allow an increasing role for multiculturalism and a grater degree of flexibility by reference to an engagement with identity and socio-cultural groups.

All of the social sciences have been subject to considerable ontological reorientation during the past 25 years. There are three main driving forces of this change. Firstly, the strength of post-structuralism and the related awareness of the tacit nature of knowledge, and, secondly, how globalisation undermines the relationship between the state and theoretical concepts. Thirdly, these are aligned with the evident disconnection

1

between theory and empirical research. This leads to substantial changes as the foundational assumptions of Cartesianism are brought into question. This is a concern for disciplines that have tended to have the rationality of the centred human subject at the heart of their theoretical problematics. It results in substantial shifts.

In sociology, there is a shift away from structure and function, or structure and agency, to a concern with social practice. In economics, the linear, equilibrium models of neoclassical arguments yield to different perspectives, including evolutionary economics and other approaches that focus on the centrality of human capital, and the relationship between social and cultural capital. In linguistics, there is a shift away from a focus on syntax to semantics, and from language to action and discourse. Concepts such as that of 'communication strategies' now involve cultural rather than rational determination, and are increasingly related to how learning by doing insists on a dynamic conception. Psychology is subject to similar refinement, particularly as a consequence of Lacanian and other influences. Thinking is no longer understood as a mechanical process conducted according to procedural programmes, rules or instructions, but involves considerable emphasis on flexibility. Such notions as identity, attitudes or motivation tend not to be understood as the effects of determinants of the centred, rational human subject, but as part of the transformation of the individual into the subject of discourse (Williams, 1999). In a sense, language and the objects of the social sciences converge.

These developments overlap with three recent phenomena which have a profound influence on how we understand society – globalisation, the new technology and modernisation. Globalisation rearranges relationships between polities and their relationship to economic activity. The new technology has significant implications for communications and their role in a range of different practices. These two developments overlap with changes in the nature and organisation of society. These are three topics that will receive considerable attention below. The objective of Chapter 1 is to elaborate on a broad understanding of how social scientists understand current developments, thereby setting the context for the subsequent discussion.

The Westphalian State[1]

What is known as the Westphalian state was marked by the strong correspondence between society, the state and the nation. Each state was framed by strict territorial boundaries within which a single society, a single economy and a single labour market was claimed to exist. The political involved social groups constituted around the regulating activity of the state. The state was designed to serve and protect the interests of a citizenry which it was obliged to mould into a strong sense of commonality. Problems were formulated in terms of the right of the collective to intervene in the individual or private space – the idea that what is not forbidden is permitted, or the distinction between the moral and the legal. Simultaneously, the political constructed a group within the political dimension in contrast to a group of 'strangers'. The focus shifts from internal organisational problems and the content of the political, towards the group itself, and to the definition of the group. Belonging and identity dominate.

The ascendancy of the modern involved the equation of progress and development. This was labelled as 'modernisation'. Reason was reified as the agent of all development, and was meant to lead to the establishment of a perfect society vested with the good life for all worthy citizens. The divine was replaced by the political as the expression of the sacred in social life. Society became the field of social conflict between past and future, interest and tradition, public and private life.

There was a strong sense of universalism associated with the emergence of the modern state. This related to the claim that a particular pattern of development served as the norm for all historical development, a highly Eurocentric conception. The world was increasingly thought of as organised by the state that constituted it. It was a state constructed around the belief that it could, through legislation, eliminate any interference to progress. This progress was furnished by science which humankind could deploy in order to control and exploit nature for its own ends. Science and progress became inseparable from the polity. Progress was closely aligned with a sense of inevitable social and political evolution.

While each nation-state wishes to present itself as distinct and its history as unique, since the Enlightenment the nation-state has been the vehicle of universal values. Consequently, there is both difference and similarity across the modern nation-states. While each state lays claims to its own, unique culture, adopting a classical model has involved a uniformity according to which features of culture have been modelled as universal. It is hardly surprising that there are competing representations of 'reality', and that it is claimed that the nation-state is an 'imagined' construction (Anderson, 1991). The 'imagined' is not linked to an ethnic determinism, but to identifiable practices, especially language practices. In this respect, it links with how history inscribes practices.

In this respect, it is conceivable that whatever will be said about any part of Europe will be applicable across Europe. However, there are internal variations, and the relationships between the global and the local give these variations their distinctive contexts. This tension between the global and local exists because these objects are historical constructions within which this tension is manifest. They are not constructed by a closed history on a pre-existing community, but as a singular means of constructing human groups in interaction with others, within a dynamic where the relationship to the others guarantees the originality of a specific comparison. Thus, the meaning of the notions of 'nation' or 'national minorities' varies considerably, even though the discourses which construct these notions appear 'natural' to different constituencies.

The legitimate member of the political community is the citizen, but the relationship between the citizen and the national dimension is never expressed directly. However, the empty space that articulates the political and the private sphere already predetermines the relationship between state and culture in such a way that the preconstruction of what is political and what is private inscribes the conditions of legitimacy. It is here that we encounter the state/civil society distinction that has been so central to radical politics. It is also the place where we encounter the relationship between the individual and the state, and how this relationship is legitimised through the social construction of the 'nation'.

Consolidating a uniform citizenry involved formulating and disseminating a uniform culture that was transmitted through a single language. Language emerges as a specific object within the discursive formation that links nation and state, involving the institutional structure that can legitimise or de-legitimise discourses, and that has the right to speak about specific issues, and the role of language as an object in such 'speaking'. The issue of what is, and is not, a language is a political issue that constructs speakers and non-speakers as political subjects. It pertains directly to the setting of boundaries. Historically states standardised their state language, thereby consolidating their specificity while elaborating differences between languages. The relationship between language and territory is established in the concept of autochthony, where the spatial boundary also becomes the boundary that distinguishes the 'us' of the language group from the 'them' of 'other speakers'. There may be 'other speakers' within that territory, but autochthony involves laying claim to the territory in the name of the language group. Where the autochthonous language is also the state language there is no tension; the citizen is also the subject that belongs to the language group that lays claim to the autochthonous territory.

The industrial economy appeared at the same time as the modern state and was profoundly influenced by it. The industrial society and the associated differentiation of social classes prevailed. Social classes and the nation-state were formed together (Mann, 1993). Individuals were integrated into the institutions of industrial society in such a way that it conditioned their identity and sense of being. The individual was aligned with collective forms of consciousness. The state served as the integrated form of social consciousnesses, linking social classes with the nation. Social movements constructed against the backdrop of social class stimulated a series of social reforms that, in turn, enhanced state regulation of society. At times the threat of a regional language, unknown to the central authorities, was a feature of some such movements, leading to an enhanced drive on the part of the state to exploit a uniform education, operating exclusively through the medium of the state language. Minority languages were restricted to the private domain.

A central legitimising force involved how the state was able to safeguard its economy and the associated labour market. A specific feature of this process was the creation of a social protection that was anchored in the nation-state (Barbier, 2008). The state protected its labour market by restricting the flow of labour from outside its territory. Simultaneously, it compensated its internal periphery for its relative economic disadvantage through various regional development policies and the selective use of social protection. Many European states extended their economic interests to 'territories' in the Third World, exploiting primary resources and manipulating the labour to serve their own economic interests. The population of such 'territories' tended to be used as a reserve army of labour.

Within this context the relationship between objects such as language, nation, economy and society are stabilised, as are the practices associated with regulation. The tendency in industrial society for the state to demand the assimilation of newcomers, while relegating their cultural and linguistic dimensions to the private domain, prevailed. This conditioned ethnic relations. Similarly, the relationship between gender roles, the household and industrial society was stabilised.

It is hardly surprising that the predominant understanding of the relationship between language and the polity has focused upon the monolingual state. This is not to deny that some states did provide legitimacy for more than one language. However, such cases tended to involve the state language and one or other of what became known as *lingue franche*. These *lingue franche* were treated as the means whereby members of different language groups could communicate despite not knowing both languages of these groups. They related to the colonial activities of the relevant state, a knowledge of the dominant state language being imposed on the host society. Such languages were used for diplomatic communication and often for communication between members of the ruling classes. In time the education system extended the teaching of such languages to at least the upper echelons of most societies. *Lingue franche* also demarcated specific territories or spheres of influence, each *lingua franca* tending to have its own territorial hegemony, relatively untrammelled by any other *lingua franca*. Again these spatio-territorial extensions were stabilised.

Globalisation and the Knowledge Economy

The current economic crisis has brought globalisation and its effects into firm focus, triggering a broad discussion of its characteristics. There are those who argue that globalisation and the emergence of a new variety of capitalism in terms of what is referred to as the knowledge economy go hand in hand (Jessop, 2002). However, the relationship between them is not clear-cut. On the one hand, globalisation refers primarily to the deregulation of the economy and its markets, while the knowledge economy focuses upon the heightened role of knowledge in economic practices. There is no necessary relationship between them in the sense that the strategies associated with the knowledge-based economy are inherently global (Jessop, 2004). On the other hand, both phenomena are linked by the role of the new technology in economic activity. Also, the main players in the globalisation process are multinational firms whose activities can be said to focus on the knowledge-based economy. Certainly, the two go hand in hand within the current economic developments, but to elaborate a causal relationship between them is not easy. Nonetheless, there is a need to discuss both the globalisation process and the knowledge economy.

Globalisation can be understood as a concrete economic and cultural phenomenon that derives from change. On the other hand, it is also used as a concept to analyse the contemporary world, allowing a consideration of new or renewable processes, how collective life is organised or undermined. In a simple sense, globalisation refers to the influence of economic deregulation on the relationship between the state and economic activity, especially trade. How regulation by the Westphalian state protected internal labour markets, economies and the perceived interests of the citizenry was discussed above. In contrast, deregulation minimises the role of the state.

On a more complex plane, globalisation promotes a powerful movement of ideas, involving the unification of markets on a global scale, with the free circulation of capital allowing enterprises to localise their activities everywhere in the world as a function of their economic interests. It creates a global, interdependent economic space for capitalism, within which open, global markets relate to the power of finance, until now, untrammelled by political obstacles. In this respect it involves a deinstitutionalisation of the world through the effect of economic forces. This has profound implications for language and society, and for the relationship between them.

It also involves a passage from liberalism to neo-liberalism. It is important to recognise that neo-liberalism is not a scientific paradigm, but a political project concerned with institutional change. Neither is it a uniform discourse that prevails universally. In general terms, it involves a shift away from Keynesian to monetarist, supply side and rational expectational theories. It focuses on the type of institutional changes and related policies that are required in resolving different problems, including the dilemmas imposed on national political economies by the forces of economic globalisation. Barbier (2008) maintains that there are two central dogmas that derive from neo-liberalism. Firstly, the reduction of the distortionary presence of government in the economy by reducing its size, balancing budgets and reducing inflation; and secondly, using freed resources to increase competition through structural reforms aimed at enhancing the smooth management of the economy.

As a political discourse neo-liberalism involves the two natural orders of orthodox liberal arguments – on the one hand, an individualistic, ego-centric, interest-motivated economy; and on the other, an associational, communitarian civil society. Economy and society are divided into separate, but related, endeavours. The market is constructed as a quasi-natural domain with its own form of self-regulation. Individuals are involved in economic relations that are indifferent to membership in any particular society. Furthermore, it claims that the individual is the only observable reality that we can refer to when we observe society. However, power is mobilised in order to condition people's decisions, but, if free of these constraints, the individual is socially free to choose from among alternatives as a function of her judgement concerning the consequence of that action. The individual is rewarded or punished for her action, the responsible person being one who supports her own action. As such, the individual is a unity which possesses a personal identity.

On the other hand, society is conceived of as a collection of individuals, each carrying interests to which she seeks to assign value. These individuals are also involved in the range and scope of social relations which characterise any particular, localised civil society. These social relations fuse, in contrast to market activity, which divides. By focusing on the operations of the market as an expression of the rationality of the individual, and the simultaneous retreat of the state and government, the emphasis is on a sense of democracy as expressing the will of the people who are viewed as the sum of all individuals. While this does seem to capture the essence of normativity, it is quite a different kind of normativity than that associated with institutionalisation, if only because of how it focuses upon rationality.

The assumed relationship between a highly conservative discourse in the form of neo-liberalism and globalisation as an ongoing process presents a challenge to those analysts who find it difficult to engage with the political rhetoric while being obliged to confront the reality of globalisation. They can simply criticise the rhetoric without offering a realistic alternative, or they can seek to engage with globalisation while offering a form of rhetorical revision. Among those who pursue the second strategy the tendency is to acknowledge the role of globalisation in expanding the creation of wealth, while arguing in favour of the redistribution of that wealth. Such an argument is obliged to address such redistribution by reference to bodies other than the state. A third stance involves merely analysing the effects of globalisation without recourse to any political positioning.

There is an implication in the preceding account that the state constitutes an obsolescence. Reich (1991) describes a world where the economy is devoid of any anchorage in the state, where states lose their sovereignty, where there is no longer any political authority capable of drawing up a defence when confronted with the unbridled forces of capitalism. This issue is sometimes referred to by reference to the geographical notion of scale (Smith, 1992). Scales are treated as social constructions that are closely related to power, domination and struggle. Thus, how space is constituted in social, political, economic and cultural contexts is important. It is the articulation of these elements that provides coherence '... within a totality of productive forces and social relations' (Harvey, 2001). Furthermore, what is implied about scale by reference to globalisation is that there is a process of re-scaling that does not simply involve a single spatial entity, but the relationships between such entities (Jessop, 2002). Within this re-scaling the state is no longer taken for granted in the way that it was by reference to the Westphalian state. This does have implications for the role of culture, including language, in both political practice and the political economy, as well as by reference to specific institutions.

To an extent, the argument about the loss of state sovereignty derives from neo-liberal principles. Among these principles is the claim that responsibility and accountability should be devolved from the state to the community and the individual. Similarly, the principles of democracy maintain that whoever holds responsibility and accountability must have a direct voice in policy formation. The nature of governance changes. The community is understood as the territorially based population that shares a sense of common identity, and, to an extent, power is devolved to such 'communities'. It is claimed that such shifts in the form of political organisation organised around a sense of territory displace the conventional relationship between the state and its regions. States also become part of larger agglomerations such as the European Union (EU), which sometimes also have strong regional policies by reference to society, economy and politics (Rawlings, 2003).

Simultaneously, globalisation generates a spate of issues that are incapable of being resolved by the state, and which require international cooperation. The role of international institutions such as the International Monetary Fund (IMF), United Nations (UN), etc. is enhanced, and the various states are obliged to strengthen their link to such institutions. The classical vision of international politics as involving the Westphalian state exploiting its diplomacy as an expression of national power dissolves, and is replaced by transnational politics within a space involving the multinationals, NGO and the authorities charged with regulating the relations between them (Rosenau, 1990). Delmas-Marty (2007) shows how the crossing influence of justice and supranational law accompanies the fragmentation and the loss of efficacy of national legislative and executive powers. She argues that there is a 'jurisdictionalisation of international law' and 'the revealing of the power of judges' such that nothing seems possible without the complicity of the state in such features of international law as those involving the International Court of Justice. Similarly, Benhabib argues that developments in law increasingly derive from outside of the state, stating '. . . the civic and social rights of migrants, strangers and residents are increasingly protected by international texts on human rights' (2007: 183). The implication is that we are increasingly living by reference to cosmopolitan norms (Kurasawa, 2007). How the current economic crisis spread like wild fire across states shows that we will live or fall together. There may be no retrenchment into protectionism, but the development of a financial regulatory system that must be internationally institutionalised appears inevitable.

Such views overlap with the argument that globalisation undermines forms of state-related identity while stimulating a global identity. This line of argument is presented by Beck (1992) who claims that what he refers to as a 'risk society' involves transforming the former view of science as that which allows humankind to conquer nature into one in which science is viewed as a threat to the environment. The consequence is the emergence of the world as the focus of concern and identity. Society loses the sense of security that relates to social cohesion. The focus shifts from the legitimation of policy making to a two-way process between the public and the polity, involving the reflexivity of governing and strengthening the legitimation of governance within its multilayered complexity. Within post-industrial society Beck claims that the problem involves the over supply of goods rather than the under supply associated with poverty in industrial age society.

In industrial society the individual was integrated with the state, its society and its institutions in such a way that identities were produced without the individual having any choice. The social group was grounded in tradition and everyone was submitted to its laws. Where the frame of action is not necessarily the nation-state, and where the demands are cultural and not social, the relations of actors to the political are considerably transformed. They contribute to the reconstruction and reconstitution of the political space, leading to more international mediation, particularly in economic and juridical terms. There is an appeal for participation, and for their capacity to create the conditions of their existence beyond the classical form of the nation-state. The subject is no longer the citizen and mainly political, but is now cultural. It involves an individualism that cannot be anchored in the social or the cultural. In becoming an activist each person selects one's issue of struggle, one's mobilisation and one's collective identity.

Given that the construction of languages as objects has derived, as much as anything, from the effects of state discourse, and how it has differentiated languages into types, whether they be categorised by reference to modern/minority, *lingue franche*/state, standard/dialect or other categories, we are confronted with the question of how this challenge to state sovereignty influences how we categorise languages. The strict relationship between the state and society is loosened, as is the relationship between the state and the labour market. This has implications for how we understand the relationships between language objects as well as between the language groups as social groups that relate to these objects.

What is the Knowledge Economy?

The knowledge economy is rarely clearly defined but rather tends to be taken for granted. It is claimed to be in the process of replacing the industrial economy and, in this sense, it constitutes a new variety of capitalism. It is also claimed to involve a heightened role for human, as opposed to financial capital or natural resources in the economy. The creation of wealth is held to increasingly involve the generation and exploitation of knowledge (DTI Competitiveness White Paper, 1996). It sometimes refers to the appearance of an entirely new economic structure. Here the emphasis is on the relationship between Information Communication Technology (ICT) and work. The new technology affords a competitive advantage that links with the exploitation of scientific and technical knowledge. Associated with new organisational forms, both within and between companies, and a fundamental shift in employment relationships, this leads to the claim for something inherently 'new' in the knowledge economy.

The reference point for the implicit change is what is referred to as immaterial labour, defined as the activity of the manipulation of symbols. Immaterial labour involves two different components. The informational content of the commodity refers directly to how skills increasingly involve computer use and both horizontal and vertical communication, while the activity that generates the cultural content of the commodity involves activities not usually recognised as 'work' – the definition and fixing of cultural standards, fashions, tastes, consumer norms and public opinion.

A major architect of the more recent developments was Robert Reich, Secretary of Labour in the USA under President Clinton. Reich argued that in the long run immaterial labour would be crucial for all economies. It involves scientific and technological research, training of the labour force, development of management, communication and electronic financial networks. Those jobs operating intellectual labour included researchers, engineers, computer scientists, lawyers, creative accountants, financial advisors, publicists, editors and journalists and university academic staff. The growth of such activities would run parallel to a decline in Tayloristic activities since such repetitive and executive activities could be easily reproduced in states with low labour costs. He further argued that globalisation had removed the link between the state and the ownership of capital and the means of production. Rather, what is important is efficiency and the productivity of communication, with capital being owned by multinational corporations (MNCs). What is lost through the denationalisation of the ownership of capital is compensated for by the ownership of immaterial labour, of the control of knowledge production. Knowledge becomes nationalised, and its organisation is managed nationally. Thus, the state should invest strategically in value-creating activities, the immaterial activities that characterise the knowledge economy. Income generated by this sector would be deployed to deal with the unemployment of the unskilled and low-skilled labour, partly in order to reduce the disparity between the incomes of skilled workers and those of the working poor.

It is partly because of these features of action that there has been an increasing search for creative workers. It involves yet another shift in productive orientations. Whereas within industrial economies labour went in search of work, we now find that work increasingly goes in search of labour. Florida (2002) has claimed that what he refers to as the 'creative class', perhaps better conceptualised as a status group, is an important driver of economic growth. According to Follath and Sprol (2007), this 'class' '...is a diverse and colorful group, exemplified by the ability to create ideas that can flow into companies – that will in turn attract return-hungry investors with plenty of start-up capital'. They claim that it is divisible into three groups: 'rational innovators', including engineers, scientists and computer experts; a 'creative middle', such as businessmen, advertising people and designers; and then the 'artists', including musicians, actors and painters. The so-called class is held together less by relations to the means of production or income similarities than by the sharing of a common culture.

Certainly there appears to be broad agreement that the three essential ingredients of a successful knowledge economy are technology, skills and a highly educated labour force (Powell & Snellman, 2004). Increasing human capital is key for innovation and growth. The creative class is claimed to be attracted to locations with open, diverse, communities which champion diversity, including linguistic diversity, and make cultural creativity accessible. There is general agreement that creativity is increasingly becoming an important part of the economy. Consequently, the market value of creative people has risen, and large industries have sought to adapt to how idea-creation assumes ever more importance.

The new technology, together with a growing complexity within an integrated system, does enhance the increasing use of information that can be transformed into knowledge. This expansion in knowledge intensity within the socio-economic system, according to Porter (1990: 73), is accompanied by the importance of rapid learning. He argues that competitiveness involves enhancing the capacity to learn, including learning to learn. Where neo-classicists treated learning as involving the flow of information into the memory banks of the individual, Hayek (1948) was the one who insisted that information was always perceived through the cognitive framework. This constituted a break from the empiricist conceptions of knowledge. Hayek also placed considerable emphasis on tacit knowledge. The relationship between information and knowledge rests on the difference between 'knowing how' rather than 'knowing that' (Polyani, 1967). Whereas information can be exchanged, knowledge cannot. Knowledge is also practice-specific. That is, it is something that is contextualised by reference to specific social practices. However, it also pertains to much broader contexts, be they historical, social or institutional.

Learning, on the other hand, is the process whereby knowledge becomes known. This involves far more than the sequential accumulation of codifiable knowledge. As a feature of human experience, learning reconstitutes the individual (Hodgson, 1999: 77). That is, learning involves far more than encountering information, and focuses on the reconstitution of individual capacities. This now is viewed as a continuous process. Consequently, unbeknown to the individual, she holds a vast repository of knowledge that is constantly dynamic, but which, simultaneously, must be capable of being shared with others. Shared knowledge and shared meaning assume a central importance for any economy. It is in this sense that knowledge is conceived of as an economic good.

The argument shifts towards the intensification of knowledge, and to an emphasis on knowledge-intensive industries, and knowledge-based organisations. Learning plays a central role, and the development of organisational structures that accommodate learning is paramount. Investment in knowledge generation and knowledge management is also important. This leads to an enhanced interest among policy makers in the role of institutional frameworks set by product market regulation, in science–industry links and in rethinking the basis for organisational innovation and management quality. Evidence indicates that high knowledge investment economies tend to pull away from the rest.

Innovation tends to be discussed by reference to product innovation and process innovation. By reference to the knowledge economy, emphasis is placed on process innovation. The emphasis on the search for new processes of production, new workflows and team work relates to the quest for the relationship between knowledge and innovation. Building on what has been said above about the dynamic nature of knowledge, innovation can be seen as an expression of productive knowledge, involving the relationship between new and existing knowledge and how they contribute to the value added. This implies that innovation occurs on the basis of knowledge.

Nonaka and Tekuchi (1995: 10) maintain that thinking of knowledge as tacit provides the basis for a new way of thinking about innovation, which now becomes an individual process of what they call '. . . personal and organisational self-renewal . . .'. Viewing innovation as the means whereby the world is recreated according to an ideal or vision, they claim that this involves recreating the entire organisational framework of companies, as well as the employees. Since learning changes a range of attributes including preferences, goals, capacities, skills and values, the individual is in a constant process of self-reformulation. Hence, we have the notion of 'lifelong learning'. More importantly, perhaps, this undermines the orthodox approaches to welfare economics that views the individual as given and constant. It is this process of reconstitutive development that is the ground-breaking feature of the knowledge economy.

The Industrial Economy and the Knowledge Economy

When the state dominates the economy, it dominates the public through its imposition of the circumstances within which the individual enters the labour market – language, qualifications, location, etc. When this is relaxed, and the state involves itself in a globalisation of the economy such that economic choice involves more than political decisions, there is a separation of the state from its society. It is argued that the state is there to ensure the welfare of the people, as a benevolent guardian, rather than as a leader (Touraine, 2007: 45). It is evident in how the EU has moved from its earlier ambitions, and moves towards the incorporation of different states, cultures, languages and nations. It is obliged to support a multilingualism and cultural diversity.

Such developments oblige an analysis in terms of systems, and an analysis in terms of actors, or those who can be considered as subjects. Within industrial society the actor and the system constituted the two faces of the same coin. The new order is a system where the categories that define the system are totally disassociated from those that define the actor. This means that the form of nationalism that creates a new state as the mirror of the former state no longer applies – it makes collective action redundant. A focus on the state means that social facts are thought of only in terms of the political, and this leads to a sociology without actors and without subjects. It leads to seeing solutions simply in terms of the state and of power – more powers to the Assembly etc. – paying little attention to the people as social actors. Yet the knowledge economy, placing as it does an enhanced importance on human capital, pulls in the opposite direction.

The organisation and management of work in the industrial age economy was based upon principles founded by Taylor and exploited by Ford.

In many respects, the work of Taylor was conceived of as a radical development, involving investing workers with responsibility and seeking to eliminate poverty through enhanced productivity. Scientific management was an attempt to apply scientific principles to the management of labour. It was Braverman (1974) more than anyone who viewed these principles in terms of the exploitation and control of labour. Nonetheless, it became the cornerstone of management theory during the 20th century.

Taylor noted that controlling labour by orders and discipline would not work, since the worker retained control of the actual labour processes, and thereby could retain part of the full potential of their labour power. Thus, control over the labour processes had to pass to management. This was achieved by controlling and dictating each step of the labour process. However, this would have to involve management having the same knowledge of the various labour tasks and performances as the collective knowledge of the workers. The ultimate goal was the control over the decision-making process in work. By carefully studying the various tasks of labour, to the point where management knew even more about these tasks and processes than the worker, management was able to determine for itself how much work could be undertaken within any unit of time. The labour process was disassociated from the skills of the worker.

The next step involved appropriating any brain power associated with work. This severed the link between the conception of the task and its execution. It allowed management to impose both methodological efficiency and the pace of work, while simultaneously divesting the worker of responsibility and planning. The planning involved management designing tasks for each worker, one day in advance. These tasks were carefully timed for their implementation, and were implemented through the supervision of the foreman. Thus all elements of the labour process were pre-planned and pre-calculated. Braverman (1974: 119) emphasised how management had a monopoly over knowledge, and used it in order to control each step of the labour process and its execution.

Taylorism, as the management process became known, was regarded by the founder of the Matushiab Electric Industrial Company (Matushita, 1988) as the main drawback in the ability to implement the knowledge economy:

> Your companies are based on Taylor's principles. Worse, your heads are Taylorized too. You firmly believe that sound management means executives on the one side and workers on the other, on the one side men who think, and on the other side men who can only work. . . . We are aware that business has become terribly complex. Survival is very uncertain in an environment increasingly filled with risk . . . Therefore a company must have the constant commitment of the minds of all its

employees to survive. . . . Only the intellects of all employees can permit a company to live with the ups and downs and the requirements
of its new environment.

The reasons are fairly obvious. Within the knowledge economy the
process of work and the associated practices change. The emphasis in
industrial age economy on information hoarding, command and control
thinking, and departmental competition that escalates costs and sub-
tracts value from goods and services yields to new ways of working.
Within the competition for markets, profits and growth, organisations
must be committed to information sharing, flexible processes, continuous improvement and new work styles. Collaboration, knowledge sharing
and organising around customer-centred processes will be evident.

The main components of industrial age business involved striving to
manage physical assets and physical capacity, while managing money as
capital. Markets had to be identified and serviced, while the link between
production and markets involved seeking locations close to transportation
centres. Similarly, access to commodities and energy had to be guaranteed. Workflows were organised according to Taylorist principles, focusing upon the assembly line. Within the knowledge economy, knowledge
becomes the source of capital, and the new technology becomes the means
whereby information and collaboration are organised and accessed. The
emphasis shifts to processes, knowledge and continuous improvement in
increasing effectiveness and enhancing flexible work practices.

The entire process demands the creation of new business environments;
a work environment that focuses on collaborative processes using shared
resources; process models that encompass knowledge mixing and sharing;
and the ICT scaffolding that can service these new processes. Communi-
nities of Practice are claimed to be the means whereby these working
processes are best organised (Wenger, 1998). These involve aggregates of
workers in face-to-face interaction who learn from one another through
involvement in work practices – learning by doing. While what they learn
is tacit, and thereby not easily expressed, it is crucial for the creation of
new knowledge.

Consequently, we are encountering a form of working that drastically
changes the relations of production. Specifically, clerical and blue collar workers are transformed into knowledge workers. The industrial age
economy emphasis on business processes based on division of labour concepts is obliged to yield to team working. Since firms increasingly rely on
ICT to develop and deliver products and services, it becomes increasingly
difficult for companies to compete simply on the basis of efficiency. They
must become more effective. This is claimed to occur through collecting,
sharing, disseminating and enhancing corporate knowledge that leads to
better products and services, and customer-centric business processes.

Workflow pertains to how different tasks or features of the work process are organised in such a way that the production process is efficient and adequately managed. Some have argued for conceiving of workflows by reference to value chains. Porter (1985) used the notion of a value chain as the basis for a model useful for examining the value that a company creates, measured against the costs associated with creating that value. Any business activity is divisible into the generic core activities and support for those activities. The emphasis is very much on activities involving value-adding activities, and activities that add no value, but generate cost. Such a chain may be in-house, or it may involve numerous firms or companies involved in the activities. The problem we confront here is that the value chain remains a concept that relies upon Taylorist principles, and fails to incorporate work as a process constructed out of team working and interaction.

By reference to our focus on language and culture the most significant change between industrial production and production in the knowledge economy lies in how the organisation of work changes. In Taylorism the individual worker was isolated, operating entirely separately from her co-workers. She was, essentially, a silent worker, interacting very little with other workers. Within the knowledge-based economy this is transformed. Team working obliges interaction, and interaction involves the essential incorporation of both language and culture. Furthermore, learning is through interaction, focusing as it does on learning by doing. It does not require any great imagination to recognise the link between language, culture, knowledge generation and creativity. Work becomes both a social process and a language process, and the challenge of this book is to elaborate how language contributes to the operation of the knowledge economy.

Language and Creativity

The essence of creativity lies in the essential ambiguity of meaning, and how meaning is socially constructed. This is in line with an understanding of the use of language as social practice. What is of interest is the creative process, its relationship to the creative environment and the role of multilingualism in both. In using language we are constantly engaged in creative, imaginary activity. This involves the creative and symbolic dimensions of the social world, that is, the dimensions whereby humans create ways of living together, and of representing their collective life. It involves the importance of signification in the expression of the social imaginary. The focus is very much on meaning and how we extend the meaning of words, how metaphor plays a role in creating new meanings, how interpretation is an essential ingredient of communication. The symbolic constitution of the socio-historical world is created by individuals through speaking and acting, individuals who strive to engage with others who are involved in their world.

However, meaning is also a source of division. It can be argued that the excessive focus of linguistics on syntax as opposed to semantics sustains such a form of division. The emphasis on the meaning of 'correctness' implicit in what is regarded as standard forms was sustained by the state, in how it has referred to a language purity that seeks to impose an oral and grammatical 'standard' that is not shared by all members of the specific society. This is the essence of Bourdieu's (1979) notion of symbolic violence. It raises the question about how globalisation involves a reassessment of the role of the state in all forms of regulation, including language regulation, and the implications for language standardisation.

What is clear is that conceptions of creativity are conditioned by the prevailing discourse of the relevant disciplines. During 1950–1970, creativity tended to be discussed by reference to personality, cognition and the stimulation of creativity in individuals, whereas after 1980 the focus shifted to the emphasis of environments and social contexts on the creativity of individuals, groups and organisations. Jeffrey and Craft (2001) argue that recent years have encompassed a concern with economic and political fields, with individuals being empowered to develop effective learning. Similarly, the emphasis on tacit knowledge, and the impact of the decentred arguments of post-structuralists have led to a focus on social practice and on a downplaying of rationalism.

The sharing of culture through practical engagement can lead to sharing different cultural influences, to challenging received thinking or to developing the means for expression, critical thought and problem-solving skills. However, it would be a mistake to understand culture by reference to static models. Culture has a dynamic quality, even though different aspects of culture may change at different rates. The focus therefore should be on the sharing of cultural creativity. It is in this sense that we understand value change.

It should be evident that insofar as the knowledge economy is concerned, it is futile to consider creativity by reference to the individual, in that the essence of knowledge creation lies in the shared meaning associated with team working. Rather, the focus must lie on the social construction of creativity and its relationship to culture. Both the social and the cultural are contexts for variation. It involves the ability to produce work that is both novel and appropriate, and leads to resolving issues associated with work. This obliges a focus on different features of the working environment, and the use of language within interaction associated with the context. Where individualist approaches tend to divorce the individual from the social, treating her as an autonomous subject, social perspectives relate to the normative social order. There is a debate here about how creativity relates to deviance, and about how the normative order inhibits creative behaviour. This is particularly relevant for Florida's (2002) work on the creative class.

The preceding discussion leads to an awareness that the use of more than one language and culture in interaction involves an intensification of the goal of sharing meaning, and that this process of sharing meaning across languages and cultures is an inherent feature, not only of creativity, but of reflection on the nature of that creativity. Yet there is an obvious need to embed an understanding of the relationship between language, creativity and interaction with the socio-cultural context. Much of the work currently undertaken focuses on poetics, building on the work of Jakobson (Tannen, 1989). Sometimes (Cook, 2000) reference is to 'play', without making any specific reference to Wittgenstein's notion of the play of language. In some respects this reference to play pertains more to how, in language learning, play draws attention to linguistic form while being relevant for advanced proficiency. Such work also points to how applied linguistics has at last started to recognise language use as something other than the reproduction of static rules of language use.

This body of work also suggests that creativity relates to context. That is, there is the implication that discursive practice is conditioned by the context of its unwinding. This is particularly characteristic of Carter's (2004) work that relies on the division of a discourse corpus into 'context types' and 'interaction types'. His main claim is that creativity is particularly associated with the collaborative sharing of ideas with friends or family, something that is supported by the work undertaken on communities of practice. A major critique of this body of work pertains to its static nature, something that is inevitable as a consequence of resorting to the analysis of corpora. Its strength lies in how it allows comparisons of settings and interlocuteurs. In fairness to Carter he does recognise the importance of socio-cultural and socio-historical dimensions of creativity.

Structural Changes

It should be accepted by now that the limitations of a sociolinguistics that focuses exclusively on the details of social interaction should be tempered by the study of the structural features that interaction reproduces. It should focus on the link between the characteristics of the linguistic practices and the social and historical conditions of their production, and how they are accepted. This involves how communities constitute objects, how the uses of such objects are contextually determined and how they reflexively interface with other interpretive fields. I have already emphasised how language has been constructed as an object primarily through the mediating force of the state. Changes in the role and nature of the state open up the space for a reconstitutionalisation of the language object.

However, there are also structural changes that have an influence on both language and culture. These derive from two sources – globalisation and the new technology. It is self-evident that a reduction in the regulating capacity of the state by reference to the economy has stimulated a complete reorientation of markets. Capital has tended to flow unregulated around the world, capable of being moved in a matter of seconds using the new technology. Whenever there is a new circulation of capital there is a new circulation of people, or new migration flows as they are referred to. This relates to the opening up of labour markets which become much more flexible. This also has profound implications for languages and the relationship between them.

The new technology opens up networks and the space of interaction. It involves what Harvey (1996) calls new constructions of 'space-time'. The social construction of space and time involves the construction of the social life of the community. In this sense it can be argued that the three deictic dimensions of time, person and place are all realigned as a consequence of the new technology and its relationship to globalisation.

It seems clear that language has played a role in the location of the new economy, and the role that different locations play in the overall context of different enterprises. It is also increasingly evident that while there has been a tendency for English to emerge as the global language, there is much more to language use within the knowledge economy than the mere incorporation of English as a working language on a global basis. Given how the relationship between specific languages and language groups and specific *lingua franca*, as well as the relationship between different *lingue franche* change, then language group relations also change. Change in the sovereignty of the state, and how it is able to control and regulate both their internal economy and the associated labour market, has profound implications for the relationship between languages and language groups.

The new technology also transforms how different materials attain a relevance for the economy. That is, it allows the commodification of what were previously regarded as non-material objects. Not only do these materials become exploitable, but there is also an expansion by reference to how they can be exploited. The relevant materials for the case I will focus upon are cultural materials. The various cultural and art forms that tended to be treated as museum objects are capable of being digitised, archived and transported, allowing a transformation in their use and their value.

This means that library and museum collections assume a different meaning from the public service context of the industrial age. Steps are already under way to create a massive online archive of library and museum artefacts that spans all of Europe. When this is in place, it will allow the creation of new content for the new media. It is important that the media industry transforms itself to accommodate multimedia activities in such a way that the potential value of the new products can be realised. It will reduce the cost of film location work through the creation of sets that can be imposed on any digitally created background, it will allow cultural materials to be contextualised according to audience and it will also allow the emergence of a new regional economic focus.

Evidently, this will require the collaboration of teams, working online across Europe. This begs the question of how language fits into such working environments. Creating online teams will be no easy matter, especially by reference to promoting their internal coherence when translation tools derive more from syntactic structures than they do from semantic coherence. If the sharing of meaning lies at the heart of knowledge economy working environments, much more understanding of the relevance of language for work will be required.

Conclusion

It seems clear that we are discussing a new variety of economy where the focus is very much on creativity. There is acknowledgement that there is a link between culture, learning and this creativity, but there is also an apparent lack of understanding among economic developers as to what its precise nature constitutes, and how it can be harnessed. On the other hand, it is equally evident that there is a strange silence about the relevance of language for the knowledge economy. This may be partly because of an ignorance about the nature and potential of language, or it may derive from the assumption that the best solution for the new transnational nature of the economy lies in the adoption of a single *lingua franca*. Given the relationship between language and culture it should not be impossible to conceptualise the role of language in this potential development.

The subsequent chapters discuss the issues referred to briefly in this opening chapter. I begin with an account of the macro changes that are occurring on a global scale, and how they effect the construction of languages as objects, and how we understand the relationship between them. Thereafter, the focus shifts to a concern with the various processes that operate at the regional level and within the working environment, beginning with how language and culture are conceptualised by reference to the knowledge economy. It involves a focus on the role of what is referred to as social capital. This discussion allows me to clarify the centrality of language and culture for how the knowledge economy is conceptualised in relation to the social. Such a starting point is essential if we are to comprehend the potential of language and culture for economic practice.

I then consider some of the principles that are claimed to operate at a more local level by considering how the changes discussed in Chapter 4 lead to a re-evaluation of regional culture and language in the process of economic restructuring. This, in turn, leads to a focus on the micro processes that allow knowledge to be created and exploited. This work focuses on the notion of communities of practice that is discussed in Chapter 5, and on the creative role of language within the working processes. Thus, having considered the relevance of regional processes for the knowledge economy, as well as how work draws upon regional and local social capital, I consider a case of how this understanding can be applied to the exploitation of specific regional cultural resources. I conclude with an exploration of how these developments pertain to arguments about a new form of society within which the nature and role of language change.

Note

1. This term derives from how the Westphalian treaty of 1648 which gave the nation-state sovereignty by reference to international law.

Chapter 2
Language as an Object

Introduction

Lundvall (1992) has argued that as knowledge increases in importance within the economy, so the role of 'national' culture, and presumably language, in its generation also increases. As we will see in subsequent chapters, similar claims are made for the role of regional culture. In contrast, current educational policy across most of Europe appears to be focusing on the teaching of English, often exclusive of other 'foreign' languages (Williams *et al.*, 2007). This has been characterised by one economist as being '... inefficient in terms of the allocation of resources, unjust in terms of the distribution of resources, dangerous for linguistic and cultural diversity and worrying by reference to its geopolitical implications' (Grin, 2005: 8). Such is the perceived prestige of English that it can be argued that once an individual has mastered English, the need to master other languages decreases. This preoccupation with English derives from a belief that social mobility within the global economy will involve an essential knowledge of that language. In some respects, this is an extension of the earlier principle whereby priority was given to state languages over other languages spoken within the state territory. An intermediate position involved how some languages, most notably in Europe – English, French and German – became *lingue franche* as a consequence of the colonial aspirations of the states where these languages were the mother tongue.

The central issue involved in such processes is that of language prestige or the value of a language for social mobility (Williams *et al.*, 1978). It relates to the role which language plays in the labour market and, in this respect, the focus is on language as an object rather than on how the subject uses language. This conception of language derives from how the state has constructed language as an object that links with other objects. In this sense, the language object is separated from the subjects who use it. These subjects are treated as citizens and workers. The nation-state was premised on the unification of the population within a political territory into a single 'nation', based on the homogenisation of language and culture so that all citizens could enter the labour market regulated by the state. Failure to accommodate the state language resulted in exclusion from vast sections of the labour market.

This relationship between languages and labour markets is currently being restructured as a consequence of globalisation. Globalisation involves the deregulation of the economy and an associated reduction in how states have been able to influence the relationship between their citizens and the internal labour market. This process should have profound implications for language in that it breaks the direct relationship between the notion of a single state language and the single state labour market. The state was premised upon universalist principles involving linguistic uniformity, so that the agencies and institutions responsible for the reproduction of most language groups remained unquestioned. The normative order of the state may lose its preconstructed, taken-for-granted nature, becoming the focus of debate. The normative order is thrown into disarray, at least by reference to how the stabilisation of discourse involves specific kinds of relationships between subjects and objects. Globalisation has led to much more fluid labour markets which span a much larger geographical space than was hitherto the case. This is not to imply that there was no role for international trade and mobility within industrial age economy, but that globalisation has significantly altered the balance between state-regulated and international labour markets. This opens opportunities which can be extremely lucrative, but which may involve a greater degree of geographical mobility, and a knowledge of specific languages which can accommodate such mobility.

There is a significant body of work on the relative value of languages within economic activity, much of it focusing on the relationship between regional or minority languages and state languages. The evidence tends to be contradictory. Some studies establish that bilinguals operating in a labour market which involves the use of more than one language do not benefit in terms of earnings advantage, and may even be disadvantaged through the suggested negative impact of learning a second language on their competence in the other language (Chiswick & Miller, 1998; Chiswick et al., 2000; Grin & Sfredo, 1998; Patrinos et al., 1994; Shapiro & Stelcner, 1997). On the other hand, this is contradicted by Henley and Jones (2005) who focused on the analysis of secondary data in the form of an extensive household survey in Wales. They showed a positive raw differential of 8%–10% depending on definition of linguistic proficiency, being even higher for women who could write Welsh. This specific case appears to be the consequence of government legislation and its effect upon regional employment.

The ELAN study (CILT, 2006) has taken a different approach to the relationship between multilingualism and economic advantage, focusing upon the advantage or disadvantage that accrues to companies operating language policies. It forcibly makes the point that export companies located in Europe, both large and small, face considerable loss of business performance when they do not exploit language management strategies.

Small and medium sized companies (SMEs) that develop a language strategy, appoint native speakers, recruit staff with language skills and use translators/interpreters were calculated to achieve an export sales proportion 44.5% higher than a company without such investments. This also fed back into the internal economy, to the extent that total factor productivity was higher by 3.7% than for the industry mean.

Others have stressed the relationship between innovation and exports (Lachenmaier & Wossmann, 2005). It is argued that the opportunity to sell into foreign markets increases the returns to investment in innovation, thereby motivating an increase in such investment (Debaere & Mostashari, 2005). Harris and Li (2005) emphasise how high-tech or innovative-intensive businesses are 'born global', that is, they internationalise at a very early stage in their development. Such studies stand side by side with those which stress the importance of language on export performance, one UK study (BCCLS, 2004) revealing that companies which placed the greatest stress on language skills within their organisation had both the greatest turnover and the strongest growth in returns form exports. The relationship between language and economic activity would appear to be changing as the process of globalisation accelerates.

The goal of this chapter is quite simple. It involves seeking to explore the effect of globalisation upon the relationship between language and the economy. To an extent globalisation destabilises, in that the role of the state in the economic order is modified. More importantly, perhaps, the setting of boundaries changes through the process of globalisation. In treating language as an object one is, simultaneously, dealing with the speaker of a language as a subject who is also an economic agent. This brings the notion of labour market into play through how the individual uses language in confronting the economy. It should be no surprise that some interesting changes in the social construction of languages are associated with globalisation.

Globalisation and the Labour Market

Capitalism has grown and been driven since the 18th century by the state. State regulation has been that which has organised much of economic behaviour. This has involved regulating not only the economy, but also the labour market whose boundaries corresponded with the state boundary. That is, the division of labour was largely confined to the state. While there was little attempt to control the movement of labour out of the state, rigid constraints were placed on the in-migration of workers. Industrial policy aimed to sustain full employment by influencing the ability of firms to lay off workers, retraining, investment incentives or the fixing of capital so that firms were unable to relocate. Similarly, regional development as a feature of industrial policy was aimed at levelling out regional disparities in employment and income. Its main goals involved sustaining employment growth, opportunities and incomes, while also generating productivity increases. In time within Europe, this was transformed into a concern with European competitiveness in global markets. Within states, the focus shifted towards enhancing national competitiveness. The concern remained the same – promoting the prosperity of its citizenry.

The global restructuring process involves the enhanced distribution of goods, technologies and the promotion of new conceptions of social and economic operations that sometimes come under the umbrella of 'culture change'. When we also include the goal of establishing fair principles of labour rights and human rights, we begin to come to terms with an understanding of what is involved in globalisation. Unfortunately, there is an increasing tendency to equate globalisation with a trade liberalisation whereby agricultural, manufacturing and service sector markets of poor and developing countries are opened. This process rarely serves the interests of the poor, partly because of how it fails to accommodate the rights of poor countries to choose their own economic path involving the choice of the best trade policies for their own interests.

In this respect, it is important to recognise that globalisation is not an ideology, but that which structures economies, societies, institutions and cultures. Furthermore, while we relate globalisation to the economy, only the core of any economy is global.[1] This means that only part of any labour force pertains to the global economy. Nonetheless, the governments of the various states place considerable emphasis on inclusion within the global economy, knowing that it is here that future growth and economic development lie.

State-organised education involved two functions. Firstly, the development of a citizenry located in a territory that corresponded with the hegemony of the state. This resulted in the formation of a common state culture that was sustained and reproduced primarily through the educational system. Secondly, it aimed to produce a labour force that could operate within the confines of the state's economy. This economy often overflowed beyond the confines of the state to accommodate its imperial or colonial interests or, in more recent times, the interests of the multinational companies (MNCs) that were tied to the state. That is, social and cultural reproduction was conditioned by the circumstances of the industrial age economy and the associated discourse.

The relationship between education and the labour market was not simply one in which the needs of the labour market were fulfiled by a labour force which was educated to fill the different positions that opened up in that market. It also closed its boundaries by focusing upon a single language, the language of the state. The language practices within the labour market tended to focus almost exclusively on the state language. While multiple identities were engendered, of prominence was that which focused upon membership of the labour force, and how it involved various features of signification and representation that derived from state legislation. It tended to have priority over any local or regional identity, largely because of how it was fostered within the education system. This homogenisation of society existed within a territory that was also constructed as politically, cultural, economically and linguistically, homogenous.

The discourse of the state was not merely political, in the sense of expressing the centrality of the state as an object, but also focused upon a pronounced nationalism that was integrated in the notion of the nation-state. Citizens were granted membership of the political community within an order where the public and the private, the state and civil society, influenced legitimacy. It is here also that we recognise the centrality of community for civil society. However, since the time of Condorcet, this community, while being the essential component of civil society, has also been constructed as pertaining to the state. Indeed, the state has always consisted of the sum of communities within its territory. This accommodation of community ensured that the construction of the state/community relationship was such that they could never be in conflict. It is also the place where we encounter the relationship between the individual and the state, and how this relationship is legitimised through the social construction of the 'nation'. Social groups were constituted around the regulating activity of the Westphalian state, and the social was privileged over the integrity of civil society. Beyond the law, the moral normative order determined what was permissible.

While these principles are retained, much of the context changes with the advent of neo-liberalism and globalisation. In Europe the notion of 'people' is contested as state citizens are given European citizenship, and the notion of a single Europe is brought into place. The direct link between state and identity construction is loosened. A tension emerges between state-based and broader bases of identity, including those that are constructed by corporate forces that operate within a global context. Much of this is the consequence of the restructuring of the economy and its influence upon labour markets. This has a great deal to do with language practices, and their relationship to work. Language practices are redefined and reinterpreted. In this sense, it also has a bearing upon how language is constructed. Castells (2006) argues that globalisation leads to a crisis of political representation, which has a profound influence on the restructuring and reconstitution of identities. I shall return to this issue.

Restructuring: Mergers and Acquisitions

Given how neo-liberalism places so much emphasis upon the rolling back of the state, and the role of market-led determination, it is tempting to consider that the global economy consists of an undifferentiated system of firms and capital flows which operate independently of any regulation. However, economic organisation is precisely that, the economy remains organised by some form of regionalised authority consisting of older state institutions and new supra-state entities. It is also evident that most economic activity and the associated employment tend to operate at the state, regional or local level, involving competition that is organised at these levels. Nonetheless, the core of the economic activity involves the increasing activity of the MNCs that are integrated globally through electronic networks employed to exchange commodities, capital and information. These core economic activities also promise to be the main features of future economic growth. The financial and currency markets are part of these core economic activities. As Castells (1998: 349) has underlined, the establishment of the euro was a reaction to how the new technology facilitated the exploitation of profit opportunities from the floating of exchange rates. The harmonisation of the European economy is a consequence of globalisation. What is emerging is a series of high-tech and other firms that are increasingly dependent on global networks of technological and economic exchange. They include MNCs and medium-sized firms that work together by reference to research and development (R&D), production and distribution.

A feature of these core activities is the increasing tendency for capital to move in search of investment in the activities of the global economy. It is estimated that there is $46,000 billion of investment funds around the world looking to invest in these activities. This leads to numerous mergers and acquisitions. In 2000 there were deals worth £174 billion in the UK. During the first 10 months of 2005 the figure was £120 billion. During the first 10 months of the following year European takeovers were 38% higher than during the same period in 2005, and 27.5% higher in the USA (*Times*, 2.11.06). The dotcom fiasco generated a temporary slowdown in these activities, but once again they are expanding. Prior to the current financial crisis, the number of private-equity houses generating buyout funds was on the increase. A major incentive involves how low interest rates means investment in equities offers steady yields at twice the rate of the cost of borrowing the money to buy them. Companies in some countries are more susceptible to takeovers than others. It is argued that the ease of borrowing within the London financial market makes the UK a key location for such developments. Furthermore, most firms can opt for organic growth rather than growth by acquisitions, but, in contradiction, the size of the global telecoms infrastructure generates urgency for firms located in that sector.

Nor are these developments divorced from the process of privatising the utilities in the different European states. The freeing of the state from a firm commitment to retaining firms within its territorial framework allows the state to privatise its public holdings. Simultaneously, the arguments associated with the emergence of neo-liberalism revolve around the supposed impossibility of states being able to regulate the activities of public holdings in order to provide the maximum advantage for the end-user. Increasingly, the role of government involves assuring social justice and regulation, but it procures services from the private sector. Thus during 2005, France privatised public assets worth $30 billion, the highest value of such activity of any of the Organisation for Economic Co-operation and Development (OECD) states. Between 2000 and 2005, as many as 900 French companies had been sold to foreign investors for $350 billion (*Times*, 28.2.06).

Increasingly, companies seek to create European continental champions through cross-border mega deals. European mergers and acquisitions exceeded $1 trillion during 2005, with companies such as O2 and Allied Domeq merging with Telefonica. This is the greatest level of activity since 1999. A 58% surge in cross-border deals is mostly responsible for the growth in mergers and acquisitions as European companies seek to compete in an increasingly competitive global market by buying foreign companies. Two years ago, cross-border deals accounted for 38.4% of European transactions; this has now increased to 58.7%. The euro had removed currency risks associated with buying another company within the Eurozone, while trade barriers are also coming down. The appeal of mergers and acquisitions involves how multinational networks of businesses built over decades seek to incorporate a ready-made global company for the price of a normal one, something that would be very expensive to create by organic growth or piecemeal acquisition (*Times*, 25.1.06). Deals of mergers and acquisitions involving European companies have been running at $10 billion/day, and all global deals at about $20 billion/day. Companies which cultivated their local and national markets are now keen to globalise their operations and, thereby, to tap new markets.

The relative value of mergers and acquisitions for the major states involved in such transactions is shown below (Table 2.1):

Table 2.1 Value of mergers/acquisitions realised in 2005 by country of origin of the target company

State	Value of mergers/acquisitions (in billions of US dollars)
USA	1,165
UK	305
JAPAN	156
GERMANY	111
FRANCE	109
CANADA	105

Table 2.1 (Continued)

ITALY	97
SPAIN	96
AUSTRALIA	55
THE NETHERLANDS	40
RUSSIA	35
DENMARK	33
CHINA	31
SOUTH KOREA	27
SWEDEN	25
BELGIUM	24
HONG KONG	21
CHINA	20

Source: Thompson International

Many of these were internal transactions, and others, such as the merger of Shell and Royal Dutch worth $100 billion, were very large. Nonetheless, Table 2.1 does serve to show the importance of USA and UK companies in these mergers. The value of foreign direct investment (FDI) in the UK increased by 182% between 2004 and 2005. British companies have high levels of profitability, with a return on equity of about 19% compared with 11% in Germany and 16% in France, and the euro area as a whole. In 2006 overseas companies acquiring British companies spent more than twice the amount spent by British companies in buying other businesses. As a result of their higher profits, British companies enjoy bigger cash flows that make them attractive. Furthermore, the *laissez-faire* attitude of government also makes it easy to close down plants if capacity has to be rationalised. In contrast, American companies are de-leveraging, that is, they are paying down outstanding debts while buying their own shares so as not to pay so many dividends, while also keeping share prices high. (*Sunday Times*, 2.4.06).

During the same period, FDI worldwide rose 29%, fuelled by cross-border mergers and acquisitions. Mergers and acquisitions including cross-border deals jumped 40% to $2.9 trillion, partly driven by the high stock market prices. Inflows to the 10 new European Community (EC) members rose by 36% to $38 billion (*Times*, 24.1.06). As much as $271.9 billion of mergers occurred during the first two months of 2006, nearly three times the value of a year earlier. However, the number of transactions did not increase markedly (*Times*, 7.3.06).

Much of this activity involves technology players. Ericsson acquired Marconi, and considered acquiring Lucent after an approach from Alcatel. Lucatel and Alcatel are major telecom equipment manufacturers. Their role in equipment standardisation makes them a good goal for bundling the delivery of telephone, television and Internet services. This merger, worth $36 billion, would create the world's biggest telecoms equipment company worth more than £12.6 billion, and employing 90,000. A combination of Alcatel and Lucent would provide better economies of scale than those of Ericsson, and would put pressure on them. Alcatel has market capitalisation of $21.9 billion and Lucatel $12.6 billion. This merger has generated considerable debate around the issue of protectionism. US protectionism revolves around national security, and the fear that defence technology will fall into the wrong hands. Lucent owns Bell Laboratories, a major US military research establishment. On the other hand, French protectionism revolves around the fear of losing firms that play a significant role in employment and development. Lucent is currently spread over 10 countries, and if the merger with Alcatel went ahead, the headquarters would be in France. It is predicted that the new firm would reduce its global workforce by 88,000 or 10% of the total. The convergence of high-speed internet, television and voice services is behind the telecoms tie-ups. In the USA, MCI was acquired by Verizon, and AT&T by SBC. These kinds of mergers force equipment makers to tie-up (*Times*, 25.3.06, 3.4.06).

When this occurs the global nature of financing leads to the large corporations usurping the customary regulatory function of the state and they can hold them to ransom. There is no compulsion on global firms to retain their headquarters in the 'home' country, and they will increasingly tend to move in search of the most beneficial taxation regime. In 2005 the most competitive countries in this respect were, in order, Finland, USA, Sweden, Denmark, Taiwan, Singapore, Iceland, Switzerland, Norway and Australia (*Times*, 17.1.06). Oliver Tant, global head of financial advisory at KPMG, claimed that 'The growing integration of Europe is a real challenge for national economies and pride. In the smaller countries such as Denmark and Finland, there is a serious threat that their stock markets will evaporate in the next 5–10 years.' He added that after companies are snapped up by foreign rivals, their domestic listings usually disappear, and their headquarters are often scaled down or moved abroad. As a result, the local provision of legal and financial deal advisory services will wither in some countries while Britain, France and Germany should benefit.

Yet there are voices that oppose these developments. Poor countries claim that globalisation undermines democracy because the states cannot control multinationals. On the other hand, the multinationals link up with local industries through a network of customers, services and markets. In the dash for European consolidation, national firms are available and unprotected. City and big business set up corporate governance that keeps boards and institutional investors at an arm's length. Cross holding and joint venture are discouraged. Groups are split into chunks, and governments sell stakes in privatised groups. The value of multinationals as business assets is rising as the world economy moves from Europe to Asia and America. A nationalist view claims that losing company head-quarters and all the professional functions that go with them is bad for jobs and wealth (*Times*, 10.2.06).

This is further complicated by the role played by the EU in promoting the single economy. Neoclassical economists have always argued that cor-porations should relocate in search of more competitive advantage. They argue that a failure to do so will jeapordise the corporation's ability to withstand foreign competitive pressure. Even attempts by the state to leg-islate against such mobility are resisted, on the grounds that it merely delays the inevitable. Furthermore, such 'artificial' support will merely drive up prices for the firm's goods. As a consequence, so the argument claims, the dislocation that derives from the relocation of capital, corpora-tions and work can be redressed through the re-training and re-skilling of the labour force. As the intensity of such shifts in economic activity pro-ceeds, it leads to a demand for educational practices that will constantly adjust to the shifting demands of the labour force, to a demand for lifelong learning.

The competitiveness of any location within the global economy revolves around the willingness of capital to move and invest, and the availability of the technology, and how these two factors relate to the prin-ciple of, first, to market and, second, to continuous innovation. The fact that a great part of the economic activity of the large corporations involves intra-firm interaction across locations means that it is a mistake to think of competitiveness simply in terms of the industrial tendency to relate competitiveness to specific states.

While the MNCs are by no means new, their rise to a position of global economic dominance is recent. By 1995 the north–south flow in FDI accounted for $100 billion, almost a third of the world total. Much of this involves intra-firm trade, involving subsidiaries and branches of the same corporation. However, the nature of MNC activity has changed, from natural resource-based commodities towards manufactured goods and services. A key feature of this shift is the intensification of outsourcing, with firms seeking the lowest cost location for each stage of produc-tion. Intra-firm activities are also giving way to an increase in inter-firm activities involving subcontracting, licensing, the creation of spin-offs, consultancies, etc.

Many of the larger MNCs recruit their graduate level staff globally. This tends to happen early in the individual's university career, with the com-pany paying their fees, offering them lucrative long-term packages and locking them into work placements. Any complaints about the quality of university graduates in one location are balanced by the availability of the best in any other. Simply because the headquarters of a company may be in one state does not mean that the company will necessarily recruit its labour force from that state.

As suggested in Chapter 1, this globalisation of capital and technology changes the terms of trade and investment. Mergers involve either companies or capital from various parts of the world entering what was previously the economic context of nation-states. It becomes increasingly difficult to identify a company as pertaining to the UK or France, for example. The various companies, or parts of them, are locked into networks so that the integration of strategic economic activities occurs through the networking of nodes, and involves the exchange of capital, commodities and information. Currently, the technology is insufficient to allow virtual communities of practice to operate across space, but even this is within reach. The financial and currency markets certainly operate globally, and are capable of an integrated operationalisation that has demonstrated its capacity to override any state controls.

States cannot insist on the use of language within private firms. As firms become denationalised, delocalised and merged into multinational outfits that recruit their labour globally, so the tendency for firms to focus on the use of *lingue franche* increases. Given the propensity of firms from the USA and the UK within mergers and acquisitions, the likelihood of English being the *lingua franca* increases. For those companies from states that do not have an international *lingua franca*, it is almost inevitable that English will prevail. However, there is evidence that language 'problems' arise from these mergers and acquisitions, and that they are likely to continue, at least by reference to human resource management (Angwin, 2001; Cartwright & Cooper, 2000).

The Circulation of Capital

Until recently, western firms focused on technology transfer as a way of developing the poor countries, and of conquering new markets. This may not happen by reference to strategic domains such as telecommunications, nuclear and aerospace because, while states object to cross-border mergers and acquisitions involving these domains on the grounds of national security, they really want to protect their monopoly on innovation. Areva refused to transfer technology for the construction of four nuclear reactors in China for fear of upsetting Westinghouse. Boeing Airbus was offered to sell 150 A320 planes on condition that a construction location was built in China. They refused. The fear was that they would acquire the technology and use it to conquer future markets. When such transactions do occur, the multinationals often impose restrictions such as limitations on re-exporting, or an insistence on abiding by the rules of IPR and global standards. Yet, acquiring modern technology is a central step of development for the poor countries. Thus China offers concessions to capture a link in the production chain of the multinationals that constitute the major axis of strategies of development.

Only the countries that invest massively in education and research can appropriate the foreign technologies and seal a veritable process of catching up. The United Nations think tank on economic development United Nations Conference on Trade and Development (UNCTAD) claims that the developing countries are the origin of only 8.4% of the spending on R&D in the world, with 97% of this being in Asia where it is related to what is necessary in order to install foreign companies. Most of the Asian states have acquired a level of development during the 1970s and 1980s that has only occurred in China and India during the last 10 years. Japan and Korea are protecting their internal markets by allowing their national industries to develop the mastering of copied technologies before launching on the international markets where their competitiveness pertains to assuring from the outset the low cost of labour linked to technological research. China and, later, India were protectionist from the start: they copied technology, and entered the global market by concentrating on a number of industrial niches. Lacking a long-term investment in R&D they relied on the adaptation and amelioration of existing technologies in order to respond to internal demand and to the congruence of western firms in the technological markets of imitation as well as innovation. (*Le Monde*, 11.4.06).

Nonetheless, a recent report by the UNCTAD (UNCTAD, 2006) indicated that, in their view, the states of the south are to become the key players in global investment. Of $916 billion of foreign investment in the creation or redemption of enterprises, the developed world attracted $542 billion, leaving a record $334 billion among the developing economies or the economies in transition. At the head of this list of countries were China and Hong Kong, Singapore, Mexico and Brazil. This is no less spectacular when one considers the emitting states, with investments emanating from developing states accounting for $133 billion or 17% of the global flux, considerably more than the 5% that was registered in 1980.

The enterprises of the developing countries accounted for 13% of the global mergers and acquisitions in 2005. The extent of investment in 'southern' states by other 'southern' states increased from $2 billion in 1985 to $60 billion in 2005. These south–south investments are regional, with Asia essentially investing in Asia to the tune of $48 billion, and with South Africa investing more than half of the foreign investment in Botswana, Lesotho, Malawi, Swaziland and the Democratic Republic of the Congo. However, there is also a flow from Asia to Africa and from Latin America to Asia.

The main southern investors are South Africa in Africa; Brazil and Mexico in Latin America; Russia in Eastern Europe; China, India, Malaysia and Thailand in Asia. The transnational companies in these countries seek to invest in energy and primary materials, for example, Petrobras or CVRD from Brazil, CNOC or CNPC in China. However, they also invest in telecoms (ORASCOM in Egypt), electronics (SAMSUNG in Korea) or information technology (INFOSYS in India). As with similar companies in the developed world, these companies want to establish abroad in order to facilitate their access to basic products, to extend their commercial openings, but also to increase their competitiveness since, in developing countries such as India or Korea, labour costs are pushing up their prices and limiting their competitiveness. In the field of electrical appliances or PCs, companies such as Acer from Taiwan, Arcelik from Turkey or Lenovo from China are achieving a global reputation because they are investing outside of their country of origin.

The report suggests that this south–south flux is growing. It notes that recent investments can lead to an external domination of domestic markets, while also limiting what local authorities can do to control the working conditions in the large enterprises. Furthermore, numerous companies from the developing countries retain shares that pertain to their governments, notably by reference to China and Russia, as an important part of their capital, something which can unbalance the relations with the state where they operate.

This should be a major concern since what we are witnessing is a consolidation of the global division of labour. The collusion between the states of the developed countries and multinationals in the various trade negotiations works against the poorer countries. It is estimated that the Doha round of trade talks will benefit the rich countries by $80 billion, and the developing countries by $16 billion, while the poor countries will lose. The picture is even bleaker when one takes the loss of trade tax revenue into account (*Times*, 8.11.06).

The report also claims that the technological firms are the easiest to integrate within the developing states since they derive from the enterprises from the north. On the other hand, the capital that originates from the developing countries is invested in factories and offices rather than in the shares of the enterprise, in the capacity of production rather than in merger–acquisitions; and they also involve simple technological industries and recruit a large labour force. The subsidiaries of the transnational firms that originate from the developing states also create more employees per million dollars than those from the developed countries. Furthermore, one advantage from the perspective of the receiving country is that they can benefit from playing off investors from the developed world against those from the south. These are developments which are likely to endure and constitute a new phase in global development since they involve countries which both receive and emit investment, thereby occupying both sides of the negotiating table.

Restructuring: Outsourcing and Offshoring

It has already been emphasised that there is no necessary relationship between the process of globalisation and the emergence of the New Economy. Nonetheless, what is evident is that the new technology can sustain the expansion of the Old Economy. Similarly, Old Economy organisational structures can benefit from the emerging process of globalisation, as well as from the new technology. To this extent, it is interesting to recognise the role played by language in the selection of locations, both for outsourcing and for the direct relocation of production.

Outsourcing tends to replace the corporate model that has dominated business life for over a century – the vertically integrated industrial company. Most activities were carried out within the firm, with the firm making what it sold. Increasingly, this is giving way to a tendency to develop fluid partnerships that constitute a network of related activities and personnel. This is partly because of how Information Communication Technology (ICT) allows information to make markets more efficient, thereby shifting the advantage to those who are best at playing the markets. Indeed, it can be claimed that the more high value activities placed outside the firm, the higher the value that is generated. Also, the liberalisation of international trade means that the average level of tariffs in industrial countries is now less than a tenth of what it was before the Second World War. The lowered cost of transactions over the internet heightens global competition, leading to cost cutting through outsourcing and offshoring. There are various ways in which this can be achieved. A single producer or provider may sell its goods or services to more than one company, allowing that company to label them with their own brands. Other companies are often little more than a brand name, and all of the production and marketing activities are outsourced. The company effectively makes nothing. They do assume legal responsibility for what is sold, even if this is done through a range of suppliers.

Outsourcing is not new, but the rate at which it has expanded has been of a different scale than previously. The international nature of the outsourcing has also increased so that outsourcing becomes what is referred to as offshoring. This is accompanied by a shift from manual workers to knowledge workers, and from manufacturing to services. The supply chain is becoming globalised. The various processes of economic activity can be broken down into a few functions which can be directed from anywhere in the world. The danger is that the workforce will not only be outsourced, but that it will be obliged to work under conditions which would simply not be tolerated in the 'home' state.

The Ricardian thesis of comparative advantage claimed that in a global market rich countries would retain their blue collar workers, and would gain new markets for high value services. Poorer countries would provide cheap goods to the wealthy countries. Wealthy countries would lose manufacturing to low-wage competitors. However, it is evident that this is an oversimplification, and that the process of global integration does not conform to such a simple conception.

One feature that tends to be associated with globalisation involves the creation of production facilities outside of the 'home' country, with the goal of marketing in the location of production. US facilities abroad which produce for overseas customers rather than for shipment back home amount to $2.2 trillion annually, dwarfing the US export figures of about $1 trillion. This has doubled since 1990. Outsourcing is not in order to bring products back to the USA, but rather, in order to expand the market as new locations or potential locations open up. Clearly, this is facilitated by the process of global neo-liberalism. At the same time US manufacturing has shed 2.7 million jobs. It is argued that in order to be competitive US companies need the beachhead abroad that allows them to expand their sales abroad. This became a major issue of contention in the 2004 US elections. As has already been stated, this is seen as an extension of industrial age economy action that is facilitated by the opening up of new markets, largely as a consequence of globalisation.

This contrasts with the outsourcing of key aspects of New Economy activities. This requires a highly skilled and educated labour market in locations where labour costs are lower than in the 'home' country. The extent of this relocation of activity is significant, but remains considerably less than the extent of comparable employment in the 'home' country. Thus, India's technology industry employs 800,000, while the US technology industry employs 10.2 million. Of these, 300,000 work in Indian call centres compared with 6 million in the USA. Nonetheless, it is a process of labour relocation that is claimed to be growing. A study by Deloitte (2003) – *The Cusp of a Revolution: How Offshore Trading will Transform the Financial Services Industry* – claims that as many as a quarter of workers in the technology sector of the developed countries will be delocalised into the emerging markets by 2010, and India, in this respect, remains the most attractive location. They believe that the zone of delocalisation will grow around the Indian Ocean, including South Africa, Malaysia, Australia and beyond that China, but that India will remain the central point. It is also a delocalisation that focuses upon specific activities associated with how employment is redefined within the New Economy. Deloitte estimates that in the next five years the following number of jobs in financial services will be delocalised to the Indian Ocean belt – US = 850,000; Europe 730,000; Japan 400,000; giving 2 million jobs in total, out of a total global workforce of 13 million. The probable scenario is one in which new jobs will be located in such places in contrast to the earlier process of the re-localisation of jobs.

This is referred to as a 'third industrial revolution' that will result in 40 million jobs heading overseas (Blinder, 2006). It will involve not only all manufacturing jobs, but also many service jobs such as the laboratory work for healthcare, examination marking, etc. This creates images of vast job losses in the west, and a vast jobless population that will have to be sustained by the state. On the other hand, 5 million jobs were created in the USA in the past three years, while 300,000 manufacturing jobs were lost. It would appear that for every cheap job created in India, it creates one in the developed world. There are those who argue that while distant Asian companies can handle relatively simple tasks such as credit card applications, they are unsuited for more complex transactions that western employers can deal more effectively with. The reasons given revolve around the centrality of nuances such as languages and cultural sensitivities. Nations will still be better at doing some things than others. This kind of national and cultural arrogance disappears when services assumed to be impervious to global competition become tradable. While initially it was felt that only back-office data processing roles and software development roles could be moved to countries such as India, services which were once assumed to be impervious to global competition have become tradable. Investment banks are hiving off high-intellect equity research and high-end development work to Budapest, South Africa and India. In 2003 about 25,000 US tax returns were handled in India; now it is closer to 500,000. The Indian branches of Cisco, Intel, IBM, Texas Instruments and General Electric have already filed 1000 patents for goods ranging from microprocessors to aircraft engines (Friedman, 2005). This is innovation. The big technology players are now investing in India to the tune of $5 billion: $1.7 billion by Microsoft who will hire 3000 new employees during the next four years; $1.05 billion over five years by Intel; $1 billion by Cisco, the world leader in internet networking technology; a similar sum by Advanced Micro Devices (AMD) linked to a group of non-resident Indians in order to develop low-price PCs.

A predominant reason for these developments is that India has a vast resource of educated English-speaking labour. Furthermore, an engineer costs 30–40% less than in the west so that developing a PC costs $18–$26/hour compared with $55–$65/hour in the USA or Europe. Between 400 and 500 companies have research centres in the country, having delocalised the work to Indian companies (Fortune, 4.5.09). The revenues of that sector grew by 34.5% during the 2005 fiscal year, and industry expects $22.5 billion dollars of revenue from exports during 2006. These returns could rise to $60 billion by 2010, becoming the main motor of economic growth, and representing 7% of GDP, compared with the present 3% (Report published 12.12.05 by Nasscom and McKinsey). This employs 2.3 million direct employees and 6.5 million indirect employees. Such development requires large educational investments, especially given that currently competition between firms for engineers among the informatic companies has led to an increase of 25–30% of salary which could undermine the competitive advantage (*Le Monde*, R&D, April 2006).

It is argued that India is best placed to win the race to provide high-intellect services. It has a widespread command of English, and is regarded as an open society. India has far more executives with the requisite skills and sensibilities to work across borders at the top level necessary for running a truly international business than does China. They join a global elite that moves seamlessly between countries, an elite that has studied in the same business schools, and worked for the same consultancy firms. They speak a language of tolerance, opportunity and performance indicators. They have more in common with one another than with people in their own country (*Times*, 9.3.06). They pertain to what Hernandez (2002) refers to as cultural deterritorialisation.

However, it would also appear that this depends on how the relationship between the outsourcing company and the offshore company is developed. There is an argument that letting go of key business functions introduces rigidities into an organisation, and makes it more difficult to respond quickly to changing circumstances. Some companies, including Sainsbury and Prudential, have brought outsourced deals back in-house. Sainsbury ended its 10-year deal with Accenture three years early in order to revamp its supply chain. It is argued that the successful cases do not require specific business knowledge, but involve significant economies of scale. It is equally likely that failures are a consequence of not having envisaged the necessary changes of operational practices that will guarantee flexibility. As product cycles become shorter, and companies expect to deliver to ever more condensed periods, flexibility became more important. This flexibility of operational structures needs also to accommodate online working environments specifically designed for enhanced flexibility, rather than existing systems that merely provide rigid information flows (*Times*, 21.2.06).

Possibly as a response to these kinds of issues, the MNCs are operating an 'offshore, onshore' model in which they recruit workers in low-wage economies and transfer them to operations in the west without putting them on western pay scales, and providing comparable job security. During 2004, 22,000 IT workers were provided with work permits to work in the UK, of whom 85% were from India. A growing recognition among outsourcing companies that they also need a British base has encouraged Tata Consultancy Services, WIPRO Technologies and Infosys, the large Indian outsourcers, to increase their presence in the UK, with an inevitable impact on the flow of workers between the two countries (*Times*, 21.11.05).

This is leading to a transformation in the activities of many such companies. KPMG estimates that within three years 10% of the work of Indian ICT companies will derive from outside of the country. Tata Consultancy, the largest provider of ICT services, already generates 5% of it revenue externally. Since 2002 it has opened offices in Uruguay, Brazil, Chile, China, Australia, UK and Japan, and will open another in Morocco before the end of 2007. Infosys, whose revenue has risen to $3.1 billion, employs 20% of its workforce outside of India. This leads to a shift from 'offshoring' to 'nearshoring' where production occurs close to the client. Much of this work involves activities where the client needs to be close to the service provider. In order to retain price competitiveness they install their production centres on the edge of their target markets. 'Nearshoring' is thus a compromise between maintaining low salaries and a relative proximity to their clients – Morocco, Hungary and Poland for Europe; Brazil, Mexico and Chile for the USA. This proximity also overcomes the reticence of some clients. Thus French banks, which have not offshored their work to India, are more open to operating through an experienced Indian company located in eastern Europe. In recruiting abroad, Indian enterprises are preparing for an eventual shortage of engineers in their own country. Accenture aims to increase its Indian workforce to 35,000 by the summer of 2007, and Capgemini has announced the hiring of 27,000 additional engineers by 2010. By 2012 it is estimated that there will be a shortage of 260,000 ICT workers in the country. In adopting the 'nearshoring' model India is also striving to retain its comparative advantage vis-à-vis newcomers to the offshoring market such as Vietnam and the Philippines (*Le Monde*, 4.5.07).

What is interesting by reference to the topic under discussion are the reasons given for this delocalisation and the locations chosen. A recent survey placed India and China as the most attractive locations for locating centres of production, laboratories and service activities. These were followed by Malaysia, the Czech Republic and Singapore. It is claimed that India is attractive because of low salary costs and a mature market. Of course labour costs are similar to other Asian countries, but a favourable taxation system and competitive infrastructure costs give it the edge. Equally important is the existence of the English language. Labour costs do not explain everything, and a firm weighs up numerous factors when the number of candidate countries increases. Labour savings are less for qualified labour and managers, and there is a tendency to look at productivity rates, risks of Intellectual Property Rights (IPR) piracy, education, turnover, intercultural management, etc., all of which may give a 20%–40% saving. In the case of China the possibility of accessing a new market plays an important role. While this implies a distinction of location choice in accordance with the nature of the enterprise and the function being delocalised, it is also relevant that the number of students from China accessing English language Higher Education is constantly increasing. The presence of foreign firms in a market persuades others to do the same. East European countries such as the Czech Republic, Poland and Hungary are also favoured, largely because of cultural similarity and the good level of English language ability within the workforce, their technical competence and a minimal juridical framework.

Certainly, these developments are sufficiently pronounced to result in a debate concerning the impact such processes are having on the 'home' labour force and labour market. The implication is that jobs are moving away from 'home', with the result that there is a shrinking of the domestic labour market. However, the argument has yet to be resolved. A study by Global Insight for the Information Technology Association of America (ITAA) claims that the delocalisation of informatic activities to foreign countries has contributed to creating twice as many jobs in the USA as in the delocalising country. The reasoning is simple – the use of cheaper foreign labour allows the US enterprise to increase its productivity and to reinvest its profits and create new jobs in the USA. That is, the argument conforms with the orthodox argument against outsourcing – that it merely exists as a means of exploiting a defenceless labour force in order to increase the profits of the owners of the means of production. It is the dependency argument revisited. Within the general process of restructuring associated with globalisation, the west loses industrial age economy occupations, especially those in the manufacturing sector. These occupations are replaced by New Economy service sector occupations.

This complex picture of economic restructuring and its effect upon the global distribution of labour is being criticised. The German president of the Chambers of Commerce and Industry encourages German firms to delocalise to Eastern Europe in the belief that the increased productivity of German firms will save jobs in Germany. It is claimed that each month 50,000 jobs leave Germany for countries paying lower salaries – the average hourly pay in the acceding countries is €5 compared with €25 in Germany. Where other factors such as qualifications, productivity or quality of infrastructure are strong, the temptation is even greater to delocalise production. It leads the owners to increase pressure on workers in Germany to be more flexible, especially by reference to working hours, with some firms having negotiated an increase in working hours with their workers without any increase in salary. Siemens claims that 10,000 of its 167,000 jobs in Germany are under threat. They claim that the costs of production of telephones in Germany are 30% higher than in Hungary, and demand flexible working from German workers in order to reduce the gap. There is an emerging struggle between the unions and the owners. Global processes are generating local struggles.

Legislation and the Search for Labour

The circulation of capital is, customarily, related to the circulation of people, or migration. This is complicated by two factors. Firstly, how the demands of the New Economy focus upon particular competencies that, on account of the global competition for a limited pool of labour, are in short supply; and secondly, how states confront their conventional resistance to the immigration of foreign labour.

There are several factors that have led states to loosen their essentially conservative regulations regarding the recruitment of labour from outside of their borders. In most of the OECD countries there has been a demographic shift involving an aging of the population. This has placed considerable strain on existing health services while also making it difficult for the existing working age population to meet the pension demands of the ageing population. This, together with the development of ICT and the growing importance of human capital in economic growth, has contributed to the demand for what is mainly skilled labour. As the structure of the OECD state economies shifts away from the primary and secondary economic activities towards an increasing emphasis on service sector activity, so the demand for skilled labour multiplies. Consequently, competition among OECD countries to recruit and retain skilled labour is keen. The end of the 20th century saw most states amending their legislation to facilitate the entry of skilled foreign workers and to allow foreign students to access their labour markets upon graduation. The enhanced labour market flexibility was accompanied by attempts to develop specific recruitment programmes.

Within the EU, these developments ran parallel with the development of the single labour market and attempts to enhance the mobility of labour within that market. Attempts have been made to enhance the portability of pensions, to ensure that workers in fixed employment will not be penalised for periods abroad, and other similar restrictive circumstances. However, these concessions pertain primarily to movement within the EC.

In some countries, most notably Denmark, France, Ireland, the Netherlands and the UK, labour market testing criteria have been relaxed for those occupations for which there are shortages in the respective labour markets. These occupations include IT specialists, highly skilled workers, biotechnologists, medical and health staff and education. Those countries such as the USA or Switzerland that use an annual quota system have increased their quotas for some highly qualified personnel. Thus in 2001 Switzerland increased the quota for highly skilled workers by 30% while high-skilled immigration to Japan has increased by 40% in 10 years, and tenfold in Korea during the same period.

Programmes have also been established to recruit highly skilled workers. Norway and the UK now allow highly skilled foreign workers to spend time seeking work rather than being obliged to secure a definite job offer. Germany has a programme to recruit IT specialists, and has reformed its immigration law for engineers, computer technicians, researchers and business leaders. Other countries use specific fiscal incentives to attract skilled workers. These offer either income tax free status for a number of years, or large tax deductions. In some countries this liberalisation of the labour market may apply only to new technology occupations, whereas elsewhere it extends to encompass a range of lower level occupations where there is a shortage of indigenous labour. Thus Spain, for example, has been active in recruiting health workers capable of supporting the ageing population from South and Central America.

Evidently there is a paradox between the globalisation of the economy, the enhanced tendency to relocate work and the continued existence on the state's ability to control the flow of labour. This paradox revolves less around restricting emigration than around controlling immigration. Within this context it is less about prohibiting immigration than about selective immigration. Where all states appear to be competing to obtain the most highly qualified labour from the poorer states, especially where it involves new technology competencies, there are some states which also place considerable emphasis on obtaining the labour to undertake the work which their own citizens are increasingly reluctant to assume.

Migration and Labour Markets

The relationship between immigration and the equilibrium and dynamics of labour markets cannot be understood without reference to the characteristics of the immigrants and the economic conditions of the host country. The labour market of foreign workers varies according to the stage of the economic cycle, and the nature of the links between immigration and the labour market depends upon the timescale of the analysis. Above it was indicated that the concentration of the New Economy tends to be uneven and focused. Thus there will be variation in the role played by the New Economy within the economy of the state and, consequently, the role played by the New Economy by reference to the labour market. Such factors contribute to how there has been an increase in the international movement of highly qualified workers during the past 10 years, and how this also varies from country to country.

Much of the movement of workers tends to involve temporary employment, and thereby contributes to the tendency to stimulate a higher degree of flexibility within labour markets. In this respect, foreigners increasingly play a buffer role in how the labour market confronts cyclical fluctuations. There is little doubt that much of the recent economic growth in the capitalist core of the global economy has focused upon the New Economy, and that this does give rise to labour shortages in ICT-related occupations. This has contributed to how these states have amended their immigration legislation in order to enhance their human capital in these occupations. In Europe this also focuses upon the goal of developing a single labour market that will serve an increasingly mobile European labour force.

There is little doubt that there has been a significant increase in the number of immigrants into the countries that constitute the core of New Economy development, and also in their proportion of the total population of such countries. Yet there is also considerable variation from one country to the other, both in the incidence of immigration and in its composition. In countries such as Luxembourg, Belgium, Ireland and Portugal, the proportion of EU citizens in the total foreign population is very high. Furthermore, it is also clear that much of the immigration focuses upon highly qualified human resources associated with the relationship between the knowledge-intensive economy and economic growth. In some respects, the struggle involves retaining qualified personnel and repatriating qualified expatriates. Several countries have taken steps to respond to these challenges. In France and in Portugal, the foreign-born population includes a significant proportion of persons born abroad as citizens, and repatriated. Thus the 1999 census in France revealed 1.6 million people born with French nationality outside of France. Similarly, migrants originating from North Africa tend to be found in three European countries – France, Spain and the Netherlands.

Within the core of the New Economy – the OECD countries – it is continental Europe that accounts for the largest number of immigrants. There are nearly 2 million immigrants from the EU in each of Canada, Australia, France and Germany, and over 4.5 million in the USA. Emigration from the UK accounts for 20% of this last figure, while emigration from Germany, Italy and Poland account for close to 15% each. In contrast, France maintains its reputation as a country whose citizens do not emigrate, with only 3% of people born in the EU who reside in other OECD countries being French. The variation in the different OECD countries is shown in Table 2.2:

Table 2.2 Percentage of foreign-born and non-citizens in the total population of OECD countries

State	Percentage foreign-born	Percentage of non-citizens
Poland	2.1	0.1
Slovak Republic	2.5	0.5
Finland	2.5	1.7
Hungary	2.9	0.9
Czech republic	4.5	1.2

Table 2.2 (Continued)

State	Percentage foreign-born	Percentage of non-citizens
Spain	5.3	3.8
Portugal	6.3	2.2
Denmark	6.8	5.0
Norway	7.3	4.3
UK	8.3	–
France	10.0	5.6
Netherlands	10.1	4.2
Greece	10.3	7.0
Ireland	10.4	5.9
Belgium	10.7	8.2
Sweden	12.0	5.3
Germany	12.5	–
Austria	12.5	8.8
Switzerland	22.4	20.5
Luxembourg	32.6	36.9

However, this undifferentiated information betrays internal differences. Thus for example, of the 20% or more than 3 million from the UK who reside in other OECD countries, or of the similar 3 million German-born who reside in other OECD countries, a large number are retirees.

Table 2.3 presents the total numbers of foreign-born in each EU state, together with the proportion of that number which derives from either the EU25 states or the rest of Europe:

Table 2.3 Proportion of immigrants deriving from different locations by state

State	Total foreign-born	% of total popn.	EU25 born	% of total	Rest of Europe born	% of total
Austria	1,002,532	12.5%	364,624	36.4%	527,007	52.6%
Belgium	1,081,098	10.7%	621,471	57.5%	117,787	10.9%
Czech Republic	448,477	4.5%	344,256	76.8%	75,989	16.9%
Germany	8,668,698	12.5%	2,552,578	29.4%	5,244,548	60.5%
Denmark	361,053	6.8%	118,004	32.7%	77,355	21.4%
Spain	2,172,159	5.3%	597,948	27.5%	194,676	9.0%
Finland	131,447	2.5%	51,681	39.3%	44,764	34.1%
France	5,868,237	10.0%	1,978.923	33.7%	412,539	7.0%

Table 2.3 (Continued)

UK	4,975,133	8.3%	1,493,235	30.0%	175,577	3.5%
Greece	1,121,758	10.3%	191,038	17.0%	733,183	65.4%
Hungary	292,926	2.9%	65,057	22.2%	209,815	71.6%
Ireland	399,677	10.4%	291,340	72.9%	16,408	4.1%
Luxembourg	140,207	32.6%	116,309	83.0%	11,855	8.5%
The Netherlands	1,615,376	10.1%	340,220	21.1%	269,158	16.7%
Poland	756,881	2.1%	248,868	32.9%	483,223	63.8%
Portugal	651,472	6.3%	159,008	24.4%	34,000	5.2%
Slovakia	119,072	2.5%	99,931	83.9%	16,097	13.5%
Sweden	1,077,596	12.0%	456,262	42.3%	215,241	20.0%
TOTAL	30,883,799		10,090,753	32.7%	8,859,222	28.7%

There are almost 31 million foreign-born within these 18 states, of which 63% live in France, the UK and Germany. Similarly, of the 10 million migrants from within the EU, almost 60% reside in these three states. There are some interesting variations. Some states derive a significant proportion of their immigrants from their former colonies, this in no small way being related to language and culture. This partly accounts for the relatively low proportion of EU migrants in such states. In other states, most notably Luxembourg, Slovakia, Ireland and the Czech Republic, the proportion of foreign-born residents from within other EU states is high. On the other hand, on the eastern borders of the EU the proportion of immigrants from non-EU countries is high.

We can now consider the different flows of population within the EU by looking at the place of origin of expatriates from the EU resident in another EU country. What stands out is the heavy concentration of movement across neighbouring frontiers. Also, countries which practice selective immigration policies based on human capital criteria tend to be among the countries which have the highest percentage of highly qualified immigrants (Table 2.4):

Table 2.4 Number and distribution of OECD expatriates by level of education

State	Total expatriates	No. with tertiary level qualifications	Percentage of total
Austria	366,024	105,149	45.9%
Belgium	321,544	108,797	33.1%
Czech Republic	215,879	53,084	25.2%
Denmark	173,009	59,905	37.4%

Table 2.4 (Continued)

State	Total expatriates	No. with tertiary level qualifications	Percentage of total
Finland	265,245	67,358	26.3%
France	1.013,581	348,432	36.4%
Germany	2,933,757	865,255	30.4%
Greece	735,430	118,318	16.6%
Hungary	314,922	90,246	29.6%
Ireland	792,316	186,554	27.5%
Italy	2,430,339	300,631	13.0%
Luxembourg	27,164	7,115	27.9%
The Netherlands	616,909	209,988	36.1%
Poland	1,276,482	328,058	26.6%
Portugal	1,268,726	82,938	6.7%
Slovak republic	374,570	51,798	14.0%
Spain	763,013	137,708	18.7%
Sweden	206,604	78,054	40.1%
UK	3,229,676	1,265,863	41.2%

Source: Dumont and Lemaitre (2005)

Thus Australia, Canada and New Zealand have 45.9%, 40.6% and 44.6% of OECD expatriates with tertiary level qualifications. However, the UK, Korea, the USA and Japan have between 40% and 50% of OECD expatriates with such qualifications. In the USA, more than 440,000 foreign-born persons hold a PhD, a number that equates to 25% of the total stock of PhDs in the country. The proportion of foreign-born doctorates in Sweden is similar, while in Australia and Canada it is 45% and 54% respectively.

It does seem that some EU countries are losing a disproportionate number of their graduates, with 36.4% of French expatriates being graduates compared with 16.9% of the native-born population, and 18.1% of foreign-born residents. The comparable figures for Germany are 30.4%, 19.5% and 15.5%; for Hungary 29.6%, 10.7% and 19.8%; and for Sweden 40.1%, 22.8% and 24.2% respectively. In all EU countries other than Portugal, the proportion of the population who are highly skilled expatriates is higher than the proportion of the population who are expatriates. This is a measure of the greater propensity for those with higher qualifications to be geographically mobile. However, this loss tends to be made up by the number of highly qualified immigrants who enter the country. The net loss of those with tertiary level education is found only in Poland, Ireland, Finland, Hungary and Slovakia. The proportion of expatriates who are graduates exceeds 50% in the USA and Japan. Evidently, most OECD countries are benefiting from the international mobility of the highly skilled.

It is only Spain, Sweden and Luxembourg of the EU countries that are net beneficiaries of highly skilled migration from other OECD countries. The UK has 700,000 more highly skilled expatriates in OECD countries than it has highly skilled immigrants from other countries. The figures for Germany are 500,000, and for Poland 300,000. France and Belgium have almost as many highly skilled immigrants from OECD countries as they have expatriates to the same countries.

When we consider the difference between highly skilled emigrants to OECD countries and highly skilled immigrants from all countries, the USA gains more than 8.2 million people. France and Germany also gain. Highly skilled immigrants account for more than 20% of the highly skilled labour force only in Luxembourg. The percentage of the highly skilled who are expatriates is less than 10% for all EU countries other than the former Czechoslovak Republic, Portugal, Germany, Luxembourg and Ireland. On the other hand, more than 10% of the highly skilled born in Portugal, Austria and the UK live in other OECD countries, and more than 20% of those born in Ireland and Luxembourg.

In contrast, of the foreign-born population in Belgium, France, Finland, Italy, the Netherlands, Portugal and Spain, at least 50% have less than upper-secondary education. In Austria the difference between the per-centage of low-qualified among the foreign-born and the native-born populations is 16%. The situation is similar in Poland and the Czech Republic.

Within the 29 OECD countries, 36.3 million or 46% of the foreign-born population derive from another OECD country. For the EU states there are over 17 million expatriates, of whom over 4 million are highly qualified expatriates. Of these, 31% derive from the UK, and an even higher propor-tion is from states where almost all graduates are fluent in English. Over a third of the expatriates from the UK, Sweden, Belgium, Denmark, France and Latvia are highly qualified. In the host countries Luxembourg, the Slovak Republic, Ireland, the Czech Republic, Switzerland and Belgium, the share of the foreign-born from other OECD countries is between 65% and 85%. In contrast, in Hungary and Poland it is close to 24%. A high proportion of the native-born population of some states is expatriates in another OECD country. Thus Ireland has almost 24% of the people born in the country living in other OECD countries, while Portugal has 13.7% and Luxembourg 12.8%.

There are also some specific nuclei of foreign-born in the OECD coun-tries. Thus the Korean community in France (13,400) is larger than those of all the other European countries, most of them working in high-tech industries. Other similar communities are the Japanese in France (14,300) and the UK (37,500), or the 450,000 US-born living in Europe. Of the

4.6 million European-born living in the USA, almost 50% have tertiary level qualifications. When we consider the issue of the selective migration of highly qualified personnel, we find some countries with a higher proportion of highly qualified immigrants than there are highly qualified native-born people. Thus in France, Austria and Switzerland, there is a 20 percentage point difference between the numbers in the respective categories, while Hungary and Denmark also stand out in this respect. They contrast with Portugal and the Slovak Republic (Table 2.5).

Table 2.5 Proportion of highly qualified native-born to foreign-born by state

State	Tertiary/ native-born	Tertiary/ foreign-born	PhD/ native-born	PhD/ foreign-born
Austria	10.9	11.3	–	–
Belgium	22.9	21.6	0.4	1.1
Czech Republic	10.2	12.8	0.4	0.7
Germany	19.5	15.5	–	–
Denmark	18.8	19.5	0.2	0.2
Spain	19.4	21.8	0.5	1.0
Finland	23.4	18.9	0.5	1.0
France	16.9	18.1	–	–
UK	20.1	34.8	–	–
Greece	13.4	15.3	0.9	0.9
Hungary	10.7	19.8	–	–
Ireland	22.7	41.0	0.3	1.2
Luxembourg	12.8	21.7	–	–
The Netherlands	19.5	17.6	–	–
Poland	10.4	11.9	0.3	0.9
Portugal	7.7	19.3	0.1	0.5
Slovak Republic	10.0	14.6	–	–
Sweden	22.8	24.2	0.7	1.5

Source: Dumontand Lemaitre (2005)

The biggest expatriate population from non-OECD countries involves the former USSR with 4.2 million, the former Yugoslavia with 2.2 million, India with 1.9 million, the Philippines with 1.8 million and China with 1.7 million. Among persons with tertiary level education there are 1.3 million from the USSR and 1 million from India. Some of the smaller countries lose as many as 80% of their highly qualified population to such migration. The highest brain drain rates are found in the anglophone countries in Africa. It is also high in Central America whose population tends to move to the USA. Emigration of highly skilled personnel from former USSR countries to OECD countries remains moderate relative to the total stock of highly qualified personnel.

While many Third World countries are losing from the population flows, they are gaining in another way. According to the IMF, their emigrants send more money back to the Third World than is received through direct foreign investment, a sum of $160 billion in 2005, and $200 billion in 2006. This does not include any informal transfer of funds which could be substantial for Muslims who use the hawala, or to China and India which have other mechanisms of transfer. In the poorest countries for every dollar of international aid, the emigrants contributed 6 dollars. In Senegal it is estimated that these sources constitute 50% of the domestic budget. Similarly in 2004, in Tonga they accounted for 31.1% of the GDP. The largest beneficiaries were China, India and Mexico (Table 2.6):

Table 2.6 Principal sources and beneficiaries of emigrant money, 2004

Source state	Amount in US dollars (in billions)	Beneficiary state	Percentage of GDP	Country	Sum received in billions of US dollars
USA	38.8	Tonga	31.1%	India	21,727
Saudi Arabia	13.6	Maldives	27.1%	China	21,283
Switzerland	12.8	Lesotho	25.8%	Mexico	18,143
Germany	10.4	Haiti	24.8%	France	12,650
Luxembourg	5.6	Bosnia-Herzegovina	22.5%	Philippines	11,634
Russia	5.5	Jordan	20.4%	Spain	6,859
Spain	5.3	Jamaica	17.4%	Belgium	6,840
France	4.9	Serbia-Montenegro	17.2%	Germany	6,497
Italy	4.7	Salvador	16.2%	UK	6,350
Malaysia	3.5	Honduras	15.5%	Serbia-Montenegro	4,129
The Netherlands	3.3	Philippines	13.5%	Pakistan	3,945
UK	3.0	Dominican	13.2%	Brazil	3,575
Belgium	2.7	Lebanon	12.4%	Bangladesh	3,372
S. Korea	2.5	Samoa	12.4%	Egypt	3,341
Kuwait	2.1	Tajikistan	12.1%	Portugal	3,212
Austria	2.0	n.a.	n.a.	Vietnam	3,200

Source: Global Economic Prospects 2006; Economic Implications of Remittances and Migration. World Bank (December 2005)

However, it can hardly be claimed that this offsets the enormous loss that the poorer states experience by reference to the value of the highly qualified emigrants for internal economic development.

Language Use

The preceding discussion has presented a picture of a new economic order within which there is a profound restructuring of economic organisations across state boundaries. This is related not only to facets of the New Economy, but also to how it leads to new alignments of firms and corporations that link within networks which transcend states, societies and cultures. Furthermore, given that many of the corporations that have derived from mergers and acquisitions are not obliged to retain even their head office in any given state, but can move in search of fiscal advantage, there is a churning of the labour market associated with these kinds of firms and corporations. The flow of population partly relates to these developments, with states and corporations cooperating in establishing the legal conditions whereby international labour markets can become much more flexible. Given the global recruitment practices of many of these firms we are discussing a truly multinational labour force. A rather obvious question pertains to how members of such a labour force communicate and, more specifically, which languages are used for which function and operation.

As labour markets are deregulated and many New Economy companies are purchased, and often relocated, there is an enhanced need for employment in these companies to demand a knowledge of one or other of a limited number of *lingue franche*. English predominates in this respect. These companies recruit their labour force globally, employing the best graduates and offering them significant financial incentives while they are still studying. However, Castells (2006: 58) estimates that only some 200 million of the world workforce of 3000 million workers find work through the 53,000 or so MNCs and their ancillary networks. Yet this workforce is responsible for 40% of global GDP, and two-thirds of world trade.

It seems that just under 4.5 million European citizens with tertiary level qualifications are mobile across state boundaries within Europe. This constitutes about 1.4% of the total population. Countries that have selective immigration policies have the highest proportion of highly educated persons among immigrants (30%–42%). Clearly, the picture of the international movement of highly skilled and highly qualified personnel is complicated. One factor that does prevail is the tendency for much of this movement to focus either on countries whose state language is English or on companies who use English as the primary language of their activities. Given such a cosmopolitan labour force, at least at the higher occupational levels, there will be a tendency to resort to specific *lingue franche* as the working languages of many of their activities, regardless of location. Among these languages English is by far the most common. This cosmopoliteness is the consequences not only of heightened geographical mobility within more open labour markets, but also of the massive extent of takeovers and mergers referred to above. Clearly, there is a profound circulation of highly skilled labour moving globally. Much of this movement is related to the New Economy. While the numbers may not be massive, they are significant. While it is evident that there is a degree of exchange across all states, there seems also to be a general trend towards the movement of highly skilled European personnel from Europe to North America, the net loss being made up by the movement of other highly skilled workers from the rest of the world to Europe.

As early as 1988 it was reported that English is used by Danish companies in over 80% of their international business contacts and communications (Firth, 1996). This is partly a consequence of how the large multinationals tend to establish or sustain previously established joint ventures with local companies, using English as their *lingua franca*. Elsewhere in Europe, particularly in the new east European member states, German is widely used. Hagen (1993) claims that in some locations German is widely used in informal communication, but less so for the formal activities of reading and writing. This implies that any company must recruit staff which have competence in more than one of the *lingue franche*, preferably in three of the four such languages – English, French, German and Spanish. Given that companies will increasingly engage with transactions outside of Europe, it would appear that English predominates in such transactions. The German Chambers of Commerce recommend the use of English as the sole language of communication for transactions with 64 countries. German is recommended as a co-language for 25 countries and Spanish for 17 (Ammon, 1995). In this respect, it leads to conceiving of English as a global *lingua franca* and English, French, German and Spanish as European *lingue franche*. Given the extent of trade involving Japan, the USA and Europe which, between them, accounted for 55% of world wealth in 1990, it would appear that this is fully justified (Graddol, 2000: 29).

Among the more comprehensive surveys of language use among multinationals is the 2003 OFEM Survey of 501 enterprises operating from France. English is reported as the principle language spoken by the non-francophone clientele (89%), followed by German (44%), Spanish (36%), Italian (17%), Arabic (6%), Chinese (4%) and Japanese (4%). The mastering of English was sufficiently important for a third of the companies interviewed to organise or finance an English language course for their employees (http://www.ofem.ccip.fr/documents/

Linguistique.pdf). How languages are used by a multinational workforce is a more complicated issue.

The ELAN study (CILT, 2006) drew together the results of three studies on language use in European business that covered 10 states. Where fewer than half the companies in the UK used at least one foreign language, the percentage was between 82% and 98% in the other states. Polish companies relied heavily on the use of German whereas Portuguese companies tended to use French and Spanish. English prevailed as the most common language, but German also held a strong position. Ireland was the country with the best figures for fluent, bilingual speakers, which is surprising, given the restricted profile of language teaching and learning in its schools (Williams *et al.*, 2007). A high proportion of the companies indicated that they undertook language training, and that this was likely to increase in the near future. In addition there emerges a picture of cultural miscommunication, especially between European companies on the one hand, and Middle East and Asian companies on the other.

This tendency is accompanied by a parallel tendency for English to become the international vector of academic visibility in the various social and scientific disciplines. This is linked to the validation of scientific credibility in the sense that publication becomes highly targeted and specific, involving validation in the 'best' journals which increasingly involve the single use of English. Scholars are integrated into an international network which operate increasingly through the medium of English (Table 2.7):

Table 2.7 Number of works – articles, books, chapters, communications – in economic science by political unit

Political unit	*Number*
UK	20,824
Massachusetts	12,983
Germany	11,793
California	11,164
Canada	9,764
Italy	7,368
Washington DC	7,368
New York	7,288
France	7,059
The Netherlands	6,141
Spain	5,728

Source: Research Papers in Economics, Department of Economics, University of Connecticut, April, 2006

This has profound implications for the use of language within the associated kinds of occupations.

There are signs that we are already seeing evidence of an increasing shift towards English in what have been the most linguistically intransigent states. In France, the percentage of job offers mentioning the mastering of one or more foreign languages varies according to sector, from 10% in Health, Social and Cultural to 49% in Technical Services (Table 2.8). There is little doubt that the majority of these firms have English in mind as the 'desirable language'.

Table 2.8 Percentage of job adverts requesting knowledge of languages other than French in France by occupational sector

Sector	*Percentage*
Health, social, cultural	10%
Tertiary activity	19%
Human resources	21%
ICT	24%
General management	26%
Marketing, commercial	30%
Production	32%
Communication, creation	35%
Administrative management	36%
Finance	37%
Research and development	41%
Technical services	49%

Source: *Le Monde*, 14.4.04

These developments are generating a surge of nationalism constructed out of the relationship between state and language. Almost two-thirds of Europeans believe that it is necessary to protect their own languages as this process intensifies, the proportion being even higher in Greece, Finland, Portugal, Spain and Luxembourg (EC, 2001). Simultaneously, politicians are making protectionist statements based upon language rather than the less acceptable appeal for market protectionism.

A similar picture derives from Sweden where Gunarson (2006) studied the recruitment practices of five transnational companies. The international links in the websites of all these companies were extensive. For Ericsson the language of all of these links was English, whereas for ABB both English and the state language were used, and for the other three companies Swedish was the predominant language. Between them the websites of these companies held more than 100 job adverts. For Ericsson these adverts were presented only in English, whereas for Scania they were entirely in Swedish, while the use of English in the adverts of the other three companies varied between 10% and 30%. English was claimed to be an essential job qualification for all the jobs at Ericsson and Electrolux, but varied between 40% and 80% of the positions in the other three companies. Three other languages were mentioned – Russian, German and Spanish – but the highest incidence of referencing these languages for the positions was 30%. Gunnarsson (2006) concludes that Swedish has far less prominence than does English in the recruitment practices of these companies.

This conforms with Truchot's (2002) observation about how Siemens AG and Aventis adopted English as their company language at the end of the 1990s. There is also some evidence that even Japanese companies have located in an English-speaking environment (Hood & Truijens, 1993). Similarly, Amazon has recently relocated from the UK to Ireland, partly in order to take advantage of the diversity of language skills, presumably within a general English-language environment. However, without an effective language policy (Dhir & Goke-Pariola, 2002) difficulties of communication will prevail (Knapp, 1997).

The recent expansion of the EC eastwards has been seen as the consequence of how Germany wished to stabilise its eastern borders against instability. On the other hand, there is no doubt that the German language is more widely used in these states than in the rest of Europe. Thus Hagen (1993: 14) states:

> German is, understandably, in more widespread use than English in European regions bordering on Germany, thereby underlining a common misperception of English as the sole *lingua franca* of international business. This is apparent in the Dutch and Danish samples, where German is ahead of English in the use of oral-aural skills, though this order is reversed for reading and writing.

It allows for the possibility of German becoming one of the small number of *lingue franche*. As early as 1991, Ammon (1991: 158) showed that most German companies used the state language with subsidiaries located in foreign states. However, Hilgendorf (2006) comments that English is increasingly used exclusively in job adverts in Germany. She elaborates that English is the predominant language for international communication among the business managers she interviewed, and that this is regardless of the German language competence of the interlocuteur. A study of the communication between Danish firms with subsidiaries in France indicated that horizontal communication invariably depended upon a language-dependent network of personal relationships and that language use conformed with the language of the network members (Andersen & Rasmussen, 2004).

This underlines the point that few transnational firms have a single cultural or language use policy, but rather, they increasingly emphasise the relevance of collaborative cross-cultural learning. Cultural difference is regarded as an asset (CILT, 2006). However, it also appears that the use of language skills in such informal communication is ignored in most of the literature on informal communication (Marschan *et al.*, 1997). Firms without a coherent language strategy tend to muddle through, and fail to confront regular problems of communication. Yet there is also evidence to the contrary. There is also evidence that when a corporate policy for language and communication exists, it tends not to be rigorously implemented. More common is the application of an agreed language for legal and contractual affairs, with the flat management structures and the encouragement of informal networking between employees encouraging multilingualism. This places the monoglot employee at a distinct disadvantage. Certainly, considerable emphasis is placed on language skills when recruiting labour. Furthermore, language and intercultural training is common in such companies. The CILT (2006) study emphasised that companies exporting try to use the local language of the market wherever possible. If this is not possible they will try to resort to one of the European *lingue franche*, not necessarily English. In some states a variety of languages may be used within the same company. Elsewhere there will be institutionalised preferences, with Russian prevailing in Bulgaria, Spanish being used to export to Portugal and French being used in both Spain and Italy.

The ELAN survey of European companies (CILT, 2006) indicated that exporting SMEs were more likely to need European languages, especially French and German, whereas the larger multinationals favoured global languages including Spanish, Chinese, Arabic and Portuguese. English was required regardless of company size. Among the larger companies few believed that the company preferred to use its own language with international customers and most used English, a few using the customer's own language. There was an acute awareness of a shortage of language skills among these companies, especially by reference to English, Spanish and Chinese.

Spain, on the other hand, points to the large Spanish-speaking population in Latin America, a population that in most cases occupies states which have Spanish as the primary or only state language. They also argue that the recent upsurge in the number of Spanish speakers in the USA, a state which has the dominant global economy, also argues for an important role for Spanish as a global *lingua franca*.

The extension of the Free Trade Agreements between the USA and the Central American states – CAFTA – may well accelerate the need for Spanish among US workers. Already 35 million in the USA claim to know the language. This is despite the 'English only' campaign. A study by the Modern Language Association of America indicated that Spanish is the most studied language in US universities, with 746,602 in Spanish language courses, four times as many as are enrolled in French language classes, and seven times more than the number studying German.

While the trend is nothing like as significant as that in the USA, there is also a growth in the popularity of Spanish among European students. A study of 16 countries in central and eastern Europe by the Cervantes Institute claims that 123,000 students were enrolled in Spanish language courses in 2002–2003. These are students who have chosen this language for professional as well as cultural reasons. The same report claims that as many as 3.4 million Europeans claim Spanish as their second language. Within the EU 2.6 million or 10% of all students at the secondary level study Spanish, and a further 250,000 at the tertiary level and 300,000 in adult classes. Of these 60% are found in France, 15% in the UK and 11% in Germany.

There is one significant difference between the students of Spanish in Europe and the USA. In Europe 44% of those studying Spanish claimed to do so because 'they liked the language.' In contrast, 61% of students in the USA were studying Spanish for 'practical reasons'. This later response is interpreted as an indication of the value of Spanish for social and economic mobility in the USA. The Cervantes Institute Report claims that globalisation is of benefit to Spanish more than for other languages because of how the existence of a substantial number of Spanish speakers on both sides of the Atlantic ensures the demographic reproduction of the language, while the means of communication reduce the risk of linguistic fragmentation. Similarly, the use of Spanish in commerce and culture guarantees a market for the language as a 'foreign' language. Notwithstanding the risk of bias in a report produced by an institution with a vested interest, the point that is being made pertains to the value of Spanish over French, Italian or German.

The same report makes the significant point that the strength of Spanish as a second language in Europe is dwarfed by that of English, which is by far the most popular second language on the Continent. This is significant if we consider the expansion of the EC as a feature of globalisation. This is simply because of the effect of the expansion on the use of languages in the European Commission and its activities. Hitherto there has already been a shift towards prioritising the use of English, German and French in the EC administration. It is widely accepted that something must be done to restrict the number of languages used when 20 different state languages are involved. Translating everything across this number of languages would produce 380 combinations. In practice, the tendency is to revert to the use of a pivot language, more often than not, English.

The working languages of the Commission have been reduced to three –
English, French and German. In practice, the use of German is limited,
and since the inclusion of Sweden, Finland and Austria in 1995, the use
of French has probably diminished. Certainly, whereas in 1997, 40% of the
documents were reproduced in French, by today this has reduced to 30%.
The officials certainly do use both French and English as if it were a rule.
However, among the new additions to the EU, a knowledge of English is
far greater than that of French. This will reduce the use of French even further. Some claim that the process of deferring to the use of English is also a
consequence of the deferring of Francophones to the status of English (*Le
Monde*, 18.4.04).

   This situation is not helped by data pertaining to existing educational
practice across the 20 states. The following table indicates the extent to
which children aged 10 and 11 are taught languages in school (Table 2.9):

Table 2.9 Extent to which children aged 10 and 11 are taught languages in
school by state

State	No languages	One language	Two and more languages
Denmark	68.7%	31.3%	0%
Spain	24.6%	74.7%	0.8%
Finland	33.0%	52.5%	14.5%
France	54.7%	45.3%	0%
Greece	54.4%	44.8%	0.8%
Ireland	96.0%	4.0%	0%
Italy	57.6%	42.4%	0%
Luxembourg	0%	21.9%	78.1%
Sweden	38.1%	50.8%	11.1%
Bulgaria	82.1%	16.1%	1.8%
Cyprus	47.6%	52.4%	0%
Estonia	12.2%	87.8%	0%
Lithuania	69.3%	30.6%	0.1%
Slovenia	77.9%	22.1%	0%
Slovakia	85.5%	14.5%	0%
Czech Republic	58.4%	40.4%	n.a.

These figures do not support an argument for a future polyglot Europe,
capable of operating across several languages. This is emphasised once
we recognise the extent to which the education systems which purport
to teach a single 'foreign' language invariably opt for English as the
additional language (*Le Monde*, 14.4.04).

Labour Market Segmentation and Diglossia

There is little doubt that labour markets are becoming more flexible. The integration of capital markets and the establishment of a single currency require the homogenisation of macro-economic conditions across Europe. Opponents of labour market flexibility argue that labour laws which make workers more secure will encourage employees to invest in acquiring skills which will be of benefit in the workplace. However, they can also move these skills to another firm by migrating. It is argued that efficiency is improved by leaving it to the market forces to determine the tasks of the employee. Evidently, this requires a high degree of worker flexibility. However, it also implies that somehow skills are divorced from the working context, whereas proponents of the knowledge economy emphasise how skill and knowledge acquisition occurs within a team whose members work together. Furthermore, increased flexibility is claimed to be associated with low unemployment and higher GDP per head. It is also argued that imposing a single monetary regime on economies with different structures only leads to a breakdown in coordination. This occurs when expenditure-switching effects are dominated by the income effects of a greater policy discipline. The antidote is seen to be a heightened market flexibility.

There is also little doubt that the consequences of the Maastricht Treaty has involved how European policies have taken precedence over state policies in a number of areas including technology, research, regional development, immigration, justice and policing. A major consequence of the Single Market is the removal of barriers that have inhibited and even restricted the movement of labour. The Single Market is, as much as anything, a single labour market. However, the mobility of labour has been far slower in developing than has the movement of capital. Much of production remains locked in state, regional or even local contexts, and most workers remain within their region. Indeed, despite the polarisation of labour referred to above, there remain opportunities for burgher social mobility which, even if it does not involve the individual firm or enterprise, does remain local in context. It is true that the destabilisation of some parts of the world and the poverty gap between rich and poor countries have resulted in an increase in the flow of immigrants from outside of Europe.

As national companies become drawn into the MNCs, the structure of their activities will often change. Certain functions will be devolved offshore. There are also middle-level occupational functions that are taken over by the new technology, eliminating the need for human labour. This, in turn, generates a polarisation of labour between the high skill, high qualification functions at the top, and activities at the bottom which continue to resemble the activities of the industrial age economy. Sociologists have distinguished between two types of social mobility. The first involves spiralism, or the tendency to combine geographical and social mobility, each step up the ladder involving migration to a new location. The second involves being promoted within the same location in the same company – burgher mobility. It is claimed that the new technology is changing the structure of work, with computers increasingly replacing humans in middle-ranking occupations based upon precision and routine. The absence of this middle sector polarises the labour force while also making burgher mobility all but impossible. These developments, together with the outsourcing of many back office jobs, lead to employment growth being concentrated on the top and bottom occupational levels, thereby elaborating inequality in work. This bifurcation will often be accompanied by a form of intra-firm diglossia, where the state language is used within the lower-level activities, and one or other of the international *lingue franche* at the upper level.

For over 200 years states have tended to regulate the use of language among its citizens by its control of the economy and of the associated labour market. The link between education and the preparation of the citizen for the state labour market placed considerable emphasis on language competence vis-à-vis what were perceived as the needs of that labour market. Economic arguments claimed that uniformity within labour markets enhanced productivity. The existence of a single economy, operated by a single labour force recruited from the single labour market, using the same language, was an integral feature of the definition of a state and its authority. Indeed, some states went so far as to deny the franchise to non-speakers of the state language. The construction of a language as an object was a primary function of all states.

The loss of control of part of its labour market has profound implications for this functional relationship between the state, its economy and language. It involves far more than the simple anglicisation of the economy. The enhanced polarisation of the labour force involves a segmentation that is elaborated by the role of language. The higher-level New Economy occupations increasingly tend to focus upon the determining force of the large multinationals. However, they are accompanied by a range of small regional companies which will often develop relationships with the multinationals. The nature of the employment in the multinationals implies a high level of cosmopoliteness and a degree of geographic mobility, often associated with social mobility. The predominant language of employment will be one or other of the dominant *lingue franche* that will also be a *sine qua non* of employment qualifications. In contrast, the lower-level occupations will continue to operate by reference to the state or regional language and will be confined to the territory of the state or region.[2] Many state languages, and all regional languages, have no value outside of these boundaries. This has considerable implications for labour market segmentation in those states which do not use any of the *lingue franche* as a state language. For those in locations such as Denmark or Finland, the higher-level occupations will only be open to those who have a mastery of the *lingue franche*. Those who do not have these language skills will not be able to enter this segment of the labour market. Similarly, those at the lower end of the occupational structure will only require the state language for employment.

In a sense, this situation is not new for minority language speakers since the use of the state and minority languages for work has always segmented the labour market, unless the minority language is entirely excluded from employment. What we are beginning to witness is that the relationship between some languages such as Danish or Dutch and *lingua franca* such as English begins to resemble the conventional relationship between minority languages and the state languages within bilingual states. It remains to be seen if this process will continue to the point where the state language declines in significance in specific contexts. We are already seeing this by reference to Higher Education.

We are also witnessing the impact of social class upon a knowledge of the *lingue franche* across Europe, at least outside of those states whose state language is one or other of the *lingue franche*. A recent Eurobarometer survey indicates that across Europe as many as 49% of students and 47% of managers have foreign language skills in two languages other than their mother tongue, compared with 28% of the general population. English is already the second language for many in Europe, with 38% claiming to know English as well their mother tongue. Together with those who have English as their mother tongue, this means that 51% of the population have a knowledge of the language. The figure increases to 82% among the 15–24 age group. In contrast, French is a second language for 14%, German for 14% and Spanish for 6% of the population. Given this level of English-language competence, and the tendency for bi or multilingualism to increase with social class, it is probably fair to say that most of those with tertiary level qualifications in Europe also have a high degree of competence in English. Across all social classes the incidence of knowing English does vary by state, with about 89% of Swedes, Danes and Dutch, 60% of Luxembourgians, 63% of Finns, 56% of Germans and 58% of Austrians having a good mastery of the language. English is the first foreign language in Germany, France, Austria, Denmark, Greece, Spain, Italy, the Netherlands, Portugal, Finland and Sweden. About a quarter of the population claim to be competent in more than one language other than their mother tongue. Conversely, 44% claim to speak no other language than their mother tongue. Finally, 25% claim to use foreign languages in conversations at work (EC, 2006).

On the other hand, there are several forces responsible for promoting at least a degree of linguistic diversity. It should be clear that I am not merely discussing the simultaneous entry of every segment of the social and economic structures into a global economy. On the contrary, while the majority of the population of any state will inevitably engage with the intricacies and possibilities of ICT, they will do so on different grounds. This will include their relationship to work. Not all members of the labour market of any state will be involved with the large multinational establishments that operate on a global level within a global market. Many will remain operating within regional- or state-level activities where they are more likely to operate by reference to state or regional languages. This means that while the state may lose control of the upper segment of its labour market, it will retain control over the other segments. The consequences include the emergence of a diglossia not dissimilar to that which minority language groups have long experienced. The higher segments will increasingly use one or other, or several of the European *lingue france*, whereas the lower segments will retain the use of the state or regional language. How far this process will extend will largely depend upon the extent of the respective languages in work. What is also possible in a limited number of regions is that the regional language may replace the state language, unless the state language is also a *lingua franca*.

Conclusion

This chapter has focused on the intricacies of global economic restructuring. The New Economy lies at the heart of these developments, and its emergence leads to the spatial reordering of economic activity across the world. The discussion has indicated how the neo-liberal focus on the liberalisation of markets and the associated change in the regulating role of the state are generating profound changes throughout the world. Neo-liberal discourse maintains that a state should concentrate on the production of those goods for which it is best suited, with other goods being imported from other countries. This means that it relinquishes the ability to artificially determine the price of many goods that have been produced hitherto. It also loses control of facets of its labour market, involving a break in how the respective states have sought to control labour markets. While they are still able to control the flow of population across state boundaries, they are less relevant by reference to the increased flow of highly qualified personnel out of the respective states. This is a process that is enhanced as a consequence of how there has been a marked speed up in the number and scale of mergers and acquisitions. This develops large MNCs whose tie to any particular state is, at best, tenuous. The workers in these countries constitute a highly mobile and highly qualified workforce which tends to congregate in the urban cores of the New Economy developments. The educational background and the working experiences of these workers contribute to developing a common context that separates them from both the members of their own home societies and the host society. The MNCs also extend to incorporate a vast network of national, regional and local companies.

What seems to be clear is that there is an increasing use of a few *lingue franche* among the higher-level workers of many companies, especially within the large MNCs. As these institutions expand in size, scope and number, this tendency is likely to increase. However, there is also a limited amount of evidence which suggests that this is a tendency which sits side by side with the use of other languages within the workforce. That is, what we are beginning to recognise is the existence of an intra-firm or intra-corporate network form of diglossia. This runs parallel to the more orthodox form of diglossia which occurs when the languages of states which do not constitute one or other of the *lingue franche* overlap with segmented labour markets.

One disturbing feature of these developments is that it is not difficult to predict that if the present trend continues there will be a hegemony of English within Europe. It is a development that is largely driven by a limited awareness of the value of language, one that places a disproportionate relevance on the value of a language within the labour market. While relevant, as the following chapters underline, it is by no means the only consideration by reference to the knowledge economy.

This broad-brush overview of the relationship between language and economy does furnish a picture of what is happening at a global level. However, considerable more work needs to be undertaken before the details of this picture can be provided. Such work should focus on the relationship between the principles of work within the knowledge economy and the use of language. It is this that becomes the focus of the following chapters.

Notes

1. I have discussed the articulation of the new and the industrial age economy in Williams (2000).
2. However, those states which have opened their labour markets to the new member states are also experiencing the use of a range of European languages at the lower levels of the employment spectrum.

Chapter 3

Human Capital

Introduction

Having established the relationship between globalisation and the changing role of diverse languages in the New Economy I can now begin to consider the specifics of the relationship between the organisation of work and language use. This demands attention to the concepts that have been invoked in an attempt to highlight the conditions that contribute to a heightened propensity for the generation of knowledge. It involves a focus on what is known as human capital. In subsequent chapters I will discuss arguments that pertain to the role of regional culture as human capital, and how language as a form of human capital can be exploited in the organisation of work. For the moment, the discussion will focus upon the theoretical and conceptual issues that have been claimed to be of relevance for an understanding of human capital. This involves an understanding of how human capital is operationalised such that it plays an effective role in knowledge generation. Such an objective requires rethinking the structure–agency relationship of sociology to accommodate a greater role for the human subject, and the understanding of social practice.

The focus on individual and group learning within the knowledge economy involves the accumulation and exchange of social knowledge. The implication is that much productive and practical knowledge is of a group character. The communication of knowledge is largely a tacit process that operates through interaction. As an essential basis to all knowledge, tacit knowledge must, somehow, be shared through intuitions and tacit meanings. Furthermore, knowledge is a constantly dynamic, emergent, entity that draws upon prior knowledge in developing new shades. At the heart of this process are language and culture as features of human capital.

It is important here to distinguish between social and cultural capital, since the different theoretical problematics involve contrasting understandings of the social, and its relationship to culture. Inevitably, the focus on the individual as the carrier of human capital involves a focus on the notion of culture, or how human behaviour is conditioned by the normative order of rules, values, etc. Thus the difference between social and cultural capital involves the former pertaining to the connections between people, or social networks and structures, and the associated institutional and organisational setting (Putnam, 1993); and the later to the norms, values and attitudes that relate to these connections. In many respects, there is an attempt to pinpoint the relationship between *zeitgeist*, or the social and cultural environment, and the 19th-century German tradition that emphasised the true realisation of the unique capacities of the individual.

Coleman (1988) argues that human capital pertains to the individual, whereas social capital derives from relationships between individuals and social groups. Where human capital adheres to the individual, thereby moving with that individual, social capital remains embedded in the context. The fundamental proposition which derives from these arguments is that membership in groups, whether or not they are manifestly political, builds social capital that, in turn, produces the basis for a more cooperative society, and for political democracy. Given the centrality of cooperation within the productive process of the knowledge economy, and how it relates to communities of practice, it is not surprising that this argument has become a prominent feature of much of the debate about the New Economy. It emphasises systems of trust and obligations, networks of information dissemination, norms and sanctioning systems, etc., all of which involve networking phenomena.

Much of the discussion has focused upon the state and democracy as the sites of trust. In Chapter 1, it was argued that globalisation is undermining the orthodoxies of the nation-state, promoting a form of multilayered governance, involving a shift in focus to the transnational and the regional. This has profound implications for the nature of civil society and its relationship to the state. It has equally profound implications for the nature of a democracy within which the paternalistic, all-protecting state constitutes a form of trust constructed around social protection. There is a shift to the local as the site of trust.

These developments overlap with changes in the nature of modernity. Tradition, in the form of the stable institutions that define the individual, was important for the formulation of local communities as mutually bonding social aggregates. Meaning, morality and justice were preordained. They give way to a strong sense of individualism around which the notion of free choice prevails. Each individual is now obliged to engage with their communities of choice in elaborating their quest for trust and solidarity. Given these developments we are obliged to consider their implications for the generation and promotion of human capital. Many of the concepts and social evaluations discussed below derive from an understanding of society that has been undermined. What form of alternative can we provide? One such direction is offered by a shift in the understanding of behaviour away from its conception as the consequence of position within a social structure to a focus on the ongoing processes of social practice.

Culture

Since at least the 18th century, culture has been treated as the cement responsible for creating the social cohesion that is the essential basis of the notion of citizen. Culture is understood as shared customs which contribute to social cohesion. Much of the discussion involves how shared values condition the existence and practice of trust. This is a theme which preoccupied Durkheim who emphasised how social rules and norms are essential features of even market-based economies. In contrast, neoclassical economics has tended to conceptualise trust and culture by reference to how they derive from utility maximising, individual agents. This position has been criticised for how it misses the specific cultural aspects and social relations involved in the generation and exploitation of trust. Both Weber and Veblen claimed that labour and business are tied into the system of cultural values and the associated normative structure of society.

This criticism is also an argument that is made against how market individualism emphasises that the individual is the best judge of her own welfare (Hayek, 1944: 44). While acknowledging that there are individual variations in personal knowledge, perceptions and values, it is also essential to recognise that the individual is an organic part of society, and behaves in accordance with what is learnt through interaction with others. Learning and practicing categories of thought and action that are necessary in order to make sense of the world, and to constitute each individuality within the social, derive from how we experience the world through others. How we invest information with meaning relies on conceptual frameworks and categories that derive from language and culture. However, this is not meant as an expression of cultural determinism.

Culture tends to be conceptualised as the set of shared interpretations that members of society learn about, the values, beliefs and norms and how they influence most members of that society. In most definitions, culture is linked to communication and a wide range of human experience, including feelings, identity and the construction of meaning. Thus identity is conceptualised as a process wherein individuals draw on culture in constructing meaning in life. Communication is the vehicle by which meanings are negotiated and conveyed, identity is composed and reinforced and feelings are expressed. It is argued that since we communicate using different cultural habits and meaning systems, both conflict and harmony are possible outcomes of any interaction. Such processes do not necessarily operate through rational calculation on the part of individuals, but tend to be thought of by reference to social practice as institutionalised behaviour. Whatever the theoretical construction, culture is characterised by an organic unity that imparts a distinctive and shared meaning to every aspect and event. It is something that lies beyond those who construct it, but it is also that which defines them per se. The heuristic value of the notion involves how it focuses on crucial aspects of social and cultural relations that influence economic and political life, but which are difficult to incorporate into an explanatory model based on the rational pursuit of individual self-interest. That is, it incorporates non-market factors into accounts of the political and economic behaviour of individuals and groups.

Despite the overriding emphasis on the relationship between the state and the uniformity of a culture that is shared by all citizens, there has also been a school of thought that emphasises the importance of class culture. Given the prioritising of 'national' culture this is sometimes treated as a sub-culture. Others assign the totality to social classes rather than the state. This emphasis on class culture does allow an understanding of class relations as social process, including an elaboration of the social processes of cultural production. To an extent it also overcomes the tendency for the universalism/particularism debate to involve a polarisation between a liberalism that has no time for culture and a communitarianism that places the entire emphasis on the group and its culture. Where culture is understood as a signifying system '. . . through which necessarily (though among other means) a social order is communicated, reproduced, experienced and explored' (Williams, R., 1980: 13), the relationship between culture, sub-culture and social structure is highlighted. Evidently, this relationship must be understood as a dynamic process whereby culture contributes to the social while also being influenced by it. Thus the signifying practices, whether they involve language or culture, or both, are also subject to change.

There is also a relationship between language and culture. This relates to how the social sciences have adopted the principles of universalism and the role of the state in that universalism. Thus the tendency for each state to proclaim a single language and a single culture leads to a simple correlation between the two. However, this relationship is not an easy one to operationalise. It can be argued that culture is transmitted through language, that is, as a means of communication, language conveys the features of the culture of the interlocuteurs. On the other hand, it is also argued that culture informs the social and political nature of language. Again we are confronted by the distinction between language as an object and language as the basis for the constitution of the subject. The two are brought into relationship in the claim that communicative interaction is an autonomous area within which cultural traditions are historically transmitted, and social relations are institutionalised (Thompson, 1984: 256).

Two further points remain to be made by reference to culture. The opening chapters discussed how globalisation restructures the economy and the relationship between languages, referring to language as an object. This involves a discussion of how the nature of specific languages changes in relation to changes in the political economy. On the other hand, in discussing the role that language plays in the working processes of the knowledge economy I will focus on the role that language plays in the constitution of the subject, and its relationship to the social construction of meaning. The argument here focuses on the different processes involved in meaning construction and how they vary across languages. Culture intervenes in how these processes relate to creativity.

This emphasis on culture has often involved extrapolating some fundamental principles that operate at the micro-economic level, and elaborating them within global contexts. The net results are grand theories about the relationship between political systems, their capacity for promoting specific forms of human capital and relevant social practice and the potential for economic growth. That is, the notion of culture is acknowledged as something that pertains to entire populations, but which, on the other hand, is operationalised by individuals. It is a manifestation of structure and agency, and reflects many of the issues that pertain to this dualism.

Trust and Cooperation

There is broad agreement about the importance of trust and cooperation for successful knowledge generation. It is argued that trust in someone leads to voluntarily engaging with them in a particular course of action. This, in turn, relies on reciprocal action by the other party. Even in situations of high risk, trust plays an important role. This trust relies on shared values and the sharing of a moral code that is conditioned by culture. The cooperation based on trust is beyond financial calculation, even if such a calculation is not entirely absent (Williams, 1976). The debates tend to divide between those that focus on the nature of the best socio-political system for the promotion of trust and cooperation and those which emphasise the significance of how the resources of human capital can be exploited within specific working environments and the interactive processes that they encompass.

The difference between human and social capital informs how social capital pertains to cooperation. Norms and values do not pertain to the individual, but they are viewed as resources for individuals who have access to particular social contexts. The norms of reciprocity and trust, characteristic of a specific group in a specific context, help to promote the appropriate behaviour within the appropriate context, and will only apply in that context. They are not features that can be transferred to other contexts within which they may be of little or no value. Norms and values held by individuals only become social capital if they facilitate action by others. Consequently, not only is each form of capital dependent upon specific contexts for its realisation, but both the capital and access to it will not be evenly distributed within any society, and not all individuals will have equal opportunity to access the various forms of capital. Spatial or regional variation in supply and demand influences the salience of social capital. Thus, the value of cultural competence that pertains to a particular language may apply in one location, but not another, where it may even be devalued.

Economic relations rely heavily upon trust if they are to operate effectively. That is, social practice is dyadic in nature, relying upon the conformity of the other with the expectations of the actor. Outcomes are beyond the control of any individual, and rely upon trust in the other. This is as true of business relations as it is of any other kind of relationship. Denzau and North (1994: 20) state:

> ...a market economy is based on the existence of a set of shared values such that trust can exist. The morality of a business person is a crucial intangible asset of a market economy, and its consequence substantially raises transaction costs.

Here they are linking trust and culture. Indeed, Fukuyama defines social capital in such terms when he claims that social capital involves '... the ability of people to work together for common purposes in groups and organisations' (1995: 10). Others (Nahapiet & Ghoshal, 1998) claim that trust is only one component of social capital, stating that innovation is the product of collective problem-solving, leading to the development of new ideas which are facilitated by three dimensions of social capital – the structural which involves network ties and how they are configured; the cognitive where codes, meanings and narratives are shared; and the rational involving trust, norms, obligations and personal identity which often derive from shared networks. Institutional and cultural bonds have an important role in underpinning trust.

The emphasis of neoclassical economists on the link between culture and utility maximisation by individual agents ignores how trust does not derive simply from individual rational calculation. Calculation by reference to the maximisation of individual utility would miss the cultural context, and the social relations involved in the production and reproduction of trust. This is delicately put by Schumpter (1976: 423–424):

> ...no social system can work which is based exclusively upon a network of free contracts between equal contracting parties and in which everyone is supposed to be guided by nothing except his own utilitarian ends.

Capitalism has relied on non-contractarian norms of obligation that are largely determined by local or national culture.[1] An overly individualised market system is simply not feasible. This relates to Durkheim's insistence on a *conscience collective* that explicitly elaborates the claim that society is not simply the sum of the individuals within it. It is here that the norms of loyalty and trust reside.

As a socially embedded notion, social capital focuses attention upon social networks and organisation. There is a danger that operationalising social capital by reference to trust and participation ignores social structure. The emphasis on norms and values results in networks being conceptualised as merely the bearers and sources of individual-level attributes. Where trust is claimed to play an important role is in the micro-processes of the organisation of work. The shift away from Taylor's organising principles of work, towards collaborative work involving team work and integrated workflows, provides the possibility of opportunistic collective behaviour constructed around trust. When work is organised within formal controls such as sanctioning and monitoring systems, the incentive for opportunistic behaviour has to be reduced in order to sanction enhanced cooperation. The mere presence of a control system causes decision makers to view the collaborative setting as non-cooperative, and other collaborators as untrustworthy.

It is sometimes claimed that the simple fact of sharing a common language generates trust. On the other hand, there is little theoretical support for such a claim. It implies that there is some emotive context involved in sharing a language that somehow pertains to common identities, and that shared identities are indicative of common trust. It is a view that is encapsulated in the notion of a 'speech community', where community is conceptualised in consensus terms as the essence of cooperation and trust. This is perhaps not surprising given how universalism has stimulated a view that the national culture invokes a commonality that is shared by all citizens, and how this is integrated with the sharing of the 'national' language. Furthermore, since the 19th century the understanding of the state has incorporated the understanding that the state is constructed as the sum of all communities within its boundaries. Consensus and commonality are the essential ingredients of such discourses. What it ignores are the bases of division and power that are internal to the 'national' society. This is a theme pursued by Bourdieu, as discussed below.

A more sophisticated expression of such a view is inherent in Habermas's argument that the speech-act is the source of '. . . intersubjective mutuality of reciprocal understanding, shared knowledge, mutual trust and accord with one another' (Habermas, 1979: 24–25). It is a view shared with the exponents of ethnography of communication. On the other hand, in contrast to the arguments of the ethnography of communication, Habermas focuses on the relations of production and a social integration unified through values and norms. His fundamental assumption is that society is constituted by communication, and that '. . . other forms of social action – for example, conflict, competence, strategic action in general – are derivatives of action orientated to reaching understanding'

(Callinicos, 1983: 143). Thus his anti-naturalism stance separates communicative action involving language and culture from instrumental action. Furthermore, like Bourdieu, the importance of universalism for Habermas results in an emphasis on assimilation by reference to non-state languages.

Habermas's work encompasses an attempt to formulate a universalism that is not encompassed by Hegel's philosophy of consciousness. In pursuing this goal he substitutes language for consciousness. This allows him to elaborate a form of normative totality that pertains to an ideal speech situation, structured in language itself. Communicative action derives from the rules of linguistic competence, while also serving as the framework for the legitimation of public space in society. Complexity becomes a liberating force that frees the individual from the dictatorship of instrumental reason. On the other hand, this complexity is grounded in, and is also the surface manifestation of, simple generative rules. Complexity is a problem of rationality.

He argues that there can be a sphere of communicative action of uncoerced, ideal speech situations that does not try and artificially erase boundaries between social systems, yet makes the diverse systems of modern rationalisation intelligible to individuals in the lifeworlds, while providing them with norms that are discursively developed. Here he conforms with a privileged view of society as a whole without giving up on the notion of a differentiated society. This leads him to elaborate a Wittgensteinian framework that emphasises language play as a localisation of rationality that makes rationality context-specific. Each form of rationality is determined by the system of language games of which it is a part. However, each form is constituted by the community of each particular game, and by the rules that are tacitly agreed. Again we confront the notion of a totality that consists of a multiplicity of communities. Furthermore, each community betrays an implicit or explicit consensus that derives from an identity with the community that legitimises its activities. Each community is bounded and thereby excludes while also including. Local reason is restricted to the community.

The overlap between different language games and a proliferation of social systems is subordinated to an ideal speech situation in which a discourse that is abstracted from the needs and actions of daily life grounds assertions through an argumentation that is agreed upon by the participants. This merely allows the presentation of arguments rather than transmitting information, influencing actions or presenting experience. Habermas then argues for a 'better argument' that is determined through communal consensus. This consensus serves as a formal model of non-coercive argumentation whereby knowledge reflects a rational common will remote from private interests.

Locally grounded language games give way to a metalanguage game or an idealised speech situation. This metalanguage game is grounded in a critical form of reflexivity. Reflection takes the form of reconstitution and allows Habermas to base normative discourse in the structure of language. He proceeds to identify two kinds of reflection. Self-reflection involves '... the reflection upon the conditions of potential abilities of a knowing, speaking and acting subject as such ...' (Habermas, 1987: 377). This makes the tacit rules that determine competence explicit. On the other hand, self-reflection as critique involves the '... critical dissolution of subjectively constituted pseudo-objectivity' (Habermas, 1987: 377). There is an engagement of rule-competence and practical consequences such that unconscious elements are made conscious.

These views of Habermas betray a great deal in common with the work of Chomsky on deep and surface systems as they relate to 'competence and performance' (Chomsky, 1965). However, Habermas goes out of his way to play down the essentialism on Chomsky's arguments. It is particularly evident in how sentences are transformed into speech acts. He identifies the possibility of undistorted speech in the underlying formal structures of language. In this respect, it is very much an engagement between theoretical and practical reasoning. It is also an argument against the claim that language reflects reality.

The work of Garfinkel involved the process of breaking the rule in order to establish the nature of the rule. That is, the intelligibility of discourse provides a sense of ontological security for the subjects of the discourse. The subjects that are constituted in and through discourse sit in specific relations to other subjects and a plethora of objects. Whether or not one treats the tacit rules of discursive relationships as a structure, there is no denying their institutional forms, and it is this form that provides the ontological security to which Giddens (1984: 50) refers. Habermas's ideal conception of the ideal speech context provides one perspective on such contexts for shared meaning in the routine of social life. It provides the basis whereby interaction between subjects that relate to the thread of discourse is elaborated as the positive and constructive meeting of selves and identities.

There appears to be a consensus concerning the relationship between trust and the organisational and institutional context within which it is fostered and promoted. This is expressed in a variety of ways and involves a range of institutional contexts, ranging from the state to the work team. The following discussion strives to consider the relevance of changes in the understanding of this organisational and institutional context and how they influence our understanding of trust.

Democracy and Growth

Some of the debate about the relationship between democracy and economic growth is a reaction to the demise of state socialism and its focus upon centralised ownership and control. Neither Lenin nor Trotsky had much enthusiasm for markets, even though they recognised the need for them, at least within the transition to socialism. It was perhaps Gramsci (1971) who contributed to a more tolerant and pluralistic Marxism, leading to arguments in favour of a democratic socialism involving decentralisation and local autonomy (Hodgson, 1999: 25). This led to integrating a democratic and decentralised socialism with decentralised property rights and a role for markets. Nonetheless, the tendency has been to oppose democracy and markets on the one hand, with socialism, common ownership and central control on the other. The demise of socialism has led to a form of triumphalism, and a new enthusiasm for a debate about the relationship between democracy and economic growth. Indeed, some may even claim that the demise of socialism and the adoption of neo-liberalism have generated a missionary thrust for a global democracy.[2]

Trust, social cohesion and cooperation are claimed to be the essential ingredients of democracy. Consequently, it is hardly surprising that the relationship between democracy and economic growth is at the core of many of the discussions about the successful generation of knowledge. On the other hand, a major problem associated with the claim for a relationship between democracy and economic growth is how the market fosters competition and individualism as opposed to trust and cooperation. An awareness of such issues has been responsible for specific forms of political economic structures such as the Third Way, or the networking of firms that collaborate and cooperate in production and marketing.

At the heart of the neo-liberal argument in favour of democracy is the notion of the autonomous individual who accepts responsibility and accountability, whether this is in civic or economic activity. Such an individual operates by reference to an open market, with market activities placing constraints on behaviour, while also offering opportunities. There is a need for the state to promote the opportunities for such behaviour, while also withdrawing from any control of markets. This rolling back of the state should leave the individual in control of her resources, both human and capital, and in a position to develop the enterprise by reference to market forces.

In a sense it can be claimed that the rolling back of the state leads to both politics and politicians being little more than planners whose main goal is that of sustaining the market, and the role of the individual within that market. The preoccupation with state regulation disappears. It is up to the individual or the enterprise to produce new commodities for the market, aiming to generate sufficient buyers to keep production viable. In this way diversity is sustained and innovation guaranteed. Hayek (1944: 46) advocated precisely such a perspective in arguing against the need for any centralised planning system because of how it led to excessive discussion and debate. He claimed that within a market system no one is '...forced to produce agreement on everything in order to that any action can be taken at all'. A mix of private property, exchange and market relations are held to be the creators of institutional diversity. While the market alone may not be a sufficient guarantee for democracy and pluralism, democracy and pluralism cannot prosper without markets.

By reference to the individual, neo-liberals argue that competition and inequality are the stimulants that drive the individual to innovate and to operate effectively within the market. Production and investment decisions are made atomistically through reflection on existing circumstances. The existence of multiple, potentially conflicting, plans of numerous production units obliges each individual unit to retain flexibility, and to be aware of the need for constant innovation. Learning becomes an essential ingredient of such dynamism, but it is a 'learning by doing'. Flexible learning institutions would appear to be the *sine qua non* of a learning economy.

This is an argument in favour of an attempt to favour a planning that operates through consensus, albeit a consensus that is tacit in nature. That is, it derives from the normative social order and divorces itself from any authority, other than that of society. Yet, at the same time, innovation breaks with normativity, planning is time consuming and should be abandoned. This leads to claims in favour of flat management, devolved decision-making and team working. It involves a search for the kind of relationship between decision-making and production that integrates decisions into the operational procedures of production. It relies on the awareness that markets create zones of partial autonomy within an interrelated socio-economic system.

In pursuing such debates a link is made between democracy and cooperation. Giddens (1994) has emphasised how the New Right accepted the economism of classical liberal thought and, as a consequence, replaced Durkheim's emphasis on the '...non-contractual element in contract' with conservative ideas. He proceeds to state: '...market institutions, as an Oakshottian conservative would also argue, cannot prosper in an autonomous way. They imply norms and mechanisms of trust, which can be protected by law, but only to a limited degree by legal formulations.' Durkheim's (1984) criticism of market individualism saw the limitations of a contract-based system within the contract itself, arguing that any contract depended upon much more than rational calculation. Within a contract there are factors that are not reducible to the intentions and agreements of individuals but which, nonetheless, have regulatory and binding function for the contract itself. They consist of rules and norms that may not be codified in law. Inevitably they involve social practice as tacit behaviour which the respective parties take for granted, and may not even recognise in explicit form. Nonetheless, there is always the assumption that this 'taken for granted' is shared with the other party. Such simple practices as the writing of a cheque imply the existence of a dense network of established institutions and routines which constitute institutionalised social practice.

Veblen referred to '... knowledge and practice of ways and means' (Veblen, 1919: 343), recognising that production relied upon '... the accumulated, habitual knowledge of the ways and means involved... the outcome of long experience and experimentation' (Veblen, 1919: 185–186). Identifying and owning the myriad of immaterial circumstances and combinations of skills involved in the production and use of material and immaterial assets are far from easy. Such capacities reside in the institutions and culture of the socio-economic system so that '... the capitalist employer is... not possessed of any appreciable fraction of the immaterial equipment' deployed in the production process (Veblen, 1919: 344).

The claim of the French Enlightenment that the state could eliminate any interference to progress is evident in how the notion of democracy has been called upon as a driver of progress. In a sense it would appear to be contradictory to invoke an argument in favour of a relationship between cultural diversity and economic growth on the one hand, and democracy on the other, when the political thrust in favour of democracy as a desirable global political system has implied the elimination of existing cultures. Similarly, the argument in favour of a relationship between a polity and culture draws on an awareness that the modern state has been premised on a single state, with a single language, that operates by reference to a single labour market that it strives to regulate. That is, the normative order that is sustained by culture pertains to the role of the state in producing and reproducing that uniform culture. As such it is a unitary form that pertains to everyone, being part of that which generates a citizenry. While states may well pay lip service to the need to sustain the culture of any immigrant group that enters the country, the overriding concern remains associated with assimilation, and with the integration of new immigrants as citizens. This goal is not far removed from the need to assimilate the state's culture in order to be able to participate as an economically effective citizen.

Even if economic growth would appear to lead to democracy, it is not necessarily the case that democracy is associated with growth. The emphasis on democracy in sub-Saharan Africa during the 1990s has systematically failed to resolve the economic stagnation. On the other hand, countries such as Singapore, China, South Korea or Taiwan which have experienced spectacular growth have done so under authoritarian political regimes, or even under military regimes. One hardly needs to look any further than China to recognise that massive economic growth is possible while retaining a centralised, single-party state. Despotism and the concentration of power may appear to constitute the death knell of the economy, but this is largely because the predatory regimes are not interested in a development that they cannot control.

Democracy is less favourable for growth from a low economic base than it is at a higher level. This has led some to argue that this accounts for the existence of democratic institutions in Europe that emphasise redistribution, whereas poor states tend to incorporate dictatorships which contribute to sustaining poverty. This is the kernel of the argument made by Przeworski (1991) who shows that it is mainly the stability of political institutions that accounts for economic growth. He argues that in this respect the ability to channel social conflict is paramount. These two conditions would explain, for example, the divergence between Latin America and the USA, where per capita income was similar at the beginning of the 19th century, whereas by the end of the 20th century there was a fivefold difference between them. The authoritarian regimes have to be in power for a long time if they are to neutralise social conflicts. In this respect, Roemer (1994) argues that democracy is nothing more than an electoral, ruthless, competition between social groups with different interests.

States and Trust

Putnam (1988) and Fukuyama (1995) controversially debate the relationship between the social organisation of polities and their economic propensity. Given the relationship between the state and culture, and how the state has played a prominent role in the production and reproduction of culture, it is not surprising that the discussion leads to an attempt to develop a typology of culture based upon differences between one state and another. While the individual is conceptualised as the carrier and exploiter of cultural traits, culture also becomes a common ingredient of how the individual is integrated with broader social groups as well as the state. Locke claimed that culture was transmitted across generations, arguing that it included moral rules of conduct. Since behaviour derived from knowledge, differences of experience would generate both individual and national differences in behaviour (Williams, 1992: 15). Recent work has elaborated on this assumption by reference to differences between northern and southern Europe. That is, the contrast extends even beyond the level of the state.

It is argued that social institutions create rules, incentives and sanctions that engender trustworthy behaviour, a precondition of cooperation (Gambetta, 1988), and the facilitator of the exchange of information and knowledge, and coordinating action aimed at goal achievement. The individual is incorporated into society through adherence to the normative structure that is created by social institutions. Since there is only one society within each state, it is only a small step to claim that both the nature and degree of trust vary from one state to another. Variation in the nature of trust is accommodated in the relationship between states and culture. However, the explanation for variation in the degree of trust from one polity to another is more complex.

Putnam claims that a richer organisational life correlates with more effective governance and a vibrant local democracy. Trust is the primary linkage in the chain of events that relate individual membership of civic institutions, thereby becoming an effective citizen in a democracy. Beginning from the assumption that the dependent variable, democratic involvement, was a consequence of the independent variable, trust, Putnam concluded that states in northern Europe had a higher degree of participation in civil society than the 'less developed' states of southern Europe which had a low degree of such involvement. Arguing that '...a nation's well-being, as well as its ability to compete, is conditioned by a single pervasive cultural characteristic, the level of trust inherent in the society' (1995: 33) Fukuyama builds on Putnam's work. High-risk societies are characterised by the development of large-scale corporations out of family firms by exploiting a rich and complex civil society. The emphasis is on how the actions of individuals facilitate the working of institutions. In contrast, within low-trust societies, trust is restricted to the family.

As that which organises society and influences the techniques and characteristics of a socio-economic formation, culture constitutes a framework for conducting economic activities and, thereby, innovation. It is an argument that has had considerable influence, the World Bank having incorporated it into its programme of economic restructuring and state reform in the developing world:

> Social capital refers to the institutions, relationships, and norms that shape the quality and quantity of a society's social interactions...Social capital is not just the sum of the institutions which underpin a society – it is the glue that holds them together. (The World Bank, 1999)

Nonetheless, it is a conservative and depoliticised version of civil society that argues that since the market fails to generate social cohesion, such social cohesion remains the prerogative of civil society.

A major critique of this work involves the tenuous link between individual involvement in voluntary associations and political consequences at the level of society. It is difficult to determine if group membership creates trust, or if existing trust merely facilitates group membership. Given how much of the use of the civil society notion has presented it as the basis for resistance to the power of the state, adopting such an understanding of civil society would result in a total rejection of Putnam's thesis. The emphasis on civil society as the source of social capital is also at odds with the role of social capital within organisations.

Similarly, the use of the notion of social capital is both excessively narrow and excessively broad. Its narrowness involves the focus on asso-ciational membership and norms of reciprocity and trust, the former as a source of social capital, and the later as akin to human capital vested in individuals rather than contextualised social relations. There is also an exclusive focus on the positive outcomes in how social capital pro-motes civic engagement. There is no reference to how social capital is socially embedded. The associated empirical exercise in Putnam's work leads to ignoring important aspects of the social capital argument, and the notion is transformed into a characteristic of individuals acquired through social networks which focus on the voluntary associations of civil society. It ignores how the effects of social capital at the individual level cannot be reduced to a set of individual properties (Bourdieu, 1987: 256), and how common norms can create a degree of conformity that can stifle busi-ness initiative (Portes & Landolt, 1996). Social capital becomes something that validates an entire society, while valuing it by reference to a desirable political objective.

Some of the claims put forward by Putnam and Fukuyama are remi-niscent of the romantic discussion of language as that which consolidates communities wherein the sharing of a common language is argued to gen-erate an awareness of an inherited commonality, rooted in a past and sustained by a common culture. It ignores internal divisions based on social class or other dimensions of inequality, and emphasises the total-ity of the language community. As with all communities it is very much an 'imagined community' (Anderson, 1991), one that is elaborated by the various agencies that serve as the means for conveying information and knowledge across all members of that community.

Evidently, such claims have relevance for the argument concerning how globalisation has influenced the salience of the state, and how the change from modernity to reflexive modernity involves an enhanced individual-ism. Before such a consideration it is necessary to note the contradiction between how individualism prevails in economic activities and how poli-tics emphasises the collective imposition of decisions. Market choice relies on individuals choosing what suits them, and democratic politics has been imbued with the notion that the goal of life is self-actualisation, leading to the belief that it is only through the rational choice of the individual that we can express ourselves. Yet, as a collective decision-making process, pol-itics has been highly centralised. This tension that rests its claim on a sense of a single 'people', nurtured by a state culture that generates normative practice, is problematic for those who seek an engagement on the part of the citizen in the affairs of politics. There is a sense in which those involved in this debate are striving to rearticulate the individual with the collectiv-ity, while having rejected many of the notions and concepts whereby this has been theorised within orthodox social science.

However, there is another meaning of individualism. It involves Beck's (1992) argument about the change from modernity to reflexive modernity. He argues that the undermining of modernity and the associated way of life of industrial society in terms of the binding roles of social class, gender, family, etc. promote a form of individualism. This does not involve isolation from collectivities, nor an atomisation of society, but rather, refers to how the individual is freed from the constraints of how tradition enforces an integration with the institutions of industrial society. This disembedding is accompanied by a re-embedding in a new order such that individuals are now free to choose the nature of their social alignments and allegiances. Such decisions are not free and open decisions, but are influenced by the need to take moral, social and political commitments within specific political contexts. Beck argues that whereas in industrial society individuals were forced into togetherness, within reflexive modernity they are obliged to build their lives on their own, with all the risks that this entails.

This means that the former basis of solidarity has been undermined, and that the notion of trust is recontextualised. Similarly, there is a new relationship between the individual and society. This does not merely relate to how globalisation has undermined the relationship between state and society, but also how social change promotes such changes. It obliges the negotiation of relationships within new contexts and heightens the relevance of new social movements from which no one is isolated. Within these relationships trust must be justified and experienced. Where trust derived from the stable social position of the individual, it now must be won and work must be involved in its retention. This 'presumes a process of mutual narrative and emotional disclosure' not expected before (Giddens, 1994: 187). Within larger organisational contexts as opposed to interpersonal relations, trust requires the 'opening out' of institutions. Failure is now understood as an individual failure, in contrast to how failure involved the collective failure of class in industrial society. Lash (1999) argues that the forging of new communities is located in a shared significance rather than in reflexive interpretation, and in active experience rather than politically mediated experience, and in a confident social praxis. He thereby conceives of a reflexive community in a way that does not rely on either tradition or socially constructed identities.

This involves recontextualisaing tradition in relation to a new plurality of values. In Giddens's (1991: 105) view of reflexive modernisation, traditions – habits or relics – '. . . only persist in so far as they are made available to discursive justification and are prepared to enter into open dialogue . . . with alternative modes of doing things'. Thus, as tradition, gender, language or ethnicity become objects of discourse that are destabilised. What tradition is no longer able to do is to provide the norms and beliefs that hitherto served as the basis of trust. Since all social relations are negotiable, and since norms are subject to a reflexive justification as a feature of social practice, the norms and ethical principles that serve as the basis for economic, social and personal relationships must be negotiated. New forms of social solidarity derive from interpersonal relationships, and not from tradition. Giddens thus argues that post-traditional society is constructed and reproduced in and through social practice, in the two-way interaction between individual social practice and social institutions.

Organisations and Networks

The concept of culture enters the debate about the best form of organisation within the New Economy. It takes two forms. One argues in terms of a regional culture that conditions the capacity for firms to operate within networks. This is the topic of Chapter 4. The second, which is not necessarily unrelated to the first, involves a conception that is different from the all-encompassing argument for a societal culture, and claims that each enterprise operates by reference to its own internal culture which conditions internal behavioural norms and practices.

The network enterprise is a new form of organisation characteristic of economic activity, but gradually extending its logic to other domains and organisations. It is a network made either from firms or segments of firms, or from the internal segmentation of firms. It includes MNCs, strategic alliances between corporations, networks of small and medium sized companies (SMEs) and link-ups between corporations and networks of SMEs.

The claim for the success of this kind of organisational structure derives from the centrality of flexibility for economic practice. Evidently, flexibility derives from the benefit that is meant to accrue to the firm and its owners, and often deprives workers of forms of employment security. Nonetheless, it claims that there is a particular dynamic to a network architecture, and that this dynamic leads to an emphasis on open-ended relationships, and a high degree of flexibility. Organisations operate by reference to communication flows that are global and customised. They employ workers who are highly individualised, who tend to work on short-term contracts, often through sub-contracting from other firms. Consequently, such firms are highly dynamic and operate their various projects by reference to a relatively weak structure.

What is claimed to hold together this network structure and the social actors involved is a set of shared cultural codes involving values, categories and meanings that the network can process effectively. However, in order for it to operate, the existing cultural code must be changed, and the basis of culturally based meaning must be modified. This involves paying attention to the identities of the personnel, and to treat this as an aspect of what are called 'identity based social movements'. The net result of such engineering is a cosmopolitan democracy that regulates the network society and the network state.

This focus on 'new social movements' has relevance for the shift from modernity to reflexive modernity. As we have seen, it is argued that the role of tradition within modernity was such that individuals were incorporated into the institutions of industrial society to the extent that they defined their identity. Furthermore, this identity always bore a relationship to the centrality of the principle of organisation where the world is thought of as organised by the state. The epitome of social movements in industrial society was the working-class movement. As a consequence of globalisation, the link between social movements, enlightenment and the state is broken. The focus on contesting social actors diminishes, and no longer involves passing from social protest to political participation within the same frame, and trying to take control of the state is less evident. This means that the earlier preoccupation with analysing social movements in terms of the mobilisation of resources is now redundant. It is this understanding that is incorporated in the notion of 'identity based social movements'.

The conventional understanding of the social sciences involves how individuals draw upon cultural attributes to create meaning in their lives. The associated cultural construct can pertain either to the individual or to the group. However, it is customary to link identity with the historical context to which they pertain. Even if we draw upon the post-structuralist arguments about how becoming the subject of discourse positions that subject in relationship to a plethora of objects and other discourses and how this constitutes identity, it is still the case that identity is constructed out of personal experience (Williams, 1999: 300–304).

It is sometimes argued that how states have been losing their sovereignty as a measure of multilayered governance and associated loss of political legitimacy is a contributing factor in the enhancement of collective identities (Castells, 2006). The alienation that derives from this process involves the state being distanced from the building of meaning in the lives of the citizen. The separation between the state and the nation that it has striven to create expands. The same argument can be made by reference to political parties which increasingly are linked to the state but not to the nation. Consequently, people increasingly build their identities on historical foundations.

What tradition is no longer able to do is to provide the norms and beliefs that hitherto served as the basis of trust. Since all social relations are negotiable, and since norms are subject to a reflexive justification as a feature of social practice, the norms and ethical principles which serve as the basis for economic, social and personal relationships must be negotiated. New forms of social solidarity derive from interpersonal relationships, and not from tradition. Giddens (1991) thus argues that post-traditional society is constructed and reproduced in and through social practice, in the two-way interaction between individual social practice and social institutions. The institutions and structures of society become both the means and the outcomes of individual action. Within larger organisational contexts, as opposed to interpersonal relations, trust requires the 'opening out' of institutions. Contrary to conventional wisdom, Giddens believes that this new demand for building organisational trust is a greater force than information technology in breaking down organisational hierarchies and 'command systems'.

Organisations can be described as massively interconnected networks of groups, departments, alliances, peripheral organisations, suppliers, collaborative joint ventures, etc. The spread of the internet and globalisation have accelerated the emergence of business networks by introducing a further layer of complexity and new business drivers and contexts. Within the global context, managing means managing networks of external resources such as outsourced agencies or partner institutions that do not belong to the organisation. It is claimed that the emergence of Asia as a major player in the global economy has involved the emergence of new organisational forms, blending Asian communitarianism with entrepreneurial individualism. At the same time, the extensive outsourcing of knowledge-based activities is transforming MNCs and organisations in the West. Competition increasingly derives from knowledge-intensive organisation in high-tech sectors with new organisational forms linked to the outsourcing policies of western companies.

Social Practice

Above, reference was made to how communicational processes that involve language and culture should be understood not so much as features of rational calculation, but as features of social practice, understood as institutionalised behaviour. It is the work of Pierre Bourdieu that has been most influential in promoting this view. This development is important because it breaks with the preceding focus on the relatively static nature of society, and the inability of sociological theory to encompass an understanding of social change as a process (Williams, 1992). It was an approach that was readily assimilated in the early work on both sociolinguistics and the sociology of language, and is perhaps best exemplified in the notions of language maintenance and language shift. These two notions imply a change that is followed by a static equilibrium involving a period of adaptation that heralds further change. It is a conception that characterises the preoccupation of early sociology with the biological analogy. In contrast, the notion of social practice allows us to understand change as an ongoing process, and links with conceptions of structure and agency wherein the individual is not only subject to the influences of the social structure, but also contributes to changes in the social structure (Giddens, 1979). It allows us to develop an understanding of language use as social practice such that there are continuous changes, both in the nature of social practice and in language use.

Social practice involves a reconceptualisation of social action away from the preceding tendency to consider action either as the consequence of structure or as the rational product of inter-subjectivity, or methodological individualism. The former tended to treat the subject as a dupe, while the later ignored Durkheim's insistence that society was more than the sum of the individuals within that society. Thus it emphasises two things – the ongoing, dynamic nature of social praxis, and its relationship to a reflexivity which may or may not involve rationality. As such it involves a social constructivism. It also involves an institutionalised form of behaviour in the sense that practices are habitual, and relate to specific institutions and organisations.

In rejecting structuralism Bourdieu adopted a form of utilitarianism wherein symbolic constructions were '. . . social activities performed from the point of view of utility maximisation' (Honneth, 1986: 56). Any particular society is thus viewed as the outcome of a struggle over rare goods. This emphasis on scarce resources dovetails with how he claims that '. . . there is an economy of practices, a reason immanent in practices', this reason being '. . . constitutive of the structure of rational practices, that is, the practice most appropriate to achieve the objectives inscribed in the logic of the particular field at the lowest cost' (Bourdieu, 1980: 50). This grounds his work in what he refers to as '. . . a general theory of the economy of practices' (Bourdieu, 1980: 122) that relates to how '. . . there exist in the social world itself, and not merely in symbolic systems, language, myth etc., objective structures which are independent of the consciousness and desires of agents and are capable of guiding or constraining their practices or their representations' (Bourdieu, 1982: 15). Such a social structure is based on Saussure's notion of difference such that positions of agents are defined by their relations of antagonism vis-à-vis one another.

Given the dynamic nature of social practice, it is constantly modifying the meaning of objects which are constructed and reconstructed (Williams, 1999: 208). However, as social practice there is an element of stability. The relationship between practice and meaning is dynamic, even if there is a relative stability to any practice. Since meaning is treated as the real effect of discourse, it is in social practice as the social construction of meaning that we locate the essential social dynamic. It involves signification, understood as the use of language and its pragmatic meaning. It also involves a confrontation between social groups over meaning. However, if we refuse to separate discursive practice from ideological practice, and view social practice as discursive practice, then we recognise that ideology

is not constituted before the act, but becomes a feature of social practice. The signification of a word is its use in language. Power is a feature of language.

Pleasants (1999: 55) has made the important point that there has been a shift from an emphasis on rationalist and empiricist philosophy to a concern with tacit knowledge, a shift from theory to practice. Consequently, rather than seeing knowledge as the outcome of theory, knowledge is seen primarily as process and activity. This picks up on the distinction between 'knowing how' (practice) and 'knowing that' (theory) (Ryle, 1945–46). To claim that any individual has more practical than theoretical knowledge is to conform with Habermas's (1991: 10) observation that '... every instance of problem solving and every interpretation depend on a web of myriad presuppositions.' I return to the relationship between social practice, language and knowledge in Chapter 6.

Language Use as Social Practice

Before concluding this chapter I would briefly like to continue the consideration of the work of Bourdieu that refers to language. The main thrust of his argument is sufficiently known not to require repetition. What I would like to do is to consider how this body of work pertains to language use as social practice, and how it relates to an understanding of language dynamics.

The essence of Bourdieu's work revolves around the standardisation of language. The state plays a central role in this process. It involves the elaboration of a pure form by reference to grammar and pronunciation. This standard is the form against which alternative forms are evaluated. It is sanctioned as the socially and intellectually desirable form, largely through social differentiation and its relationship to education. Linguistics is incorporated into this legitimisation process to the extent that syntax can be claimed to have political and ideological dimensions. The relative degradation of linguistic forms involves both class varieties of the standard language and other autochthonous languages that exist within the state territory.

Bourdieu extends the notion of capital to involve much more than economic capital. Culture capital becomes the degree of mastery of the cultural practices that a society recognises as legitimate. It is present in '... the paradoxical relationship to culture made up of self-confidence amid (relative) ignorance and of casualness and familiarity, which bourgeoise families hand down to their offspring as if it were an heirloom' (Bourdieu, 1979: 66). Evidently, this incorporates a competition between different forms of culture, with the prevailing culture being most familiar to one social class. There are also other forms of capital, including educational capital. Different forms of capital are mutually convertible, with economic capital capable of being reconverted into educational capital through investment in the accumulation of educational qualifications. Building on Mauss's (1954) anthropological classic *The Gift*, he claims that in pre-capitalist society the generosity of the rich was a means whereby the economically dominant class secured the consent of the dominated in the form of gratitude, respect and a sense of obligation. The 'objective' truth of 'economic' practices – naked self-interest and egoistic calculation – is unrecognisable, and is transformed into a symbolic capital that legitimises it. This also operates in capitalist society, and is the basis for social reproduction. Thus social class must include its 'being perceived', in addition to its centrality in the relations of production. Cultural products such as art presuppose the autonomy of cultural production that, in turn, privileges '...that of which the artist is master'. Responding to this requires a specific cultural competence that culminates in the separation of one class from the other.

The point which Bourdieu seeks to make is that since the role of language within the labour market plays a central role in social mobility, with upward mobility involving a rejection of the subordinate form or language, the complicity of the people in '...the destruction of their instruments of expression' (1991: 34) is a feature of 'symbolic domination'. That is, this complicity does not involve either a passive submission or the adoption of dominant values. Rather, accepting the legitimacy of the official language or form is a feature of the institutionalisation associated with what he called the habitus. The net result among those who cannot conform with the acceptable form of the official language, but who accept its legitimacy, is that they are condemned to a *reconnaissance sans connaisance*, so that they apply the criterion of the established order to their own social practices. Through this 'unknown recognition' the individual is party to her own subordination.

Any speech act involves a legitimation that is tied to institutions which define the conditions that must be fulfiled in order for the act to be effective and acceptable. The institution endows the speaker with the authority that is compatible with the statement and its intention. It relates to symbolic capital that is determined by the authority delegated by an institution. Bourdieu is at pains to claim that '...authority comes to language from the outside' (1980: 107). This obliges a consideration of what he refers to as the linguistic markets wherein speakers exchange statements.

The concept of a linguistic market incorporates the notion of a field that is structured as a space of positions, with the properties of the positions being determined by their location within the space, rather than by any personal attributes. Furthermore, the different fields – educational, economic, literary, etc. – carry general laws. This structure is the subject of a constant struggle between agents or groups striving to gain strategic advantage. Bourdieu pursues the economic analogy by linking markets and different forms of capital – economic, cultural and symbolic. The fields allow one form of capital to be converted into another so that, as we have seen, educational qualifications can be exchanged for lucrative employment. The struggle, which Bourdieu maintains is in operation within any field, involves those whose interests are served by the status quo in the distribution of capital, and those who will benefit from change. Despite being locked in struggle, all participants will benefit from the preservation of the field, and thereby will have an interest in its reproduction.

Evidently, linguistic capital involves both the capacity to conform with the official linguistic form and the flexibility necessary to adapt language to match a particular market. Bourdieu claims that the subject has the goal of maximising material and symbolic profit in making any utterance. However, it is not a conscious calculation, but a tacit anticipation based on an understanding of the acceptability and assumed value of the linguistic capital on the market. The value of a linguistic statement is determined by conformity with products that represent social differences. What Bourdieu calls a structural sociology of language relies on relating the linguistic differences that he claims are structured, with social differences that are also structured. Thus even the simplest exchange between interlocuteurs carries the traces of the associated social structure, and the statements help reproduce that structure. The greater the linguistic capital that an individual has, the more she is able to exploit the system of differences. This is a consequence of the scarcity of certain linguistic practices within the market.

Habitus is a tacit disposition which engenders specific parameters of action that enables a whole range of social practices. It is produced by '... the structures constitutive of a particular type of environment', but he also claims that the dispositions constitute '... structured structures predisposed to function as structuring structures, that is, as the principles of generation and structuration of practices and representations ...' (Bourdieu, 1972: 175). Thus the habitus varies in accordance with the conditions of existence where it is acquired, whether this is related to ethnicity or to social class, or to some other social parameter. The dispositions are acquired through socialisation into the institutional organisation of a particular society. This results in particular forms of social practice, but they are capable of being transposed into practices relevant to fields other than those within which they were generated. Nonetheless, the habitus does tend to generate social practices which conform with the conditions of existence from which they derive, this being a feature of reproduction. Yet they are not entirely determinant, in that through a reflective and rational practice which occurs within a structured space of possibilities which he refers to as a style of life, the individual is capable of being flexible.

The linguistic habitus is one kind of system of disposition that determines language use as social practice. The individual learns language through its use in particular markets so that the linguistic habitus governs the subsequent use of language and the understanding of the value which it carries in particular markets. This contributes to the stability of language products within the market structure. Most importantly, Bourdieu claims that the sense of value of an individual's language product is a dimension of the sense of that individual's place in society. Thus, through the inculcation of habitus, the social structure is transformed into patterns of behaviour which constitute institutionalised social practice. The overriding emphasis on socialisation within a specific habitus means that individuals are 'unconsciously determined by reference to perception, thoughts and conduct' by the dispositions incorporated during socialisation (Wieviorka, 2008: 30).

His conceptualisation of language as an instrument of power used by 'agents' who manipulate meaning in 'linguistic markets' is important because of how shared meaning is so central to the discussion of work in the knowledge economy. Different meanings are defined by clusters of meaning, and how they articulate with the market where they attain their 'most common meaning'. This tends to ignore the existence of language communities, while also failing to recognise that the significations that carry a language are not reducible to a strategically masterable code, nor are they strictly determined, as is implied in Bourdieu's work. On the other hand, what is important in his work is how the notion of habitus characterises how beliefs and discourses of agents vary with change in social divisions and inequalities within and between cultural fields. Individuals make sense of their existential situation using the available resources of a particular place and time. Yet this cultural capital is already embodied in practices and institutions that mediate individual and collective action. Consequently, the 'frames of meaning' available to different agents are resources for further social action. Individuals and social groups creatively use the potential resources of language in creating meaningful environments. However, this is not necessarily a rational process, but the product of language use as social practice.

All knowledge is framed by its institutional status. It is also grounded in the material activities and historical functions of human agents as active beings. While action involves the subjective meaning imposed by the participant, social action takes into account the interpreted understanding of the behaviour of others. That is, knowledge processes are always socially constituted. Knowledges are produced within practices conditioned by reference to pre-existing institutional fields. Consequently, all knowledge formation is correlated with some affective system of praxis. Also, each local field is bounded by wider social patterns, and collective dimensions.

Habitus '...contributes to constituting the field as a meaningful world, a world endowed with sense and value, in which it is worth investing one's energy' (Bourdieu, 1987: 127). Such a perspective on how knowledge is communicated in interaction focuses on the mutual orientation of those involved in the communication process, this involving not so much shared language as shared meaning and the cultural standards and norms that allow this meaning to be shared. While Bourdieu may not have given sufficient attention to issues of meaning and signification, his work has contributed significantly to our understanding of the relationship between language, social practice and knowledge. It has opened the way for a discussion of language use as social practice.

The pronounced emphasis on language, and on how class varieties play a role in the reproduction of social class, locates Bourdieu's work in industrial society and modernity. Given the arguments about the demise of industrial society and the reduction in the salience of social class as a tradition, it raises the question of how we now understand class varieties of language. The diminution of sovereignty and the associated appearance of a multilayered governance will have profound implications for the relationship between a 'national' standard that is devoid of place and class varieties that are distinguished regionally. Similarly, the break between tradition and social class will have implications for the social significance of class varieties per se. The nature of the 'habitus' must surely change as will the effect of 'habitus' on language and its use.

As regional governance gains ground, and boundaries are increasingly determined at the regional level, the tendency for regions to serve as the basis for comparison within the state diminishes. Judgements are increasingly framed at a regional rather than a 'national' level. Additionally, the reduced significance of social class as a dimension of social inequality and the associated focus on multiculturalism begin to remove the stigma associated with class varieties of language. In some respects, such developments involve a reduction in the efficacy of universalism that characterised the state as the centre of existence and being. On the other hand, the emerging particularism goes hand in hand with a new form of universalism where languages and language varieties are judged, not by reference to the state and its influence on standardisation and legitimation, but on global criterion. Divisions are established more by reference to different languages rather than varieties of any single language. This may well extend to accepting what hitherto would have been accepted as a variety of a specific language, for example, Singapore English as a language. It raises the question of the relationship between the state, power and the legitimation of language.

If it is Bourdieu that has been mainly responsible for popularising the notion of social practice, despite his emphasis on flexibility, his work does contain a sense of structural rigidity, especially by reference to the relationship between habitus and language use as social practice. That is at odds with how language use as social practice is understood by other theoreticians.

Language use as social practice leads us in the direction of Wittgenstein's (1988) language play, and Bakhtin's (1981) dialogism. If the transition from language (form) to meaning (social) involves an effect in terms of practice, we appreciate that the linguistic may well set constraints on form, whereas it is meaning that sets constraints on the social. The social is now understood as the effect of meaning. The stabilisation of meaning is what gives form to social practice. On the other hand, the play of language involves an arbitrary and constraining external structure. Foucault's (1994) concept of episteme underlines how the individual believes that she speaks, that speech crosses the individual, such that the knowledge on which the individual operates is extremely limited. This includes the effects of prior knowledges which cannot be known to the individual and how constraints on what can be said derive from the specifics of discursive practice. Since meaning is never fixed, social practice constantly modifies the meaning of objects as they are constructed and reconstructed.

Within this understanding of social practice thinking becomes a skilled social activity rather than a contemplative attitude. It is the central point of Wittgenstein's later work in which he emphasised that as humans we engage in the ordinary social practices of a society using skills that are exercised spontaneously and creatively without explicit reference to any official or formulisable set of rules or norms that are held to govern our practice. This was an explicit refutation of any attempt to draw on cognitive powers and tacit rules as explanation for social practice. 'There is no why ... This is how I act' (Wittgenstein, 1975: §148), '. . . it is our acting that lies at the bottom (of our practices)' (Wittgenstein, 1975: §204). This emphasis on describing linguistic practices is in contradiction to how Giddens (1979: 4) understands social practice as involving a Kantian problematic of cognitive powers, and rules that are intrinsic to language and thought. Fundamentally, it is a disagreement over the relevance of 'rules' for social action. It allowed Giddens to understand social structure as affording the possibility of social action while presenting social practice as a mediating force between them. Social practice is reduced to stabilised behaviour.

There is an overlap between the work of Bakhtin and that of Foucault, an overlap that pertains to a struggle over meaning. Bakhtin made specific reference to Benveniste's understanding of discourse as 'language appropriated by the individual as a practice'. In elaborating, he emphasised that any statement was not simply the product of an *enonciateur* that is interpreted by the *locuteur*, but involves a dialogical relationship which shapes the statement as it is made. Dialogue is only between subjects and not between sentences. Interestingly, Bakhtin treated all order as incomplete, thereby emphasising the dynamic nature of language use as social practice. It was a dynamic within which words only carry potential. This view dovetailed with the claim that languages are learnt through interaction as a consequence of which they are learnt 'already dialogised'.

Similarly, it is important to recognise that culture is also a feature of social practice. There is a danger in excessively emphasising the homogeneity of culture, and of ascribing fixed boundaries to the group with which it is associated. There is also the danger of equating culture and identity, such that culture is envisaged as a manifestation of group identity. This does not mean that to the insider culture and identity are not 'real'. Rather, it is to understand culture as a dynamic entity, constantly subject to creation and re-creation, involving boundaries that are similarly subject to creation and re-creation. If we do not subscribe to a view of any culture group as existing in isolation, it is axiomatic that culturally informed social practices are contested, and it is in this contestation that culture is elaborated. Similarly, all cultures are riven by conflicting accounts or narratives, such narratives also being constantly being modified through contact with one another, as well as with those of alternative cultures.

Conclusion

In this chapter I have sought to begin to outline the principles whereby human capital operates by reference to the generation of knowledge. The centrality of knowledge for the economy, together with how knowledge is a derivative of interaction, brings certain concepts into play. Central among these is trust. Much of the contribution that revolves around this concept views it as a feature of organisations that can be identified. It betrays an alignment with the rationalism and universalism of modernity. This is nowhere more evident than in the debate about the relevance of the state and democracy for the promotion of trust. On the other hand, it does point to how trust operates at different levels.

The shift in the importance of culture for the economy has come about because of the emphasis on the importance of human capital for economic growth. Furthermore, since the market economy relies on shared values, it is claimed that these sustain trust (Denzau & North, 1994). Hodgson (1999: 67) states: 'Institutional and cultural bonds have an essential function, even in an individualistic and capitalist economy.' While reciprocity relies on trust, it also extends to encompassing some fairly formal transactions without being a form of contract (Williams, 1976). This contrasts with how neoclassical economists view trust and culture as deriving from the behaviour of individual agents operating by reference to utility maximisation.

The economy is claimed to operate by reference to principles of normative social practice that include trust and moral obligation. What much of the recent work has sought to do is to take this observation and relate it to assumptions about how the same principles apply outside of economic operations. They then assume that these same principles also apply in the same way to the operations of political institutions within a particular form of political organisation. Capitalism has always relied to some extent on non-contractarian forms of obligation, something that is tied to regional or national culture. To imply that democracy as a universal principle constitutes such conditions would appear to be taking the point to its extreme. It is difficult to sustain the argument for an indissoluble relationship between trust and either the state or democracy, especially if either is perceived by the poor as unjust, or by a minority as based on 'the tyranny of the majority'. On the other hand, capitalism would simply not survive within a purely individualistic market system. Consequently, both trust and obligation must be grounded in the moral order of culture and society which, in turn, means that the social must be seen as something other than the sum of its individual members. The individual is socially and culturally formed.

The change from modernity to late modernity has implications for the trust that derives from the relationship between the state and the citizen. For Giddens (1994), 'post traditional trust' is a blind trust in which there is reliance on the functionality of abstract systems of knowledge and experts. It is the means whereby everyday practices are linked with the global network. It is a trust that must be transformed into an active trust that must be won. As such it requires the 'reflexive citizen' whose individual autonomy and responsibility links with her vision of activity. Such notions relate to Beck's arguments about the prevalence of risk in society (Beck, 1998).

In contrast to the attempt to ground trust in particular forms of the state, there is an increasing awareness that trust is a feature of social practice, and that social practice is an ongoing process that has considerable relevance for the construction of meaning. It is here that we begin to recognise the centrality of language and culture which are understood as essential components of social practice. The sharing of meaning involves negotiation and a degree of mutual trust. Viewing language use as social practice involves different conceptions that are conditioned by variations in social problematic. The recent emphasis on knowledge as process and activity, rather than as the product of theory, links the language, social practice and knowledge generation.

The issue of cultural or linguistic diversity tends to revolve around the relevance of these notions for the structuring of communities. It has little to do with sustaining diversity within any broader context. The value of community in the preceding argument pertains to how it promotes and reflects a trust that relies upon shared meaning and the ability to promote networks as the basis for cooperation. The strength of speech communities or language groups becomes associated with the potential capacity for democratic governance and economic development. In this respect, it turns on its head the prior notion that such language groups are atavistic, traditional survivals that will inevitably succumb to the benefits of modernism. However, as a consequence of the conservative way in which community is conceptualised, the notion of a language group is incorporated into precisely the same conservative problematic.

One theme that persists throughout the preceding discussion is that the institutions and processes of modernity which have sustained and promoted trust are undermined by the process of globalisation, and the shift from modernity to late modernity. On the other hand, there remains a commitment to the role of language and culture in the generation of trust. The changing role of the state, and its relationship to both globalisation and devolved governance, has substantial implications for the relationship between the state and its regions that was characteristic of industrial society. In Chapter 4, I will focus on arguments which claim that the nexus of economic activity revolves around the region and its culture.

Notes

1. This is the premise associated with the arguments in favour of how both state and regional culture influence the very kinds of interactions that are essential for operationalisation within a network economy. This is discussed in Chapter 4.
2. This certainly seems to be true of how Rawls sees moral and political progress in terms of the universalisation of a liberal democratic system.

Chapter 4
Regional Innovation Systems

Introduction

Much of the discussion in Chapter 3 revolved around the importance of the state by reference to its role in fomenting trust within a democratic context. The literature tended to draw upon the notion of the modern nation-state with its capacity for regulating the economy, labour markets, culture and language. Globalisation has undermined the sovereignty of the nation-state while simultaneously contributing to the development of a multilayered form of governance. Power has been devolved to the regional level and the transnational level, and there has been a reordering of governmental responsibilities. New spaces open up for a reconsideration of the relationship between languages. Also the enhanced form of individualism redefines the customary relationship between the state and identity formation, while also undermining the orthodox understanding of the relationship between the state and civil society.

Chapter 3 also included a brief discussion about how the laws of economics are bound to the normative structure of society, and the associated system of cultural values. This theme was taken up by Lundvall (1992) who elaborated the notion of national systems of innovation. His work was later elaborated by reference to regional culture and its relationship to innovation. It is this theme that will be pursued in this chapter. In so doing it allows me to consider how the enhanced relevance of regional governance plays a role in the engendering of trust and the relationships between economic players.

Lundvall argued that '. . . basic differences in historical experience, language and culture will be reflected in national idiosyncrasies' (1992: 13) in the internal organisation of firms, types of inter-firm relationships, the role of the public sector, the structure of financial institutions and the nature, organisation and volume of research and development. Despite the tendency for most economic theory to ignore this variation there is ample evidence of such diversity. It is perhaps most evident in a comparison of Japan, where the transition from feudalism to capitalism was fairly abrupt, and parts of Europe where this transition took several hundred years (Dore, 1973). Japan has retained many of the Confucian codes of loyalty and chivalry within the capitalist order. The consequence involves the appearance of quite different systems of industrial relations. It is this level of difference that has been rethought by reference to regional culture.

Chapter 3 also made fleeting reference to how regional culture is invoked as the basis of the capacity of firms to operate within networks. This appears to contradict the argument that global forces are homogenising the effects of language and culture. The work considered here largely derives from among geographers whose discipline has always emphasised the spatial component, and a concern with regional issues. It is axiomatic that a region is part of some much larger component, whether it involves geographical space or a politico-territorial entity. However, the work on regional innovation systems (RIS) explicitly emphasises the state–region and, in this respect, maintains that the state culture is by no means homogeneous. Given the reorientation of the state/region relationship as a consequence of globalisation, it leaves many issues unexplored.

The process of globalisation is being interpreted by many as a force for the elimination of diversity in all its forms. Thus the arguments concerning the impact of the predominant role of English as a global *lingua franca* on other languages is often interpreted much in the same way as the explanatory arguments concerning how minority languages have been subject to an evolving process of erosion. The exclusion of these minority languages from the economic process, and their relegation to informal networks associated with the family and the community, was viewed as an expression of their subservient role outside of the confines of reason and its relationship to politics and the economy. A simplistic equation of the role of state economic regulation and the process of globalisation leads some to make claims, not only for the homogenisation of the economic process, but even for the demise of the state. Given how culture has, to a great extent, been produced, structured and reproduced by the role of the state and its various agencies, it is only a small step to generating arguments about the demise of cultures. This is not to deny that processes of homogenisation, standardisation and deregulation will have an important impact upon both language and culture, but there are compelling arguments that this will involve new forms of relationship between the local, the regional and the global. Thus Graddol (2000) argues that while many of the world's minority languages are in danger of disappearing, there will also be a new process of linguistic hybridisation that will generate new varieties of language.

Networks, Regions and Culture

Modern organisations can be described as massively interconnected networks of groups, departments, alliances, peripheral organisations, suppliers, collaborative joint ventures, etc. The spread of the internet and globalisation have accelerated the emergence of business networks by introducing a further layer of complexity and new business drivers and contexts. Within the global context, managing means managing networks of external resources that do not belong to the organisation. The new organisational forms that blend Asian communitarianism with entrepreneurial individualism insert new contexts into new forms of networks. At the same time, the extensive outsourcing of knowledge-based activities is transforming MNCs and organisations in the West. Competition increasingly derives from knowledge-intensive organisation in high-tech sectors, with new organisational forms linked to the outsourcing policies of western companies.

The tendency to refer to culture in an all-encompassing way, making it a shorthand for that which determines behaviour, without giving it any universal causal frame of reference, allows the emergence of such notions as corporate culture. This relates to new forms of organisational structures with their own organisational logic. The focus of the structure is the existence of networks of relationships, involving firms or segments of firms, or even the internal segmentation of firms. Such networks may include MNCs, strategic alliances between corporations, networks of SMEs, or links between corporations and networks of SMEs. Adler and Kwon (2000) argue that formal institutions and rules which help to shape network structure and influence norms and beliefs also influence social capital.

These networks are claimed to be highly dynamic and thereby liberate the participants from the constraints and controls of society by constantly reconstituting values and the institutions. This partly relates to how the multinational networks transcend society, obliging the formulation of new moral codes of conduct and paying attention to cultural diversity. It is claimed that networks and the associated social actors require a shared cultural code based on values, categories and meanings that the networks can process effectively. Nonetheless, many of the arguments around which this understanding of how the so-called network economy will operate, and how its constituent participants will behave, are also relevant at the regional level. While all members of the regional business network will, by and large, derive from the same society, they still require a degree of cultural coherence in order to be able to operate by reference to the demands and needs of the knowledge economy. It is argued that the cultural context pertains as much to the region as it does to the state.

For some time it has been recognised that the ability of a language group to produce and reproduce itself is dependent upon the extent to which it is incorporated into the economic order (Williams, 2005). Currently, service sector activities within the New Economy appear to be highly sensitive to the need to develop and modify products that can reach local and regional consumers, at least by reference to regional languages, if not by reference to regional culture (CILT, 2006). At the political level in Europe there is a sense in which European integration is conceived of by reference to regional differentiation. This implies a willingness to accept a broad range of specific regional cultures, while providing space for promoting individual paths within a common framework. The creation of Nomenclature of Territorial Units for Statistics (NUTS) regions within hitherto highly centralised states, and the integration of Europe's historic regions into this new regional structure, is accompanied by an enhanced process of political decentralisation.

Cultural aspects of regional development and innovation have tended to be ignored until recently, when reference to culture has appeared in the literature on industrial districts (Amin, 1999; Asheim, 1996; Garofoli, 1991; Piore & Sabel, 1984) and on innovative milieux (Aydalot & Keeble, 1988; Crevoisier, 2001; Maillat, 1998). More recently it has been adopted in studies of clusters of high-tech or knowledge-intensive industries (Cooke, 2002; Keeble & Wilkinson, 2000; Saxenian, 1994). It is perhaps even more prominent in work associated with what are referred to as RIS (Cooke *et al.*, 2004; Tödtling & Trippl, 2005) that ask how a unique regional/national culture can be used to create competitive advantage in specific sectors, for example, in Japan (Freeman, 1987), Denmark (Lundvall, 2002), Silicon Valley (Saxenian, 1994), 'The Third Italy' (Sabel, 1989) and the Uusimaa region in Finland. The debate about 'regional cultures of innovation' is closely linked to the debate about conditions for creating a 'Knowledge Economy' (Cooke *et al.*, 2004). This body of work argues that attention to regional structures influences economic competitiveness and innovation because regional differentiation enables complementarities and synergies to emerge in facing global competition. It incorporates the need for a strong commitment to local/regional traditions and specialities. The argument claims that regional culture has a strong potential for innovation and knowledge generation, and that this potential can be realised through paying sensitive attention to cultural change.

In these studies regional culture is seen as sets of traditions, common values, understanding and a common language which makes it easier to interact with others. Considerable emphasis is placed on how trust is constructed around regional culture; this trust is regarded as a facilitating factor, or even as a precondition, for effective knowledge exchange, cooperation and collective learning. The notion of a regional culture extends to include the behavioural routines of companies, of organisations and of policy actors. An awareness of these routines reduces uncertainties, helps in decision-making and, thus, gives rise to the formation of technological trajectories. They also have influence on the willingness to undertake new ventures, to assume risks and to establish new firms. In some respects, although constructed out of quite a different problematic, there is a sense in which these ideas overlap with the notion of communities of practice.

It is important to recognise that whereas corporate culture is embedded in a more or less clearly defined organisation, regional culture is the result of historical experience and a range of different, often polarised, interests. That is, regional culture is constructed as diffuse and heterogeneous. In certain terms, it is this heterogeneity and its related cognitive diversity that works as a positive framework for an innovation culture. It is argued that if fragmentation is to be avoided, this diversity requires a shared vision and a clear sense of its relationship to history as the prior discourse (Boschma, 2005).

The spatial division of labour is changing from that determined by the contingencies of industrial production, and new agglomerations are appearing (Pianta, 2000). While all regions are accommodating a shift to the New Economy, the transition is moving at a different pace, and in different ways within and across regions (Vivarelli & Pianta, 2000). It is also clear that some spatial aggregates will be slower in making the transition than others. Indeed, there is already evidence that the peripheries of the Old Economy are those which are slowest in taking up the New Economy (Cooke, 2001). The 'death of distance' (Cairncross, 1997) is in demise.

The New Economy does not open up new opportunities that apply equally across space. Locations outside of the hardware core in Europe that focuses upon Stockholm and Helsinki, and the software core that extends in an arc from Dublin through to Milano, are obliged to consider alternative routes of entry into the New Economy. The principle of path dependency argues that such routes will largely depend upon the nature of the already existing economic activity within the different regions. All regions are likely to have Knowledge Intensive Business Services (KIBS). However, each region looks to its existing strengths in developing its own initiative.

It can be argued that neo-liberalism opens the space for a discussion of the relationship between regions and their economies. The arguments in favour of limiting the regulatory role of the state and focusing upon the centrality of community for development lead to a focus on decentralisation and the devolution of political power. The relationship with democracy involves arguing that if political decisions are made closer to the people whom they influence, the degree of involvement in the democratic process will be enhanced. Certainly, recent years have seen an expansion in the devolution of centralised power, this being accompanied by the practical application of the principles of neo-liberalism.

The argument in favour of RIS refutes the orthodoxies of the democratic state and cultural uniformity. The assumptions associated with this particular development are straightforward:

- as the emphasis on economic development shifts to the micro level, innovation has to be thought of in terms of interaction;
- the convenient level of interaction is the locality;
- innovation is a systemic process based on social systems, and innovation is the basis of competitiveness;
- that which integrates localities into meaningful spatial and identity-based aggregation – as social rather than interactional forms – is the region;
- the region is not uniform, but is conditioned by history and culture;
- thus the region and its institutional structures become the basis for developing and promoting innovation.

In this respect, they derive from Lundvall's (1992: 13) claim that the same factors responsible for generating national systems of innovation are also applicable by reference to regions. However, this conceals a variety of intriguing issues worthy of analysis.

Silicon Valley

I would like to begin with a discussion of the work of Saxenian (1994, 1999) on development in Silicon Valley, work that has attracted considerable attention in recent years. Indeed, for many, the location which her work focuses upon – Silicon Valley – has become the master model to which most regional developers aspire. The key argument of her work is that there is a strong connection between the internal structure of firms and the broader structure of the region in which they are embedded, that the structure of the firm mirrors the structure of the region. Thus she cites Silicon Valley as the location in which the boundaries between firms are porous, blurred, fluid and open, leading to open, hierarchy-free firms. This basic insight has important implications for public policy – that it is insufficient to direct attention to inter-firm relations and the construction of institutions that promote openness, cooperation and collaboration, if one does not also address questions of transforming the internal structures of firms. She contrasts Silicon Valley with Route 128 in Massachusetts that she claims has bound hierarchical and secretive firms. Consequently, new institutions alone would not be sufficient to bring about real change in the performance of Route 128's firms. The implications for the rapidly multiplying state and local 'network-building' programmes are obvious.

What matters most, according to this analysis, are firstly, how boundaries between firms are defined, that is, whether they are rigid and closed, or flexible and porous; and secondly, the kinds of relations between firms, especially those between large and small firms, but including relations between firms of a similar size, regardless of their scale. Both regions had large firms: DEC and Wang in Route 128, and Hewlett-Packard, Apple and Intel in Silicon Valley. Yet the patterns of response and adjustment to crises diverged radically in the two locations.

Saxenian's conception of the regional 'industrial system' assists in the analysis of production systems in general. This concept is based on three elements:

- local institutions and culture, viewed as that which shapes shared practices and understandings;
- industrial structure and how it conditions the social division of labour;
- corporate organisation and culture.

Between them, these three components provide a holistic view of the constellation of forces that define a region's economic trajectory through time. It appears that under certain circumstances the latter comes to dominate, and even to define, the former.

Saxenian's notion of regional culture is understood in an encompassing way as '... the shared understandings and practices that unify a community and define everything from labour market behaviour to attitudes toward risk-taking' (1994: 7). In order to understand what is involved in the causal connections in the 'embedding of the economy', we actually need to make a distinction between regional culture, regional industrial culture and organisational culture. If we take the notion of embeddedness seriously, these aspects of culture assume a necessary causal interlinkage. But they are not the same thing. Despite lacking an adequate theoretical perspective, these distinctions help to analyse some of the processes that shape localities and regions, while also assisting in relating aspects of the corporate and regional dynamics that are interlinked.

The currently popular notion of embeddedness (Granovetter, 1985) emphasises a conceptual interconnection between action and structure. In the context of Saxenian's narrative, it helps us understand firms as actors in regional development, in the sense that as actors they are obliged to operate in a pre-existing regional culture that they must largely accept as given. They also operate as actors within that wider culture by creating their own internal organisational cultures, while participating in the formation of a regional industrial culture that, in turn, supports their operation, and ultimately leaves its imprint on the overall regional culture. It would appear that there is no room for any universal blueprint of New Economy development, but that each region must employ the basic principles of the knowledge economy, while accommodating the regional culture. Furthermore, the operational principles of communities of practice will, similarly, operate within the firm by reference to how regional culture influences interactional contexts.

Tying together the notions of 'regional', 'regional industrial' and 'organisational' cultures or sub-cultures may well help in understanding the origin of certain processes of change. This is particularly important since '... we still do not know what makes regional development happen' (Pudup, 1992: 195). If, as is implied, Silicon Valley provides a model for other regions, in order to become competitive, the firms within any region should break off their embeddedness in the regional culture of the past, and intentionally try to change their ways of organising and behaving. In so doing, they should create organisational cultures reminiscent of those of Silicon Valley firms. That, in turn, should affect the way inter-firm relations work, thereby changing the region's industrial culture. Thirdly, this should have an effect on the regional culture, involving how employees shape the relationship between their work and private lives, on how risk-taking is perceived and so forth. The idea of embeddedness suggests that a change in the majority of the organisational cultures of firms is not possible without a change in a region's industrial culture, and in the overall culture. A region attempting to adopt the particular model provided by Silicon Valley would need to create a regional culture that supports continuous innovation as a feature of rapid socio-economic and socio-cultural change.

It would appear that regional development presupposes, but is not reduced to, cultural change. The importance of understanding various aspects of culture and how it changes becomes evident. Saxenian acknowledges that '... regional institutions and culture are difficult to change' (1994: 162). Culture tends to be inert and also to persist. The power of key agents of change thus becomes ever more central in understanding the cultural aspects of regional development. In some respects, this is not too far removed from the arguments which characterised much social science thinking during the 1950s and 1960s, when various arguments were put forward about the desirability of persuading 'under developed' cultures to abandon their existing languages and culture, and to adopt those of the 'developed' world. While it is inevitable that culture changes, it would also appear to be necessary that regional cultures should retain their uniqueness while accepting the link between culture, social practice and economic activity.

What Saxenian refers to as the industrial culture of local industrial systems involving something beyond specialisation and interlinkage constitutes the cement that holds the system together. A successful industrial culture is embodied in a language of communication and self-understanding of the community of producers. This industrial culture provides the strong interpretative and communicative channels for the information essential to innovation to be developed and communicated in the face of constant uncertainty. Saxenian asserts that this culture in Silicon Valley is embodied in inter-firm relations that cannot be reduced to input–output transactions. It is also embodied in social contacts between engineers that take place outside the circuit of direct inter-firm relations. What they 'know' is tacit and intangible. Consequently, no mechanical model of network architecture can substitute for what actually makes the people in the network interact so as to be technologically innovative, and capable of constant successful adjustment to competition.

Saxenian claims that the regional culture underlying its dispersed network is responsible for Silicon Valley's success in developing cutting-edge innovation. This runs counter to those who claim that the success in basic innovation in high technology essentially derives from state-level R&D strategies, and the input of large MNCs. In Santa Clara County firms involved in the early developments both spun off and sponsored start-ups in sectoral sub-specialties, involving new companies that clustered together in Stanford Park and at other nodes. The persistent mobility of technical staff among firms, including downward mobility from failed ones, fostered a collaborative entrepreneurialism replete with informal networks, webs of contracting and constant alertness to technical and market possibilities. Taken together, these generated a culture of openness and adroit flexibility that attracted talent and enabled the district to survive the mid-1980s crisis, and to flourish.

Saxenian's comparison of Silicon Valley and Route 128 appears to be a continuation of a much earlier tendency in US regional cultural analysis, perhaps the best known of which was Clyde Kluckhon's (Kluckhohn & Strodtbeck, 1962) 'variation in value orientation'. She appears to focus on a corporate and technological culture that invested the electronics sector with eastern and western variants. The eastern one derived from 'the hierarchical and authoritarian ethic of Puritanism' (1994: 60) was profoundly conservative, having identity and social relations that focused on family and community rather than on occupation, and focused on risk avoidance, secrecy, loyalty and integrity (1994: 64). The western one replaced Puritans with 'pioneers' as its totemic referent, emphasised experimentation and entrepreneurship, yet it also featured elaborate lateral connections among professionals, a rough democracy of in-migrant men who valued craft over kin and neighbourhood.

It must be admitted that there is a scarcity of explicit theorisation in Saxenian's work that would help to understand variation in the competitiveness of firms and regions. There is a sense in which this is true of much of the work on RIS, and there is also a sense in which it represents a continuation of earlier forms of structural functionalism within which structures exist as systems by reference to their functional validity. I would now like to turn to a consideration of what has been elaborated in related work about this notion.

Regional Innovation Systems (RIS)

The adherents of the RIS approach claim to be rejecting the optimisation principles of neo-classical economics which, it is claimed, are unable to account for innovation and technological change because of the tendency to treat them as external to utility maximisation. In contrast, the emphasis is placed on much of the work that informs the emphasis on the importance of interaction involving trust, reciprocity and mutual understanding for an economy where knowledge is of paramount importance. In this respect, it appears to be arguing that non-optimal economic behaviour should not be seen as irrational, but should be contextualised in order to understand its existence.

This rejection of neo-classicism is held to derive from how globalisation has led to the demise of Fordism and Taylorist working principles, and the parallel emergence of regionalism as a predominant form of governance. It opens new space for a reconceptualisation of economic development, resulting in the emergence of new spatial alignments involving science parks and a new regional development policy, premised on how innovation is fundamentally a human process, with planning having to accommodate this premise in how it integrates space and development at the regional level. There is a strong element of both geographical and cultural determinism in the argument.

Evolutionary Economics is contrasted with modernist regional development theory in emphasising the particular over the universal.[1] It stresses the importance of environmental, institutional and cultural differences in how economies evolve. This orientation again derives from Hayek's work. His distinction between rules and the action that they generate informs how he posits an evolutionism based on a system of rules. It retains the sense of evolutionism as progressive behaviour, even if the notion of socio-economic evolution is not deterministic. Where RIS departs from this line of thinking is in seeking to integrate particularism and universalism. It goes out of its way to emphasise the relevance of cultural variation for ways of doing. It seems to go so far as to claim that interactional behaviour is culturally conditioned. On the other hand, it strives to claim that the relevance of the regions for innovation and development is universal.

The emphasis on particularism links neatly with regional variation. Core-periphery differences derive not from a lack of resources, but from different organisational and technical capabilities, and how this interferes with the ability to apply practical knowledge. This opens the way for an enabling role for the planner whose superior analytic knowledge and capacity link with the potential of regional firms, in that it provides the input for demonstrating how innovation premised on social capital becomes possible. Since the necessary abilities are not predetermined, they can be learned; all that is required is a system that can show the way. Tacit knowledge replaces culture.

However, this merely raises the issue of the relationship between tacit knowledge and the possibility of a planning process. Dosi (1988: 1131) made the point as follows: 'In each technology there are elements of tacit and specific knowledge that are not and cannot be written down in a "blueprint" form, and cannot, therefore, be entirely diffused either in the form of public or propriety information.' This leaves a vast amount of vital knowledge outside of the process of rational deliberation. It is the very argument that is made against any form of centralised planning.

The importance of the regional dimension lies in the claim that the appearance of a new regional orientation to economy in the form of regional governance, and an explicit practice of concentrating development on spatially proximate firms as clusters, creates the conditions that are necessary for innovation which, in turn, derives from social capital. These conditions promote the appearance of human potential and social capital which are the consequence of how firms within clusters develop the kinds of relationships which rely on trust, reciprocity, mutual understanding and the other characteristics associated with the new learning and development paradigms. This social capital contributes to a knowledge production that must be promoted and managed in being transformed into the dynamic basis of innovation. It relies on the willingness to cooperate, while also existing within a competitive environment. The central assumption of the entire approach is that if corporate and regional cultures match and complement each other, they will successfully capitalise on their potential and, together, they can breed an innovative space.

The intense process of interaction involved in continuously creating and recreating knowledge within social networks relies on mutual understanding. Both knowledge and innovation involve a process of social construction. Knowledge creation will rely upon external inputs, but the region remains the focus of this process of linking global and local knowledge. It involves developing and promoting the links of the network, and the role of the development agency moves closer towards that of knowledge management. It is the local context that generates a collective identity based on mutual trust.

RIS is presented as a conceptual system in the sense that it derives from a particular theoretical problematic involving '... principles or laws that explains relationship between variables' (Cooke, 1998: 11). This implies that there are universal principles that apply to every case, and that these derive from a particular logic, and conform with the need to establish the global context. There is also the need to accommodate cultural variation and particularism, and indeed, regional variation. This is resolved by claiming that while the basic ingredients of a regional innovation system will be similar, how they are put together will be subject to variation in accordance with regional cultures or ways of doing things. This allows the development of a comparative approach, involving the analysis of regional development across the world in order to establish which cases apply to the general principles, and how they vary. It is in this respect that it seeks to integrate particularism and universalism. In arguing from logical principles that inform how firms and regions should deal with a free market conditioned by tacit knowledge, there is a tendency to treat this logic as a superior knowledge, accessible only to certain actors. It is by reference to what are held to be the prerequisites of success within a free market that this logic is valid. It conforms with the claim that tacit skills can be codified by the expert, and that this codification is essential for knowledge management.

These systems are social systems in the sense that innovation derives from the social, and in this respect the conceptualisation demands a sociological input. It is there in the same sense that society is a universal principle; each state has a society of its own that is different from any other. This is more problematic by reference to region in that modernism has insisted on the state as the territorial imperative that defines the boundaries of societies.[2] The social would appear to pertain to the institutional context within which formal institutions pertain to the region. Beyond this, the institutionalised social practices that the RIS seeks to promote can be seen as another expression of the social. Furthermore, the tendency to discuss innovation by reference to social interaction or social relationships, rather than by reference to social groups or social structure, further complicates issues. Within the RIS approach, the nearest one approaches to a conception of social structure is in the sense of a regionally defined community of interest consisting of the different players who have a role in the system. Thus the system would appear to involve the rules and conditions whereby things happen within very specific kinds of social networks. These rules conform with how the current paradigms discussed above refer to the benefits of interaction for firms vis-à-vis their need to operate successfully within a market-driven economy that operates globally. Thus the system is another manifestation of what is already expressed in other orientations and perspectives on the same problem, except that it is claimed to operate at a regional level, with variation in the rules from one region to the other. On the other hand, since the focus is on network interaction, it can hardly be treated as a social system. Indeed, there is room to suspect that it shares with neo-liberalism a rejection of the social as anything more than the sum of the individuals within it.

What RIS has sought to do is to take the interactional principles of the current thinking about knowledge development, and to develop a grand theory out of it by giving these principles a frame of reference that claims to be both social and universal. The social relates not to the state, but to the region, and to a normative order which also pertains to the region. Similarly, culture pertains to the same normative order, and the same spatial and political boundary.

A perspective that emphasises the centrality of systems is obliged to explain how the interdependent parts fit together, how they are interdependent, and secondly, it must confront the problem of system maintenance. These issues appear to be incorporated in the relationship between a normative order premised upon cultural diversity, and the tacit skills that inform the market. The system is held together by functional interdependence, and by the role which regional culture plays in forging a uniform identity. It is the moral values embedded in the tacit knowledge that inform not merely the market, but also the interaction between firms. The functionalism of the argument is a clear manifestation of the Montesquiean idea of the inter-relationship of parts within an integrated whole that contributes to a social order, and is sustained by a normative order. That is, there is consensus ingrained in the system, a form of social solidarity deriving from shared identity and culture. It is an inherently conservative and cohesive view of society, one that is reminiscent of Parsonian structural functionalism. This functionalism usually seeks to show how both order and change derive from the same conditions. In so doing they substitute a rationality which appears to involve society at large for that of the individual. This leads to the problem of distinguishing between the intentions of the actor and the consequences of that action. What RIS does is to claim that intention is decentred in that it is implicated in tacit knowledge. It is this tacit knowledge, reinterpreted in terms of social practice or patterned behaviour, which gives the desired consequence, albeit only under the right conditions. These conditions are only known to the external expert, and the planner. It seems to be another expression of how both Durkheim and Weber underlined the importance of moral values in generating unintended consequences as a manifestation of the non-rational in humankind. Of course, Durkheim saw these moral values as a source of solidarity, and as the basis of pattern-maintenance – the very basis of social order!

How both culture and behaviour are discussed is highly reminiscent of a bounded regulatory social order that determines behaviour. In this respect, one distinguishes between culture as behaviour and culture as the rules that determine behaviour. What is implied in the RIS argument is that the normative order conditions a form of social contract operating at the regional level, one that is responsible for generating individual identity and self-conception. It involves the stabilisation of discourses which construct time, person and place in particular ways. Subjects and objects are constructed and constituted by reference to how the regional space becomes the basis for the boundary between the 'us' and 'them' that constitutes social identity. This is sustained by the discourse of institutions that involve both the state and civil society, as well as the relationship between them. It is also informed by the prior or historical discourses, the traces of which include a specific stabilised relationship of subjects and objects. There may well be contexts within which state and regional identities are in opposition, and others where they overlap. That is, while we are referring to multiple identities, they are related in different ways that involve different status relationships. However, it does seem to be an exaggeration to imply that regions will now sustain distinctive normative orders that somehow replace those generated by states.[3]

The region constitutes a system of collective social order that derives from mutual understanding, trust and reciprocity operating among the collective economic community. Since this order derives from the cultural distinctiveness inherent in the concept of 'culture areas' bounded by the spatial parameters of the region, this must mean that sustaining the idea of a regional normative order must involve the elaboration of a regional culture through regional institutions. It is this institutional order that will be responsible for developing and sustaining the stable and regular flow of information that, as in value-added partnerships, informs that which sustains the collectivity. However, considerable emphasis is placed on how the path dependency that informs particular regional trajectories of development depends upon '... regional industrialisation history often spanning hundreds of years', because technological knowledge is organised regionally and conditions regional behaviour. (Braczyk & Heidenreich, 1998: 415) A region incorporates its particular social and cultural capital. There is a very specific conception of culture involved in this argument – it seems to be a bounded form that conditions behaviour, while also relating to the normative order. It refers to behavioural parameters that tend to be discussed as separate from the individual and the social group, in that the main referent is to the relationship between culture and 'regions'. History plays its role in that the specific working practices associated with historical production systems become a feature of the regional social capital. It is in terms of tacit skills that the relationship between culturally conditioned behaviour and the individual is witnessed. This is consistent with the idea of a spatially bounded normative order which conditions productive behaviour.

The concept of culture is not unrelated to how the concept of community is used. Relationships are characterised by reference to the extent of equality between the protagonists. This implies that certain kinds of relationship are desirable, but that they only apply within compatibilities of scale. This corresponds with the need for equality as a basis for trust and the ability to cooperate. It frames an egalitarian community, one which must be fated and promoted by external agencies within a particular socio-cultural milieu. Community is constituted out of '... routine practices and mentalities of entrepreneurship in the context of a commercial community' (Cooke, 1998: 9). Thus, the reference is not merely to culture as social practice, or as that which conditions social practice, but also to culture as that which generates a mental condition in the form of 'identity'. Progress is an economic potential that materialises as a consequence of adopting the RIS within a correct socio-cultural milieu that will generate the routine practices and mentalities of entrepreneurship. Community is both a form of unreflective patterned behaviour and that which derives from common economic behaviour within spatially constrained boundaries. There is a sense of mechanical behaviourism, and a sense of inevitability, in the relationship between cluster formation, networking and the associated learning that promotes innovation. This is not to deny the importance of the link between interaction and learning but, rather, to claim that the kind of learning that stimulates innovation is highly specific, and involves far more than the mere existence of systems and networks.

The planning agent is not merely responsible for promoting the reflexive learning and interactional contexts that lead to innovation, but they must also inculcate a process of 'forgetting' by reference to existing behaviour. Here RIS relies heavily upon the transcendental nature of tacit knowledge. It would appear that at the heart of the ontology of individual and social life is a sense of agency involving the capacity for action rather than rational intent. There is also the implication that behaviour could be other than it is, otherwise there would be no need to 'forget'. This implies the existence of a 'free will', even if it is reliant on a sense in which the individual is unable to express what she knows, even by reference to social action – the world is not deterministic. It contrasts with the portrayal of individuals as structurally determined in orthodox sociologies. However, it is unclear if this individual agency is the necessary precondition of social structures, since no reference is made to such concepts. This concern with individual agency tends to be expressed by reference to the reification of 'the firm'. There is little reference to the individual. That is, whereas the work of Giddens and Hayek emphasise the thesis of a free market economy, RIS and the associated discourses operate a language and conceptualisation which conceives of production within associated contexts. The employed are unsuspecting 'actors', in that tacit knowledge involves the replacement of empiricist, subject-centred perspectives by the decentring of subjectivity without eliminating the reality of individual consciousness, but merely displacing it. While not exactly 'dopes' they do require being skilled through a process of 'forgetting' that links with the self-reflexion of 'learning'. This means that while scientific knowledge is accorded the status of 'knowledge', so also is non-scientific activity. This usually involves the shift in emphasis from theory to practice that permits a shift from identifying knowledge with theory as an intellectual product, to viewing knowledge as a process or activity. For RIS this is not the case, in that the expert as planner remains a theoretical expert who is distinct from the knowledgeable worker.

There is a strong sense of faith associated with the RIS. It involves the claims made for the relevance of clusters for interaction, the effectiveness of principles of co-option for sustaining reciprocal relationships, how regional institutions can develop the partnerships with firms that will transform them and even the ability of regional developers to comprehend the principle of flexible learning that is responsible for such a transformation. The emphasis upon proximity and regionalism breaks down when the discussion moves to a consideration of how regional systems are obliged to grapple with the global context. It is argued that ICT can serve as the basis whereby regional firms can integrate with similar systems in other locations. Yet, if the system relies upon the specifics of culture, and on face-to-face interaction, it is not clear how this will occur. Working online across language and culture may well be the inevitable consequence of markets which are structured by language and the elimination of state regulation, but neither the platforms and technologies for such operations nor the process itself will stimulate the conditions necessary for innovation as discussed in the RIS.

This relationship between the ideal type model of RIS and practice is handled by resorting to case studies that tend to focus on the institutional, and on the relationship between the components of the system. That is, the focus is much more on structure than it is on process. This means that the assumptions about the relationship between such components as clustering, and the learning outcome as reflexive behaviour, tend not to be evaluated. It leads to the construction of typologies that are meant to refine the universal concept. The parameters of the typological construction involve '. . . the individual characteristics of technological and regional development paths . . . and the regional governance structures that have developed in a manner complementary to these economic structures' (Braczyk & Heidenreich, 1998: 417). The resultant types constitute a continuum from the old and mature industries to knowledge-based and service-based activities.

The onus is now on those responsible to stimulate and promote Regional Innovation and Learning Systems (RILS) and to ensure that every region has the basis to develop 'advanced' economies, with political determined policy being responsible for removing anachronistic practices. The creation of a regional governance and a governmentality that is capable of operating as the basis of normative order is a prerequisite of success. It is the policy agent and the intellectual, sensitive to the system, that will lead the workers who, because of the centrality of tacit skills for the argument, are incapable of assuming the initiative themselves – they must be led. The role of the planner is clear – to create innovative regional clusters by ensuring that producers engender features of reflexivity and interaction in their working practices, with working practices becoming social practices.

In focusing upon the issues of innovation and development, the RIS argument does not focus exclusively on the New Economy, but claims that the history of the industrial age economy at the regional level sets the basis for the nature of the transformation from the Old Economy to the New Economy. This largely depends upon path dependency, and how it relates to technological capabilities as they exist within regionally based organisational structures. However, technology transfer alone is insufficient, and must be associated with the organisational change that facilitates the learning context and networking capacity. It is the interaction of learning, R&D, technological information, production and finance that is responsible for local or regional innovation 'atmosphere' (Braczyk & Schienstock, 1996: 424). It is trust, reciprocity, regional identity and learning that are the key elements of development. What is interesting is the claim that 'strategies of institutional learning or institutional borrowing' are not transferable to peripheral economic regions as a panacea in the form of new institutions. This is because they would not guarantee the flexibility and innovative behaviour of successful regions. What seems to be implied here is that the associated practices must be institutionalised as social practice. Where the regional competence for action lies, that is, how preference for regional action is sustained, is unclear, but the focus is firmly upon the strength of regional identity. Actors are operating with a rational understanding of the regional basis of their identity, and operate for the region rather than merely in self-interest.

'Region' is modelled on an ideal type that is closer to the European historic regions within polities which espouse a decentralised socio-political discourse, and a governance that is in line with the particularism discussed above. Non-historic regions do not currently operate by reference to the ideal type of the RIS thesis, and the thesis would argue that the non-historic regions must be transformed into 'Learning Regions' through the very process that the argument outlines. Where the state stands in this process is unclear, unless all of the European states are transformed into a new form of federalism based on cultural diversity.

It is acknowledged that most innovation gains, whether involving process or product innovation, derive from the interaction between firms and the associated learning process. All interactions are treated similarly by reference to the concept of networking. The various components of social capital that derive from networking relationships – trust, mutual understanding, etc. – are dealt with as if they are uniform features separate from particular personal and institutional contexts. It is difficult to accept that firms will enter relationships of trust and cooperation simply because they coexist within clusters, or even if they share similar production roles. Neither is there any necessary relationship between a shared culture, tacit skills and collaboration. Process innovation and product innovation involve separate forms of interaction.

The RIS argument claims that the importance of governance at the regional level is inevitable in that it derives from a globalisation that seems to be the evolutionary feature of economic development and growth, rather than being the outcome of neo-liberal principles. What makes the region attractive is that it has meaningful flows of economic activities determined by economic specificity and an administrative homogeneity. Yet the approach does encompass most of the principles of neo-liberalism. What the investigators have uncovered is a reorientation of economic process associated with the consequences of adopting the neo-liberal discourse on a global basis. The attempt to place these within a regional context relates to how the same neo-liberal discourse advocates the rolling back of the state, and how meso-governance involves a new form of governmentality wherein the region is allocated a greater degree of political and administrative autonomy than was hitherto the case. This process also opens the space for a new understanding of diversity. The universal principles of state discourses that insisted upon cultural uniformity give way to a more open discussion of diversity. Yet the link between language and culture is, strangely, missing.

Regional Languages

There are two arguments that are of relevance for any discussion of how regional languages can play a role within any RIS. Firstly, the claim that globalisation has promoted a form of governance, multilayered governance, within which governance is shared between international bodies and state and regional governments. Secondly, the argument that the transition from modernity to late modernity involves an enhanced process of individualisation that derives from how the individual is no longer incorporated into institutional systems such that there is little scope for the negotiation of identity. I will discuss each of these issues in turn, prior to considering the relevance of regional languages for RIS.

Castells (2006), among others, argues that globalisation leads to a crisis of political representation which has a profound influence on the restructuring and reconstitution of identities. He emphasises how the world is facing problems that are incapable of being managed within the national framework. The failure of the state to engage with multiple sources of identity creates a crisis of representation. The deregulation of the state in certain contexts, together with how devolution transfers aspects of the regulatory role to the regional level, begins to undermine the modern constitution of social groups. In political terms the EU has established what Castells refers to as a 'network state', wherein national governments work together within institutions in sharing sovereignty. This form links with the various international institutions. It involves a heightened and different relativisation of the self and society within the global (Friedman, 1992). The associated identity emphasises an undifferentiated humankind, perhaps threatened by the consequences of modernity's drive to harness nature. The individual is identified with humankind. Simultaneously, the fragmenting effect of multilayered governance on national and international hegemony foments local and regional identities whose authenticity is linked to roots and place.

Globalisation thus is a peculiarly post-modern phenomenon, different from the colonial order of early modernity. Giddens emphasises the transformation of tradition in reflexive modernity. As tradition was diluted, and humans increasingly intervened in nature, so risk increased. By controlling time, tradition also controlled space. In contrast, globalisation controls time by controlling space. By this he means that globalisation disembeds traditional institutions and extends them over 'indefinite spans of time-space' (Giddens, 1990: 124–125). Thus a global society is not conceived of as a world society, but as one whose space is no longer subject to the finitude of state closure. Social bonds now must be created rather than deriving from the past, and social solidarity insists upon opening up to the 'other'. Thus individualism does not equate with social fragmentation (Giddens, 1994). Where in modernity, trust derived from the stable social position of the individual, it now must be won, and work must be involved in its retention. This 'presumes a process of mutual narrative and emotional disclosure' not expected before (Giddens, 1994: 187). Within larger organisational contexts, as opposed to interpersonal relations, trust requires the 'opening out' of institutions.

A central argument associated with the transformation from modernity to late modernity is that individuals are no longer integrated into institutions such that their identity and sense of being derive from the associated social collectivities. That is, social actors are not institutionalised in the sense of being inscribed in a political system that focuses on the state, so that the correspondence of society and its actors of political and institutional systems is undone.

There is a pervasive argument that such changes derive from neo-liberalism, and that they are articulated through a specific discourse that supports and expresses the principles of neo-liberalism. Thus, the focus on 'exclusion' as opposed to social class or the 'unemployed' presents the main issue as involving the minimisation of deprivation while also condoning the withdrawal of the state from its responsibilities for compensating the victims through the redistribution of wealth. There are elements of the tendency to relate poverty or 'exclusion' to an inadequate culture (Levitas, 1998). If this is the case, then it begs the question of the extent to which neo-liberalism in practice is the driving force for the emergence of reflexive modernity.

Rather, it is claimed that an individualism within which an absolute value is conferred on the individual rather than the community or institutions or private life is valorized, and the intensity of relationship to the self is magnified. Cultural fragmentation, where all forms of cultural variation occupy public space, contributes to the emergence of individualism. The focus shifts to contexts wherein the categories of social life are increasingly separated from political and cultural life, both of which are less integrated, leading to a context where the nation-state is no longer afforded a situation of priority. Where the frame of action is not necessarily the nation-state, and where the demands are cultural and not social, the relation of actors to the political is considerably transformed. We witness more international mediation. The subject is no longer the citizen. The individual is now free to selects one's issues of struggle, one's mobilisation, one's collective identity, etc. That is, the basis of identity is no longer imposed on the individual, but allows a free choice. This does not imply the demise of collective identities and the associated collective action, but argues for their integration around an aggregate of individuals who have elected to identify with such collectivities.

This notion of the individual as a knowledgeable, autonomous agent that contributes to social action relates to the relationship between reflexivity, individualism and modernity. Not all action is goal-orientated, but it is monitored by reflexive practice, whether this be conscious or unconscious. It is this emphasis on reflexivity that distinguishes late modernity from modernity. This reflexive modernity is an institutional rather than an individual phenomenon. Yet social actors, through reflexivity, constantly adjust their social practices. In this respect, the regulative role of knowledge in modernity is replaced, with knowledge becoming an integral feature of how social life is constantly reshaped.

Promoting personal subjectivity is a decisive element of the emergence of modern individualism that is observed in all sectors for collective life – that which justifies what one can call after Beck (1998) the 'second modernity'. The subject has the capacity to be autonomous. That is, to resist being subject to imposed roles, norms, etc., and to be the proper source of his representation. However, modern individualism includes the subjectivity of persons, but is not limited to it. In late modernity, the social space that allows the autonomous definition of identity becomes available. The course of life is no longer determined for us, but becomes our own creation and responsibility.

Despite focusing on individualism, there is no necessary rejection of the relevance of collectivities. Thus individuals may well construct themselves, and may well be constructed as individuals, but they also engage with collective identities. The change involves individuals who are not restricted to specific identities by the centrality of tradition, but are free to engage with whichever collective identity they choose. Such a view persists with the notion of identity construction as a rational process even if it does incorporate notions of invention, creativity and personal engagement.

However, it can also be argued that this focus upon a freedom to engage with any form of identity overlaps with what has been termed 'identity politics', and how it derives from post-structuralism. Identity politics can be seen as how the left responded to the emphasis on identity among oppressed groups. Post-structuralism denies the unity of social formations, instead placing the emphasis upon the struggle between multiple points of power such that the social totality incorporates a will to power. The multiple bases of power give rise to different forms of oppression, each of which has a corresponding form of resistance. The oppressed group is unable to transcend its specific identity. Universal perspectives, including Marxism, are portrayed as the products of a Eurocentrism that derives from Christianity and which persists in the processes of modernity (Laclau & Mouffe, 1985).

The preceding arguments emphasise how the individual in late modernity is liberated from an essential engagement with tradition. However, it also acknowledges indirectly that tradition itself is an 'imagined' condition. That is, it is socially constructed through how the discourse of the state presented itself as the essence of modernity while simultaneously contrasting modernity with 'tradition'. Linguistic diversity was presented as an anachronism, as a spillover from an archaic nationalism. In the economic discourses of modernity, cultural diversity was marginalised and relegated to 'context'. The universalism of such discourses has also been assumed in the arguments of the left. Thus it was common to claim that attempts to incorporate regional languages into the labour market constituted a form of elitism that undermined the interests of the working class within the same labour market. The interests of this working class could only be served through the universal language. Minority or regional languages and their speakers have long suffered from the effects of such discourses.

While the preceding arguments emphasise how the integration of the individual with the institutional organisation is undone, thereby liberating the individual from conformity with the identity formation of modernity, there is also a sense in which the new condition liberates the individual from the negative constraints associated with the orthodox discourse of a modernity that emphasised universalism. The very discourses that promoted a 'negative identity' are reversed and diversity is promoted, especially within a region that now has access to its own form of governance.

Among the responsibilities transferred from central to regional governance are those that pertain to both language and culture. Consequently, both assume a regional flavour and significance, while also being institutionalised and legitimised through the creation of bodies responsible for their promotion. These bodies become accountable by reference to the activities undertaken by reference to promoting language and culture. It is no longer possible to ignore either. A positive environment surrounds regional language and culture. This must be transformed into practices that are relevant for extending linguistic and cultural diversity. Thus the emphasis on reversing language shift (Fishman, 1992), replete with all references to an outmoded structural functionalism as the mantra of language planning, must be abandoned in favour of a perspective that accommodates recent understandings of social and cultural change (Williams, 2008).

Much of what the regional state can achieve by reference to regional languages focuses on the public sector. While this is important by reference to the role of the regional language within the regional labour market, there is a limit to how it can influence its broader salience. There is little doubt that such developments do have an influence upon the relationship between educational systems and the regional labour market, and how this serves as a motivational force by reference to promoting the language. However, it is only when there is an entry into the private sector on a level that will have significance that one can really expect to encounter the strength of the link to the RIS.

The articulation between the regional and the global is direct and open. It is direct in that it does not require mediation by the state, and it is open in that the framework for its constitution involves its internal coherence as well as by reference to external bodies and agencies. The loosening of the constraints of modernity and industrial society contributes significantly to the basis for regional action.

If the claims about the importance of path dependency for the entry of regions into the knowledge economy are correct, then the significance of the regional language within this economy will involve a restructuring of the link between language and the corporation. We have seen a relaxation of the insistence of companies about the use of different languages in work, but we have yet to find much evidence of how firms actively promote the use of multilingualism in work, partly, one suspects, because the relevance of the role of language in creativity is not recognised. It should be self-evident that the New Economy will not be the sole prerogative of the MNC, even if such institutions do play a driving role by reference to that economy. On the contrary, there are a variety of ways of entry into the knowledge economy, some of which depend upon path dependency, and others involve entirely new regional alignments. Similarly, there are numerous examples of regional firms entering into partnership with the larger multinational firms. Within such partnerships one or other of the *lingue franche* may well prevail, but thus far, evidence suggests that there is a much greater degree of tolerance of the use of a variety of languages than one might suspect.

What is changing is the relationship between the state and regional languages. The state language no longer stands as the point of reference for the regional language within an economic world within which relationships may well be with firms from any part of the world. Furthermore, as argued in Chapter 2, many of the multinational firms owe allegiance to their shareholders rather than to any specific state. Also their locational alignments is determined more by the level of corporation tax than by any locational point of origin.

Conclusion

Despite the growing body of work on RIS it is questionable that we are any closer to understanding how and why innovation works. In such processes the role of companies is crucial. Competitive rules, the needs of capital markets, global sourcing, sector regulation and the developmental paths of specific companies all generate pressures to rationalise and standardise. Interaction between companies and regions takes place in different ways and involves different organisational structures. Where material linkages were crucial in the industrial age economy, in the future, knowledge-based interaction will be increasingly important (Amin & Thrift 2004, xvvi). Therefore, cultures in knowledge sharing and innovation are of special interest in company–region-interaction, in particular because tacit knowledge becomes more and more important, and spatial density is claimed to be decisive.

A limited understanding of culture contributes to the rationalism in the RIS arguments. Thus the focus on institutional and innovation issues involves a strong rationalist bias because the symbolic dimension of cultural change is widely ignored. As I have implied, there is also a normative bias because of the strong empirical and theoretical focus on innovative and Learning Regions and the related processes. There is very limited research on the preconditions of innovation, the bottlenecks, or the failure to build appropriate regional networks, or innovation systems. Of course, there is a strong discussion about the dangers of regions becoming conservative and closed (lock-in). However, regional culture is often regarded as a static concept, and as an exogenous variable. It remains unclear how regional culture and trust are formed, why in some regions there seems to be more trust than in others, and to which extent culture and trust are changing through the interaction of companies, organisations and policy actors (Morgan, 1997; Powell, 1996; Sabel, 1992; Storper, 2002). In this respect, we are not much further along the road of explanation than by reference to the work of Putnam that was discussed in Chapter 3.

Viewing culture as consisting of rationally accessible and observable values, it is argued that the culture of a newly established company is not coined by the initial values of the company's founder or strong leader, but rather, it is the product of mutual interaction between all relevant actors in the organisation (Morgan, 1997; Pekruhl, 2001). The weakness of this rationalism gives way to a claim that if a majority of these actors (employees) originate from the same region, it is very likely that values, beliefs and habits, created by the mutual cultural socialisation of these actors, will enter the organisation and will have considerable effects on the generation of the new company's culture (Breidenbach & Zukrigl, 1998: 81ff; Trice & Beyer, 1993). The building or activating of regional cultures can be understood as the creation of a shared reference system. There is no need for a reference system like this to be homogeneous, nor for it to be devoid of contradictions, but it does need characters and symbols.

Regions in the periphery of the New Economy are unlikely to attract the main players in the knowledge economy, and will have to rely on their own resources and ingenuity to enter this economy. Presumably, according to the RIS argument, within the path dependency process of development, regional firms will already be integrated into the regional culture, but will be obliged to modify this relationship between their organisational and productive forms and regional cultural structures, if they are to succeed in the knowledge economy. This certainly pertains to how the work on Benetton in Italy, or the work on Baden Wurtemburg, portrays the situation. Within the networking of companies, innovation is a very important motive for such behaviour, involving qualified labour, specialised suppliers, as well as research and development companies, when they are available, in the region. Similarly, a comparative study of the Swiss and French Jura implies that regional consensus, shared future visions, common habits and culture have a strong influence on the pattern of behaviour of firms, and on a region's adaptability and innovativeness (Maillat *et al.*, 1996). Such studies present regional culture as that which embeds firms in the regional economy, saying little about how such companies shape the regional context.

These processes will be quite different from the changes expected of large knowledge economy companies entering the core regions of the New Economy. They will confront problems that they only loosely understand, and will be obliged to work with regional development agents who carry highly embedded operational methods that often lack flexibility. The issues of why a company is engaged in a region, and the process of cultural integration, are neglected, as are the tensions and conflicts within the companies, and within the region. The interaction between companies and the region is not necessarily harmonious.

The limited understanding of how new knowledge is generated from within resources that are tacit in nature presents a particular problem. The regional innovation system work only touches on this issue, and appears to be struggling to identify successful processes, using a largely inductive methodology. While not wishing to deny the importance of networking and regional culture, it does appear that resolving this central issue requires a much greater attention to the details of interaction and of the role of language in that interaction.

Neither is there any certainty that companies newly locating in the region will articulate with the regional culture. They are engaged with different social spaces, which carry different cultures. While they have the option of developing a regional orientation, if it is acknowledged as being of significance, it is by no means essential. It requires a specific commitment by the company, and a regional framework which is constructed out of sensitivity to regional culture, and a commitment to its promotion. Companies, especially global players, are often discussed as footloose or fluent. Indeed, many models of orthodox economics and development, based on the arguments of capital markets and global companies, the driving force of global investment and relocation in specific sectors, openly promote this image. Many companies which have been absorbed through mergers and acquisitions will tend to relocate in seeking the best advantage vis-à-vis state-level taxation. This merely perpetuates this tendency to relocate. For them, Granovetter's (1992) argument in favour of relational and structural embeddedness is a distraction, unless they recognise how transaction costs in material as well as in socio-cultural terms are often underestimated.

Undoubtedly, the home base of the company gains in importance in terms of the quality of life for a highly qualified labour force, as well as for suppliers or customers. Nokia is a case in point. Even if companies are acting in global networks, they depend on an efficient region with qualified labour, a reliable infrastructure and a prospering economic environment. Even companies that are not engaged in the region in economic terms often sponsor regional development strategies, or local sports and culture activities, sometimes to help compensate for the joblessness caused by the company's global strategy. This has been presented as a reason why the USA should resist foreign acquisitions of its main economic players on grounds other than protectionism (*Le Monde*, 13.5.06).

Lundvall's argument leaves an important role for all of the state languages within the knowledge economy. It is not merely the *lingue franche* that should operate within the economy. Regardless of the criticism, it also leaves a role for regional or minority languages. Currently, educational policy across most of Europe appears to be focusing on the teaching of English, often exclusive of other foreign languages. As I have already remarked, this has been characterised as being '... inefficient in terms of the allocation of resources, unjust in terms of the distribution of resources, dangerous for linguistic and cultural diversity and worrying by reference to its geopolitical implications' (Grin, 2005: 8).

It should be clear that there is significant overlap between RIS and communities of practice. This is because of how social practice based on tacit knowledge has become part of the received wisdom of sociology. Given that knowledge derives from interaction or social practice, there is a need to try to at least account for the nature and process of knowledge generation associated with tacit knowledge. Where RIS relies on an abstract and weakly formulated notion of culture as the explanandum for knowledge generation, the communities of practice conception resorts to the creation of meaning as the cornerstone for understanding knowledge and learning. Clearly, both concepts are central to understanding the relationship between society and language. What neither does is to articulate these concepts with a linguistic component. Nonetheless, it does imply a role for autochthonous language groups. In Chapter 5, I will focus on the issue of communities of practice before turning to a deeper consideration of the relevance of language for these issues.

Notes

1. Evolutionary Economics implies that Fordism was an inherent conceptualisation that derived from the neo-classical discourse. It does not deny the relevance of neo-classicism, but that it is no longer relevant since an evolutionary principle is involved in the progress from the one to the other, and progress is evident in the one feature that is common to both, the need for growth.
2. Giddens (1984: 283) suggests that the relationship between society and state is no longer so clear-cut.
3. Such issues emerge when one recognises the extent to which globalisation and the role of the European Union in it is replacing the role of state by reference to society. This undermines the very principle whereby each state has its own normative order and society. Consequently, there appears to be a need to rethink the fundamental principles according to which sociology has discussed society.

Chapter 5
Communities of Practice

Introduction

In the preceding chapters, reference has been made to communities of practice and how they are regarded as the operational structure wherein knowledge generation is possible. As such it is an important concept, one that is key to several aspects related to the knowledge economy. Its focus is on learning through social practice. In this respect, it addresses how the structuring of communities involves a learning process within inter-action. However, the key to the argument is the notion of community, in that other concepts such as social networks could well be regarded as capable of generating the same process. Thus the focus is on the mem-bers of the collectivity that, together, constitute the community, rather than on the individual. Given that the notion of community has been around for as long as the social sciences have been practiced, this facet is not new. Nonetheless, the associated work does draw upon recent soci-ological theory and, to this extent, leads to a reappraisal of the concept of community.

It is important to recognise that the main thrust of this work is con-cerned with learning, and how it differs from the conventional under-standing of education. The main claim is that learning occurs within bounded, interactional contexts, without the individual necessarily know-ing that she is learning. To this extent learning is an on-going process that constitutes a fundamental part of the relations of production. This 'learn-ing' is reduced to the creation of new meanings. What is surprising is that a thesis that relies so exclusively upon 'meaning' makes so little reference to language. This is not to maintain that the orthodox conception of lan-guage is the location for an understanding of the construction of meaning, but that it would appear necessary to consider the details of meaning con-struction by reference to more than the theoretical conceptualisation of interactional practice.

While some sociolinguists (Eckert, 2000) have drawn upon the con-cept, striving to access processes of linguistic variation, little has been made of the relationship between what is treated as the key components of communities and learning – shared meaning, and language. This is an issue I will focus on in Chapter 6. Here I would like to carefully consider the ideas associated with the concept of community of practice as a prelude to that chapter.

Tacit Knowledge

The central problem confronted in the discussion of communities of practice involves how knowledge, if it is tacit in nature, can be learnt. The implication is that the person who has the knowledge is not directly capable of transmitting that knowledge to the learner within the customary context of 'teaching'. The issue of tacit knowledge has already been touched upon in Chapter 3. In that chapter it was stated that while the notion of people as knowledgeable rule followers was retained, knowledge was not explicit. This means that the normative social order that sociologists have claimed to constitute the basis of social action cannot be premised on the rational thinking subject, and her relationship to a pre-established system of knowledge. Here I wish to take this issue further in that the denial of the efficacy of rationalism obliges quite a profound rethinking of the nature of language and meaning.

The notion of learning presents a challenge to the idea that markets operate by reference to the actions of players who are endowed with a complete knowledge that informs their existence as the best judges of their interests. It implies the existence of completely formed, unchanging, knowledge and, in this respect, it is compatible with how sociology used to conceive of socialisation as limited to childhood. Clearly, the neoclassical economic understanding of learning is deficient.

Hayek and other Austrian school economists treated learning somewhat differently. In this respect, they drew heavily on the work of Polyani (1958). Rather than treating information as something that flows freely from the mind of the individual, they insisted that information is perceived through a cognitive framework. In line with psychology there was a tendency to treat cognition by reference to the individual who, consequently, was capable of an individualistic interpretation of data. Hayek's main concern was with the use of knowledge rather than with its creation or construction. It was this emphasis that allowed him to treat knowledge as a scarce resource. As we have seen this was something that was taken up by Bourdieu in his discussion of social capital. In economic terms, the focus remained on the discovery and the use of existing knowledge, most notably price information. The empiricist emphasis upon something 'out there' that is capable of discovery remains. In this respect, the work contrasts with the emphasis upon the construction of meaning which tends to encompass interactivity, adaptation and creativity. The individual is already in place, ready to discover that which she requires.

The other issue that emerges here relates to the role of planning in development. This involves the question of what planning can do in order to promote an innovation that relates to learning and knowledge. Once we recognise that information is data to which some meaning has been attributed, and that knowledge can be understood as the product of how information is used, we begin to accommodate the importance of recognising that the processes which we use to obtain and use information are tacit in nature. What stands out about tacit knowledge is that it involves *knowing how* rather than *knowing that*, and, as Polyani recognised, this is not easy to articulate because 'we can know more than we can tell' (1967: 4). It is acknowledged that tacit knowledge is transmitted through conversation and narrative.

The distinction between *knowing how* and *knowing that* involves the former referring to a skilled praxial knowledge, while the later involves a type of knowledge that refers to linguistic, conceptual and propositional knowledge. The former appeals to a form of embodied reasonableness involving intuition and common sense understanding, while the later is abstract, and pertains to the reflective model of formal rationality. The acquisition of the formal, reflective knowledge demands an immersion in the operative knowledge of a specific community. It is this understanding that Bourdieu took on board in his notion of *habitus*. *Knowing how* involves a behaviour which individuals engage with without necessarily being able to provide an account of how they perform. Language in the sense of a communicational competence is of this order, and, as such, constitutes a form of cultural disposition.

Much of the preceding applies to language use, in that we cannot be expected to reflect on every single word that we speak, which must mean that, as Bahktin (1981) recognised, we learn language already dialogised. We use language not as a grammar that is recognised and exploited in a rational manner but, rather, by drawing upon the tacit knowledge of language and how it operates that we all have. Tacit knowledge is an essential foundation of all knowledge. It might be possible to consider organisational learning as something that involves transforming some tacit knowledge into a codified form that can be communicated to others, but it simply is not possible to render explicit all tacit knowledge. This is largely because meaning is constantly shifting, so that every time something is expressed it changes its meaning.

Chomsky (1972), on the other hand, claims that if the speaker's utterances conform to the conditions specified by a language rule, then that speaker knows that rule. This involves *knowing that*. Furthermore, when it is claimed that someone knows a language rule, Chomsky would claim that there is a sense in which that person expresses belief or attitude towards the propositional content (*knowing that*) embodying that language. In this respect, knowing involves language behaviour taking the form that it does by virtue of the content of the cognitive state that supports language behaviour. That is, the content of the cognitive state represents the speaker's knowledge of language, and serves as explanation for the production of appropriate *enonciation*. This leads to the question of the extent to which the formulation of a rule expresses a speaker's belief, rather than the conditions with which the speaker's behaviour unknowingly conforms.

Searle (1972) has criticised how Chomsky argues that speakers follow the very rules which grammarians have formulated. He claims that there is a need to distinguish between actual rules that are being followed and hypotheses or generalisations that describe the speaker's behaviour. He also asserts that the person who is claimed to be rule following should understand herself to be following that rule. She should be capable of explaining why and how her speech displays the regularity that it does. This is rarely the case, and not all speakers are aware of why they produce *enonces* in the way that they do. We fall back on Polyani's (1967: 4) claim about knowing '... more than we can tell'. That is, as Chomsky claims, much knowledge of language is tacit in nature. His understanding of tacit knowledge involves how it is '... generally inaccessible to consciousness'. This understanding of tacit knowledge conforms with ordinary knowledge that is not isolated from other attitude states, and claims that how speakers use their tacit knowledge is influenced by their '... goals, beliefs, expectations, and so forth', which suggests that tacit knowledge is anything but tacit. It seems to imply that there is a value system that is already in place that determines how tacit knowledge is deployed. This system is accessible to consciousness, whereas tacit knowledge is not.

Chomsky also claims that first-person reports regarding what a person thinks she is doing are not reliable: 'We might ask Jones what rule she is following, but ... such evidence is at best very weak because people's judgements as to why they do what they are doing is rarely informative or trustworthy' (1986: 254). Indeed, he is obliged to fall back on the knowledge of 'experts'. Thus he claims that a person's knowledge includes what is known to experts within the speech community. He draws upon Putnam's (1988: 19–41) notion of the division of linguistic labour in claiming that the meaning of a term may be expressed in terms of the specialised knowledge of others in the speech community. This would appear to be little more than asking the lay person to consult the work of linguists in order to ascertain the linguistic rule which that lay person is using.

When we move from a consideration of the extent to which tacit knowledge can be made explicit, to a concern with the relationship between knowledge and learning, we are led to the conclusion that the only way in which one can 'teach' such knowledge is to provide the opportunities for people to learn it. However, the notion of communities of practice implies that individual examples of propositional knowledge, or practical skill, are more than the sum of its parts. This, in turn, would mean that the answer lies in 'learning by doing', or a 'situational learning' that cannot be reduced to standard teachable forms that would, in all likelihood, destroy it. The notion of learning by doing has been an inherent feature of apprenticeships and how they draw upon professional intuition in the transmission of knowledge by non-verbal means. This is at odds with how skill learning tends to be constructed as acquisition rather than as transmission.

The idea that tacit knowledge is shared knowledge is something that was taken up by Wainwright (1994) in arguing against the individualistic ideas of Hayek's work. She claimed that tacit knowledge is largely social, and is often held by groups of workers rather than by individuals. While knowledge may be social in nature it does not mean that it is readily accessible to any member of society, as if it was some kind of cultural codification known to the insider. It raises the thorny issue of how a knowledge that resides in productive teams of workers relates to the coordination of the associated economic organisation.

It is in this sense that there is reference to the social construction of knowledge. Constructivism implies that there exist both local and specifically constructed realities. It is an ontology that claims that reality is a relative phenomenon. Thus there are no observers involved, merely 'viewers' who carry different 'views' or representations that interact through a semantic communication process. Those who emphasise the cognitive nature of meaning emphasise the exploration and discovery on the part of each learner as central to the learning process. Knowledge remains a symbolic, mutual representation in the mind of the individual. This differs from socially oriented approaches which maintain that the context is part of the knowledge – it is based on experiences which vary from one social institution to the other, and these institutions may also be subject to change as the institutional realities change.

Clearly, knowledge is rooted in social practice, and involves conceptions and practices that are shared. It is this awareness that leads some to argue that the best that can be achieved derives from creating the 'knowledge culture' which encourages learning and the creation and sharing of knowledge (McInerney, 2002: 1014). It is such ideas that lie behind the notion of communities of practice.

Communities of Practice

Much of what is claimed by reference to the generation and management of knowledge is encompassed in Wenger's notion of communities of practice (Wenger, 1998). His work is remarkably eclectic, and it is difficult to see how his mixing of problematics does not result in epistemological contradiction. He embraces the work of Marxists such as Gramsci and Braverman side by side with the asociological work of the ethnomethodologists. He incorporates the more conservative Weberian thrust of Giddens's work, while also flirting with post-structuralists and allied thinkers, including Bakhtin, Heideggar and Wittgenstein. He embraces the work of Michel Foucault, but is not comfortable with it because of its denial of the individual subject. He does accept how Foucault's work involves '...pervasive forms of discipline sustained by discourses which define knowledge and truth...', and views discourse as '...a characterisation of practice...' while not equating the two. He is also critical of Foucault for ignoring identity, seemingly being unaware of how the relationship between the individual, the subject and identity are handled in post-structural discourse analysis.

The claim that much of our knowledge is tacit in nature is central to the notion of communities of practice. It is another manifestation of the claim of both Giddens and Bhaskar that the normative order of any society involves tacit knowledge. That is, normativity is not seen as a preordained form that relates to social order, but is to be found in the common sense of the ordinary citizen who is unable to easily express the basis of this common sense. While Polyani's work is of relevance here, so also is the more general work of post-structuralism, and how it has had a profound impact upon how sociologists have come to understand behaviour.

What Wenger does with this awareness of the nature of knowledge is to relate it to social practice. He claims that bounded communities operate social practice on the basis of tacit knowledge. Within this process meaning is constantly negotiated, not as a rational process, but as an ongoing process of interaction that draws on tacit knowledge in developing new knowledge. This would appear to be merely another manifestation of how sociology has always viewed social structure as patterned behaviour. What is different is how he relates the production of knowledge, not to a rational form of reflexivity, but rather to the relationship between identity and the social construction of meaning within social interaction among members of this community of practitioners. He argues that the task for anyone interested in organisational learning is to be able to uncover and exploit tacit knowledge.

Thus the focus is very much on knowledge management as a strategic exercise. In many respects, it constitutes an attempt to move away from how learning was conditioned by the production line of Taylorism in industrial age economy, and to develop a learning context based upon the centrality of knowledge creation for the New Economy. Where Taylorism has been displaced by business units, working as teams in dealing with markets and production lines, it still had not come to terms with the ownership of knowledge. This is a highly neo-liberal concern that involves the relationship between ownership, responsibility and accountability.

Communities are claimed to be units which share knowledge. That is, the continuous process of face-to-face interaction is claimed to result in collective learning that relates to social practice as an expression of how to behave within such communities. This involves the normative practice of a range of expected or preferred behaviour, and the range of flexibility that such behaviour can tolerate. The central point is that knowledge within such communities is not constructed as an object, but as part of their social practice, or of their ability to participate within the community.

The reference to 'community' tends not to relate to a strict definition but rather involves an interactive group which shares knowledge in common. However, in sharing knowledge, and being capable of generating knowledge, that group assumes a social character in that it is the commonality that sets the boundary for the group, while if tacit knowledge is a feature of the normative order, then its shared nature makes the group social in nature. That is, we are discussing more than a group of individuals. It may well be that Wenger's intention was to go further and assign to the community the stricter definition of group wherein differentiated and complementary roles are organised to achieve a shared purpose. Certainly, there is a sense of mutuality involved in the notion, and considerable emphasis tends to be placed on the attributes of the 'community' – mutual trust, shared identity and associated attributes. Indeed, social practice is claimed to be the source of coherence of a community. Evidently, if social practice is held to be institutionalised behaviour, then it is inevitable that the community will be defined by this sense of patterned behaviour, or ways of behaving, or of doing things.

Whatever the attractions of Wenger's work there remain two fundamental problems to be resolved. Firstly, the existence of a social structure and the relationship between such a social structure and practice. Secondly, the nature and extent of rationalism within the theoretical model. One of the problems with pinning Wenger down vis-à-vis his own position is that, whereas he gives a detailed indication of the relevant work associated with different concepts, he does not indicate his own position vis-à-vis the divergent theoretical problematics he confronts.

Theoretical Issues

Wenger claims that meaning is negotiated but, clearly, since the procedure is not necessarily a rational process, this negotiation does not involve a negotiation based upon rationally conceptualised exchanges. Interaction is discussed by reference to the notion of social practice that involves behaviour conditioned by the circumstances that are claimed to inform interaction. In this respect, he devotes considerable attention to the work of Bourdieu whose conception of social practice redressed the structural functionalism of the 1970s. While, like Wenger, Bourdieu does resort to Wittgenstein as a source of reference, it seems to be primarily secondary to his outright rejection of post-structuralism. He even rejects the work of Althusser in claiming the need to retain the notion of agents, even though claiming that practice was far removed from the automatic execution of rules which, somehow, related to structure. Rather, practice conforms with specific habitus, and the reference to Wittgenstein pertains to practice as a form of 'play' (Bourdieu, 1987). It does not exactly conform with Wittgenstein's scepticism regarding the 'explanatory power', and critical efficacy of critical social theory. It is hardly surprising that Giddens (1979: 250–251) refers to a relativistic 'paralysis of the critical will' regarding Wittgenstein's philosophy. Nonetheless, it is important to note that most of those who draw upon the notion of 'tacit knowledge' claim, not always correctly (Pleasants, 1999), Wittgenstein to be a significant influence on their work.

Wenger goes on to indicate that his own notion is more in line with Giddens's theory of structuration. This conceives of a relationship between social structure and behaviour such that each modifies the other. Individual action and social structure no longer involve two mutually exclusive metaphysical world views – one involving 'individual agency' and the other 'objective determination' – but are claimed to be intimately interlinked. Thus, social structure or system is the knowledgably produced outcome of the action of individuals. Conversely, the actions of individuals draw upon individual–transcendent structures and systems. Giddens's concept of structure involves a 'virtual order of differences', and derives from structuralist linguistics, and the associated notion of 'duality of structure' is constructed on an analogy between language and speech.

Structuration is an attempt to unify sociological theory through the concepts of the duality of structure through which it becomes possible to analyse human practice as both action and structure. This means that society is no longer conceived of as an external, constraining system. Rather, it is viewed as the result of skilled, knowledgeable and reflexive agents whose action occurs within specific social contexts. All of what have tended to be thought of as objective structures are substantiated in practice, as the agents produce and reproduce the structures that underpin and enable action to occur. Structure now becomes something that is an inherent ingredient of reproduced practices that are embedded in time and space. Consequently, it is both the medium for, and the outcome of, social action. In many respects, this argument is not unlike Weber's concept of social action that implied that social institutions and structure have no existence apart from the actions that they embody. The focus is very much on social practice.

Structure is conceived of as paradigmatic in the sense that it is conceptualised as a virtual system that is recursively instantiated as it is drawn upon by agents who act and interact on a routine basis. It differs from the social system that remains as a system of patterned behaviour or relationships involving the concrete practices of the actors. Structuration involves how structures lead to the constitution of social systems. Structure as a social object is not external to the subject, but is inseparable from her behaviour. It provides the set of rules and resources that makes social conduct possible, and its reproduction and transformation derive from the instantiation of rules in action and interaction. As elements that shape the conduct of the actor, structures both constrain and enable.

Both structure and practice are referenced by rules and resources. Rules provide the basis for an ordered and stable social life. They operate on two levels of consciousness. Firstly, the discursive, in which agents have a tacit or theoretical comprehension of the rules involved in the reproduction of social practices, thereby enabling them to understand and give reasons for action. Secondly, operating on a practical level, the awareness of the skills and knowledge which enable agents to carry out forms of action. Resources, on the other hand, are the elements that agents incorporate into the production and reproduction of social practices. They involve the knowledges and skills which allow people to interact with others and to transform relations. The rules and resources allow social life to be recursively structured, rather than being intentionally realised by agents. That is, social practices change situations, but also reproduce the social order on which the rules governing social action depend. Structure becomes both the medium and the outcome of social action. This social action involves reflexive agents capable of monitoring their actions through practical and discursive consciousness. These agents are no longer over-socialised, passive dupes, but become knowledgeable, creative and active.

The central components of this theory are tacit knowledge and transcendental rules. Giddens acknowledges that the associated ontological pictures are central to the 'decentring of subjectivity', and that this derives from the post-structural theories of subjectivity. Yet he retains the notion of the 'knowledgeable agent'. Individuals are no longer preconstituted subjects, dualistically related to an 'external' world of social structure and relations. Nonetheless, individuals are, in Husserlian terms, 'always already' social beings, and the social system becomes a recursively reproduced product of individual action. Giddens defines the actions of social actors as a continuous flow of conduct, and it is the regularity of this behaviour that constitutes social praxis. They are capable of reflexively monitoring that praxis in the sense that they can relate their actions to one another, as well as to the world within which they occur. Accounting for their actions constitutes one feature of this reflexive monitoring.

Tacit knowledge decentres subjectivity while, in Wenger's model, retaining the reality of individual consciousness and knowledgeability. As such it replaces 'the philosophy of consciousness' of rationalist and empiricist philosophers (Habermas, 1991: 387). There is a shift from 'theory' to 'practice', while the practice of scientific work, like the practice of non-scientific activity, is accorded the status of knowledge. Rather than identifying knowledge with theory as an intellectual product or state of mind, knowledge is seen as process and activity. What is confusing is that Wenger relates this tacit knowledge to Gramsci's notion of 'common sense', which not only seems to overturn the unknown nature of such knowledge but also brings in a Marxist dimension that contrasts with Giddens's position.

Similarly, Giddens acknowledges that all individuals 'know' more than they are able to articulate and, furthermore, tacitly 'know' a great deal about the conditions of their own and others' action, as well as about their social and political institutions. Indeed, structuration theory goes out of its way to deny that the institutional and structural framework of society does not operate externally, out of the reach of individuals (Giddens, 1979: 71). Rather, the existence of these 'objective', structural phenomenon depends ultimately on the totality of the knowledgeable actions of individuals. There are three kinds of knowledgeable actions – the theoretical or discursive; practical consciousness involving tacit knowledge that is continuously reflexively monitored by the individual; and the unconscious or symbolically encoded emotional experience. The only one to which the individual has no access is the last. It is possible for individuals to access some of their 'tacit knowledge'. However, translating tacit into explicit knowledge is the kind of hermeneutic endeavour requiring the theoretical and interpretive skills of the professional social theorist. Evidently, the theoretical lies at the heart of this body of theory, and stands independently of action.

It is here that we encounter the double hermeneutic. Both Durkheim and Comte wished to apply the advances of social science to generate positive social change. Durkheim also wanted the general public to be educated in the social sciences so that the conscience collective could be recast and rationalised, leading to the desired change. For both Durkheim and Giddens, theory has to articulate twice with practice. First, through the expertise of the social scientist; and second, as the creation of social scientific reflexivity among large numbers of the population.

Reflexivity depends on our not being determined by social structures or epistemology, opening the space for our being reflexive. Theories of reflexivity appear not only in the work of Bourdieu and Giddens but also in ethnomethodology. Reflexivity becomes the critique of determinate reason. Giddens's notion of reflexive monitoring involves actors maintaining a continuous theoretical understanding of the grounds of their activity.

This is a highly Cartesian position in the sense that it conforms with the paradigm of the philosophy of consciousness. That is, he claims that all individuals, as competent social actors, are intimately connected with their own practical consciousness as a feature of their everyday behaviour. In other words, we are all continuously and intimately acquainted with the conditions of, and the reasons for, what we are doing, even if it is in a tacit rather than an explicit mode. For Giddens this reflexivity pertains to what is done, rather than what is thought. That is, there is an ability to account for actions even if they are not goal-orientated, but merely intentional. This means that if the reason for action is explicit, and if the motives can be conscious, then the actors must have some degree of knowledge about their social surroundings. It is here that the reference to discursive and tacit knowledge appears, with knowledge being of this order. Together, knowledgeability and reflexive monitoring allow the actor to resist any determining power that lies in the structure. Behaviour is capable of modification, making the actor relatively autonomous, a position not unlike that of Gramsci. Constraint derives from the unacknowledged conditions and unintended consequences of social action.

It is also correct to say that Giddens operates with a Kantian problematic that involves cognitive powers and transcendental philosophy. It is the notion of practical consciousness that allows human action to be seen as 'knowledgeable', and despite the elitist claim for the significance of the social scientist, knowledge becomes an inherent feature of all humans. This practical consciousness operates through language and interactive negotiation within specific settings, and what Giddens refers to as 'co-presence'. In operating 'knowledgeably', individuals draw on and apply rules that derive from a transcendental order of 'tacit' rules which shape and inform their activities. These rules are unknown to the individual but, nonetheless, constitute that which is what social structure consists of. Consequently, both tacit knowledge and practical consciousness determine which rules to select and how they should be applied, thereby constituting the 'agency' of the individual. This must mean that social structure is constituted both by rules, on the one hand, and by individual agency in the form of tacit knowledge on the other.

It seems clear that it is from this body of work that Wenger derives his theoretical problematic, and that we can treat his references to post-structuralism as, at best, circumspect. The relationships between 'rule' and the 'knowledge of how to apply the rule' is claimed to overcome the previous relationship between 'structure' and 'agency' within which preconstituted individual subjects possess powers of agency and consciousness, but are constrained by an external order of objective structural determination. Agency now exists as a consequence of a structure of rules that inform and generate meaningful conduct. However, these structures of rules are constantly reproduced and transformed through their use.

The 'settings' within which social practices occur involve Wenger's notion of communities of practice whose boundaries are determined by the actual practices with which the community engages. Since these practices are analysed by reference to the social production of meaning, it would appear that communities of practice constitute bounded meaning systems. This may well involve direct boundary markers, or it will involve more subtle processes. Communities are defined by 'mutual engagement' that affords or denies 'belonging'. Thus it involves the historical dimension whereby specific meanings are established, negotiated and changed, to the extent that membership implies both an understanding or engagement with the relevant meanings and the ability to contribute to their changing nature. The interactions within these communities give rise to the generation of specific meanings that, at least initially, are confined to the membership. However, new members can be incorporated into the community through immersion in the interactive practices and the associated learning. It involves a learning that focuses upon doing. It also implies that these communities become part of 'structure'. The cohesion of the community derives from social practice constructed around shared interests.

However, these are not closed communities sealed by their boundaries, but link with other communities. These communities can also stand remote from other communities, or they may form part of a hierarchical structure. Thus the concept allows for membership of a variety of communities, while also establishing relationships of power and authority by reference to both communities and the members thereof. It becomes possible to straddle several communities, and to link distinctive communities. It is the sustaining of common interests over time that generates the reproductive nature of communities. Presumably, within these communities, much of behaviour or practice is institutionalised, and is not necessarily consciously reflexive. On the other hand, there is space for reflection among and across the practitioners, and it is this that is the main ingredient of learning.

Despite Wenger's attempt to distance himself from the notion, communities of practice increasingly seem to resemble Bourdieu's notion of habitus. Wenger objected to how Bourdieu argued that practice derived from an underlying structure or habitus. It is by no means clear that this is how Bourdieu intended the notion to be constructed, at least in his later work. However, the point which Wenger is trying to emphasise is that structure and practice operate in harmony, rather than as distinctive causal forms.

Habitus is a concept that was reworked by Bourdieu in order to avoid structuralism's conception of a philosophy of the subject, where the subject merely appears in and through discourse. In so doing Bourdieu drew heavily upon Merleau-Ponty's work, and especially on Husserl's phenomenology that referred to antipredictive experience. This, he claims, results in an analysis of the relationship between the agent and the world that was neither intellectualised nor mechanical (Bourdieu, 1987: 20). However, the notion has a much broader currency, appearing in work from Hegel to Weber, and Durkheim. In all cases the intention is to break with the Kantian dualism, and to reintroduce the permanent arrangement or structures that are constitutive of an achieved doctrine in contrast to an immanent doctrine. This is an issue that derives from early Cartesianism. It is the means whereby Husserl sought to uncover the philosophy of consciousness, or how Mauss uncovered the systematic functioning of the social body. Bourdieu seeks to claim that the notion of the practice of the agent, involving as it does innovation and improvisation, avoids the transcendental subject of idealism, replacing it with the notion of an active agent. This, in turn, he relates to Fichte's primacy of practical reason, and to his own attempts to uncover the specific categories of that reason (Bourdieu, 1980). He constructed the notion of habitus as a system of acquired schemes which function in their practical state as categories of perception or, at the same time, as principles of classification which, as the principle organisers of action, constitutes the social agent as the practical operator of the construction of objects.

While the notion of a community of practice is an analytical category, Wenger does go so far as to claim that it is also a familiar aspect of our experience. Communities of practice can engage with one another as constellations. These constellations can be marked by differences which relate to a lack of communication, such that the behavioural patterns and the meaning systems diverge. On the other hand, internal diversity can be engaged within constellations.

Identity

Communities incorporate the ability of the 'social configuration' to constitute identities through relations of belonging or non-belonging. The notion of separate worlds, with clear distinctions of inside and outside, associated with distinctive communities is necessary in asserting either-or rules of affiliation. However, Wenger emphasises that the boundaries of his communities of practice open and close various forms of participation. Identification becomes an important feature of communities since it lies at the heart of how we define ourselves. It is here that we must consider the notion of identity in detail. We learn that '...identity is constituted through relations of participation' (Wenger, 1998: 55). This participation pertains to living within communities and 'social enterprises'. That is, the identity is, simultaneously, both personal and social. This identity seems to retain a sense of psychologism in that it involves a rationally constituted emotional context or 'belonging' that is manifest in practical and discursive consciousness. It is this that allows individuals to be aware of belonging to collectivities. However, Wenger does not assume the individual self as the basis of identity as where 'I feel Welsh, therefore I am Welsh.' That is, he strives to ensure that the pre-formed subject/agent does not constitute the basis of identity. Rather, identity is socially constructed and constituted. Causality shifts to social configurations that are not necessarily operationalised within practice. What he is alluding to here is that identities involve a far broader elaboration of social structure than that involved in communities of practice. Identity does depend upon the negotiation of meaning within the various practices of different communities; it is the plurality that contributes to the multiple nature of identities. The rational context of this process involves the ability to 'define who we are', but this is contextualised by how '... we experience ourselves through participation...'. Thus, there is a context for identity formation that is not entirely rational that derives from social practice, and how this determines shifting identities. Identities come to be inherently involved in competence without necessarily involving either self-images or self-identification.

There is an obvious sense of reflexivity involved in identity formation. This again seems to relate to Giddens's (1991) claim that the rupture of restraining communities, with their stable and explicit codes, provides the individual with the liberty of choosing her own lifestyle within a reflexive context that directs her behaviour by reference to conscience. Self-identity is very much a psychological reality that provides the capacity of modifying her social environment. It involves non-participation as a rational decision being viewed as a basis for identity formation.

The claim that identity is constantly shifting appears problematic when one confronts the associated claim that it engages the past, present and future. It would appear that there is no stability that can be grasped. The past structures the present that is constantly subject to modification. Part of this structuring pertains to 'marks' that are left in the world. We are not told how this history is specifically deployed as a resource, nor how it conditions identity. Nonetheless, it is something that influences the ability to influence the negotiation of meaning. The modification of the past into the present becomes a feature of the constant redefinition of identities.

The individual operates within a range of communities, and identity pertains, in one way or another, to each of them. Wenger argues that this involvement allows the individual to shape the meanings produced within these communities. These two components – identity and negotiability, or the ability to influence meaning – pertain to the notion of belonging and even 'ownership'. It is here that he slips into the conceptualisation of a specific metadiscourse in discussing 'economies of meaning' and the 'ownership' of meanings.

What Wenger is trying to do here is to relate identity, both to rationalism and to its denial. This is necessary because of how he has committed himself to the dualism of Giddens's structuration theory. That is, Giddens sees social identities as associated with position-practice, claiming that they constitute 'markers' of structure. Since collectivities relate to structure in the form of normative rights, obligations and sanctions, they are relevant for roles. Wenger refutes the idea of a direct one-to-one relationship between identity and roles, while acknowledging some form of link between them. Nonetheless, it does seem that the identity of the subject is only given in relation to structure. Yet he does claim that since identification exists within 'the doing', the associated process is not necessarily self-conscious. In that it is the social engagement as participants within communities that develops or forms identities, it does not require the conscious, rational practice of reflexivity.

Identity is closely related to 'belonging', this being a crucial feature of the community. Without 'belonging' it is inconceivable that the community could operate as the generator of knowledge. However, identity is also constituted through relations of participation. Whereas 'belonging' seems to imply the existence of a pre-existing subject, the reference to identity emerging in practice implies that it is only here that the subject comes into existence. We are never told clearly how the subject is brought into existence.

It is tempting to think of these communities of practice, consisting of bounded populations with specific interactional processes, as social networks. Wenger goes out of his way to deny such an interpretation, claiming that while there is a similarity to the close ties of social networks, his emphasis on social practice as the manifestation of shared history around which ties are organised, rather than on the network of relations found in social network analysis, is important. It emphasises the structural aspect of the work and allows him to conceptualise the same interactional features by reference to his notion of communities.

Giddens's structuration thesis involves viewing structure as a constraint on action, while also being something that facilitates action. This in no way means that social agency is fully determined by structure, but that while it is a defining condition of social agency, it can act otherwise. That is, social agency can intervene in the world, and can make a difference vis-à-vis the structure. This kind of action theory relies on structure as involving the structural properties, recursively implicated in the reproduction of various praxis-forms within social systems. The associated structural analysis involves investigating the rules and resources that bind social praxis-forms in time and space. As these praxis-forms extend across time and space, so does their institutionalisation.

Such a discussion begs the question of the relationship between language and identity. This is an issue I discuss in some detail in Chapter 6. Here I would merely like to offer a few relevant comments. The most obvious starting point revolves around how the nature of society is changing, and how the grounding of identity in stable relationships to specific objects, including language, is undermined. The multiplicity of identities relate to how the rhetorical sites of identity are multiplied and diversified to the extent that no single field has any priority. The boundaries between social groups and objects such as nations, cultural forms and varieties, public and private, language and experience become blurred. Consequently, what might be termed 'being a self' can no longer be taken for granted, but becomes a feature of language use as social practice and, as such, something that is achieved.

With the demise of the rational sovereign citizen, identity is no longer anchored in a stable social self, but relates to how language use as social practice relates to specific collective forms. In this respect, the focus shifts to a concern with the relationship between symbolism and institutionalised practices. The enhanced consumerism of a global system and its relationship to signification and space play their roles. Individuals are subject to the effects of discourse in terms of how they are interpolated as subjects of a range of discursive formations. As Lash (1999) insists, 'Difference is not the opposite of identity,' but pertains to the 'neither present nor absent'. It involves the conditions of possibility of reflexivity, of the possibility of infinite meaning as it relates to the essential ambiguity of language.

This is not to deny the relevance of the collective memory and how it relates to the use of language. The self involves relating being and activities, of evaluation in self-awareness. This involves the collective memory, how it structures and conditions the relationship between objects, including an evaluation of their relative values. This reflexive capacity is intertwined with language as well as with social practice as an ongoing process. As such the focus is on modalities that are embodied in the construction of the social, and the role of language in that construction. They provide the self with a sense of being active and aware. This activity is always an intersubjective activity, the self only having an existence in relation to others, and to the detail of social practice. The sharing of meaning involves an engagement of 'the other' with the subject, and how this is constituted in and through language.

Meaning

Meaning lies at the heart of the entire conception. It structures communities of practice while allowing expression to our knowledge, and the experience of life and the world that informs learning. The framework for meaning revolves around the social constitution of meaning. This is entirely in line with the structuration theory, in that humans located in even subordinate and exploited positions are capable of finding resources that allow them to struggle, and even to transform social systems. Abandoning the negative conception of structure as merely setting limits to action gives the possibility of the actor constructing her own meaning.

It is the focus on the social construction of meaning that leads Wenger to reject any discussion of meaning by reference to technical issues, including sign and reference. The emphasis is exclusively on how meaning is generated within social practice. The relationship between practice and meaning revolves around how 'Practice is . . . a process by which we can experience the world and our engagement with it as meaningful' (Wenger, 1998: 51). Thus, practice is what contributes meaning to our experience. In pursuing this perspective Wenger draws on what he refers to as 'the negotiation of meaning'. What is not clear is the extent to which the negotiation involves the rational behaviour of the pre-formed subject.

Wenger claims that negotiation involves both 'agreement between people' and the process of readjusting the status quo. What he is trying to underline here is the constant, dynamic process of meaning construction that includes modifying pre-existing meanings. However, he also seems to be implying that this does involve the rational process of negotiation between subjects, especially in claiming that meanings do not appear in a pre-ordained form. This is modified in the claim that he does not wish to imply a distinction between interpreting and acting, or doing and thinking, or understanding and responding. Meaning only exists in practice. The social component of meaning construction relies on interaction within and across communities of practice, but it also claims that the participation of the individual in meaning construction extends beyond the boundaries of any single community, in that they carry the identity associated with each community outside of the practice associated with that community.

In line with his understanding of social practice Wenger does claim that meaning is never fixed, but is always subject to constant change. Thus, while he does acknowledge that practice involves structured patterns, the shifting nature of practice involves reproducing these patterns, and this involves an experience of meaning. The emphasis upon the dynamic nature of social practice means that what he calls 'the histories of meaning' are constantly negotiated and renegotiated. Thus he reserves the concept of meaning negotiation to refer to how actors make sense of their experience of the world, and of their behaviour in it. Meaning thereby appears as a reflex. Activities do not carry their own meanings, but are the elements around which meaning is constructed. He also makes reference to the ambiguity of meaning. This follows clearly from the preceding position, in that the shifting nature of meaning must mean that meaning must be ambiguous. However, this would also appear to imply that meaning must somehow be fixed, even if only transiently, within interaction.

This position seems to conform readily with post-structuralism. Thus, the reference to the meaning of objects and subjects being subject to constant change is a point made by Bakhtin when claiming that all discourses exist within the milieu of the 'already said' of other discourses. He also shares with Bakhtin and post-structuralists the claim that discourse involves more than the linguistic, and that the extra-linguistic is central to the construction of meaning. It is also obvious that Wittgenstein lies in the background.

The social is made explicit in the work of both Wittgenstein and Bakhtin. The former's language play involves a practice of interpretation that resolves ambiguity. It involves a practical relationship between the *locuteurs* and their *enonces*. That is, the practices within which language is placed cannot be reconstituted starting from that which is said. For Wittgenstein it involved conventions which are incapable of being made explicit – the tacit knowledge of Wenger's work. From a sociological perspective, each sector of life can be viewed as a play of language. Bakhtin's dialogism relates to the claim that the structure of *enonces* does not indicate the language play within which they are implicated. Through the notions of polyphony and dialogism he refuted both the form of idealism wherein the meaning of words mysteriously exists outside of their use and a psychologistic position. An *enonce* only achieves meaning as a result of a multitude of language plays. Meaning becomes the consequence of a practical confrontation of social groups around signification and language play. It is the product of open options at the interior of discursive organisation, organising points of view, practices and interests. Meaning is the site of struggle. Wenger is able to engage with this body of post-structuralism while retaining the notion of structural causality, precisely because of how structuration theory involves the degree of autonomy for the human subject in its relationship to structure.

Objects are reified. This implies that objects are given meaning, and that this meaning 'shapes our experience'. He claims that if meaning only exists in its negotiation, then the reification and the reified object cannot be distinct. His point is that there is no pre-existing reified object outside of negotiation. His concern is less with the objects than with how they are integrated into practice.

This seems to be a way of striving to acknowledge the post-structuralist point that objects do not exist outside of discourse, and are brought into existence in and through discourse. On the other hand, there is the suggestion that in negotiating or modifying meaning, the actor engages with reified objects. This would imply that there is an unreified 'truth', distinct from any process that involves reification. This is resolved in his discussion of the relationship between the process and the product of reification. He maintains that these two concepts should be collapsed into a single component. Yet there are reified objects that derive from outside of the specific practices, objects that are absorbed from other contexts, and which must be absorbed into these practices. This he relates to Giddens's understanding of reflexivity within modern society, where it is claimed that the world is currently engaged in a situation of enhanced reflexivity. For Wenger, the products of reifications in the form of objects become a reflection of the associated practices. He explicitly states that conversation, for example, is conscious, and involves 'reflecting on our motives'. The centred subject is evident.

There are other interesting observations on the subject. Wenger claims that participation has to do with people, while reification '. . . has to do with objects' (Wenger, 1998: 70). However, he also states that '. . . in terms of meaning, people and things cannot be defined independently of each other.' I take this to mean that 'people' achieve meaning in relation to objects. Thus the subject is brought into existence within the discursive process.

Wenger makes the point that his conception of reification does not assume correspondence between symbol or sign and referent. What he is emphasising here is that meaning is not fixed, and that it is the ambiguity of meaning that is resolved in and through practice. He does refer to the 'purpose' of reification, and to the 'assigning' of the status of object to 'something', as if this was a rational process. Also, words as projections of human meaning are treated as reifications. That is, it would appear that humans use language to project meaning. Yet it is not clear that these are separate processes. Indeed, Wenger makes the point that participation and reification go hand in hand, and should not be separated. This is the basis of his claim that '. . . explicit knowledge is not freed from the tacit' (Wenger, 1998: 67). However, he says little about the use of language as social practice. We are obliged to conclude that if language use is viewed as social practice, then reification is treated as part of that practice, and that meaning does not precede reification. Objects do not exist outside of discourse. Meaning is contextualised in and through participation. Nonetheless, it is difficult to escape the feeling that reification does involve the assignment of meaning to an object that exists outside of discourse. Even if this is the starting point for Wenger, he does make it clear that the meaning of that object is modified within practice.

There is also an interesting comment on prior discourse. Wenger claims that the marks of discourse freeze specific moments of practice which persist, to be incorporated in subsequent practice. This seems to contradict his point that practice is always shifting and that, with it, meaning is constantly negotiated. On the other hand, it conforms with how post-structuralism refers to the preconstructed and the inter-discursive. He also claims that '... what is said assumes a history of participation as a context for its interpretation' (Wenger, 1998: 67).

All of this raises the question of what, if anything, does structure contribute to the construction of meaning? On the surface it would appear that Wenger's conceptualisation of meaning and its construction seems entirely compatible with the decentring of post-structuralism. This is possible because of how structuration theory creates the duality between structure and behaviour or practice. Furthermore, any reference to social structure must involve collectivities, as opposed to individuals. Participation is viewed as a social process in that reification facilitates the coordination of action. At the same time, it shapes the individual's perception of the world, and of the self in relationship to that world. The shared meanings that derive from participation and reification apply as much to collectivities as to individuals.

The duality of structure and action means that communities of practice constitute a feature of social structure within which action occurs in the form of practice. Thus, the institutional structure of communities of practice imposes some constraint on practice but, at the same time, the outcome of practice is capable of modifying the nature and structure of communities and institutions.

Intervention

Industrial age economy involves the following components:

- Managing physical assets, capacity and finance as 'capital';
- Identifying and servicing markets;
- Location close to transportation centres;
- Guaranteeing access to commodity and energy sources;
- Organising the workforce into white collar assembly lines;
- Use of ICT for increasing efficiency while reducing costs.

The shift to the knowledge economy changes all of this, placing the emphasis on how:

- Knowledge becomes the new source of capital;
- ICT becomes the support for rapid information access and work group collaboration;
- Efficiency derives from processes, knowledge and improvement;

- Work practices develop enhanced flexibility;
- Clerical and blue collar workers are transformed into professional knowledge workers.

Wenger's work is about this transformation, as is his attempt to transform his theoretical problematic into practical implementation. Together, the hidden process of meaning production and the associated issue of tacit knowledge create a particular problem for Wenger's concern with intervention.

Any theory that places so much emphasis on a learning that relies heavily upon tacit knowledge will find difficulty in developing an intervention strategy. This is acknowledged by Wenger in claiming that there is a limit to what can be achieved by design. He claims that practice cannot derive from design, but becomes a response to design. The constantly shifting nature of practice demands that it be incorporated into design. Similarly, he claims that communities of practice already design their own learning in deciding what they need to learn, and what being a full participant involves. It is perhaps clearest in the need to incorporate new members. He proceeds to claim that design '... requires the power to influence the negotiation of meaning' (Wenger, 1998: 235). Thus, his objective is not to be highly specific, but rather to develop a framework which specifies what needs to be in place in order to achieve the desired outcome. As such it represents a perspective that is capable of being shared by those affected. However, he also seems to be implying that design cannot be imposed.

The starting point for his design involves maximising the potential for 'belonging' to the community in question. It involves supporting the work of forming communities of practice, where community building enhances the potential of learning. This includes maximising interactional facilities, whether they are based on new technology or face-to-face interaction; enhancing joint tasks; and focusing upon boundary creation and transgression. Within the community, activities are meant to facilitate engagement around issues that involve energy, creativity and inventiveness. His theoretical framework and associated conceptualisations provide the basis whereby this can be achieved.

While acknowledging that organisations are social constructions that acknowledge the centrality of practice, he also claims that the communities of practice within organisations are obliged to keep a degree of distance from the organisation. There is a difference between organisational design and lived practice. At the heart of the organisational design is the capacity to produce reflexive reifications, involving policy, standards, roles, etc. These are capable of manipulation by reference to boundary crossing. This is important because of how learning is maximised when boundaries are crossed, and also because of the need to integrate different organisations within regional planning. The dangers involve the fixing of meanings, and the inflexibility of different components or organ-isations. Each organisation consists of different communities of practice that require alignment before even considering divergent organisations and their communities of practice. The goal is partly that of breaking down hierarchical systems based on authority, while vesting authority in each community of practice. Wenger is constantly aware of the trade-off between fixing meanings, and the need for meaning to be fluid as features of social practice. The central concern involves making meaning sub-servient to practice, partly so that policy and the relations of production can be effective.

Each community of practice has its own regime of accountability that does not necessarily coincide with that established by the organisation. Indeed, any form of accountability established by the organisation is obliged to integrate with the definition of competence of the community of practice if it is to be effective. Organisations must be prepared '... to serve the inventiveness of practice and the potential for innovation inher-ent in its emergent structure' (Wenger, 1998: 245). Since practices never subsume each other, and since communities are bounded, the relationship between the local and the global does not involve what Wenger refers to as the constellation wherein interconnected practices achieve coherence. Rather, the point of engagement involves the link between the commu-nity and the organisation. Organisations connect communities of practice into an organisation by crossing boundaries. This means that it is essential to create channels of communication across practices.

In many respects, this contradicts the principles of Taylorism, with its emphasis on demarcated and separate linear functions. On the other hand, Wenger has little to say about how the New Economy obliges a reconsid-eration of workflows. Indeed, his only reference to workflows involves how they exist within communities of practice and, as features of social practice, they are capable of modification. On the other hand, some activ-ities, most notably how media is transformed into multimedia, require new organisational structures that involve entirely new workflows. Fur-thermore, transforming the workflows of industrial age economy into workflows that maximise learning and knowledge creation must be an essential feature of all New Economy organisations.

Wenger would maintain that developing end-to-end systems and pro-cesses must involve both the localisation of communities of practice and the development of a tight constellation of communities of prac-tice. This should involve the commitment of all components in a way that involves more than merely delegating key individuals to 'represent' each constituent part. This allows all components to assume responsibil-ity for efficiency. It will also require privileging certain perspectives and forms of knowledgeability over the definition of procedures. Hierarchical organisation yields to flat management.

In discussing the learning process in relation to design, Wenger over-turns the conventional picture of 'training' by emphasising the need to develop a design that can support learning. This includes communities being involved in the design of their practices by reference to learning. This is partly the essence of constructivist learning, and the emphasis on learning by doing, or problem-based learning. It also involves the sharing of information so that mutual accountability becomes possible.

Once communities of practice have been identified, operationalised and transformed into learning communities, Wenger claims that 'teaching events' can be designed around them in order to function as resources that link to their practices. This opens up the learning. His main point here involves shifting from a view of education as the source of learning to viewing it as a resource for the learning community. The community takes in charge the learning process as a feature of its practice.

Conclusion

It seems clear that there are obvious continuities between what has been discussed in the preceding chapters and the notion of communities of practice. There is a focus on the theoretical work of Giddens, but perhaps the most significant intervention is that of Bourdieu and how he approaches the notion of social practice. It is this, together with the notion of tacit knowledge, that gives the concept its transformational context. It makes it a very powerful force by reference to the role that it can play in the knowledge economy. It explains the shift in working practices from the Taylorism of the industrial age economy to the interactive focus of work in the knowledge economy. This makes the notion of central importance to any discussion of the knowledge economy. On the other hand, as a flexible system it allows for variations in language and culture and the relation-ships between them in its operationalisation. Indeed, it even allows for the possibility of working across languages and cultures without diminishing its relevance.

Despite the limitations, this remains one of the most detailed and coherent attempts to come to terms with the centrality of knowledge and learning for the New Economy, and the need to promote knowledge that lies within the tacit. Yet it is incomplete in that it barely touches on the processes associated with the constitution of meaning. It is all very well to refer to how the entire process of knowledge sharing and knowledge generation relies upon the ability of social actors to develop a sense of shared meaning, but surely this requires considerable elaboration. That elaboration would be obliged to consider the relationship of reflexivity to the social construction of meaning, and how this process depends upon a degree of mutuality across the members of any community of practice. This becomes the focus of Chapter 6.

Chapter 6

Language and the Subject

Introduction

One central feature of the knowledge economy is that where information is limited in the sense that it is fixed and given, neither skills nor knowledge are limited, largely because of how new knowledge constantly emerges from 'learning by doing'. This has implications for the notion of 'scarcity' in economics. It also has profound implications for our understanding of education and learning. Knowledge depends upon preconceptions and prior cognitive frameworks that cannot be established simply through reason or fact. One important question revolves around the relationship between social capital and knowledge. This focus on social capital has shifted the analytic to a concern with communication that, in turn, leads to a concern with language. Moving from conceiving of language as a body of technical skills to understanding language as an innate talent leads to allowing workers to adapt to local conditions. This is an implicit assumption in the concept of communities of practice.

The emphasis on shared meaning brings the use of language to the fore and, more specifically, a denial of any fixity of meaning. The dynamic quality of meaning and its potential by reference to innovation involves denying the discreetness of meaning such that new meaning becomes possible. Meaning is a multilayered and changing element that is constituted in and through a social praxis that involves both the production and reception of a statement. As a consequence it relates to the socio-historic conditions of its constitution. Meaning is constructed through the structural features of language including narrative, argumentation, discursive forms as well as syntax. However, meaning also needs to be interpreted such that the relationship between the assertion of a statement and its interpretation is performed. The complexity of meaning and its constitution varies across both linguist form and socio-cultural context. My main thesis in this chapter is that operating across languages and socio-historical and cultural contexts in the constitution of shared meaning can be a central feature of creativity.

An important feature of meaning construction is that of reflexivity. Reflexive skills and processes enable persons imaginatively to monitor their experience in creating a 'shared world' which, in turn, facilitates the reproduction of social relationships, practices and ideologies as collective legacies (Sandywell, 1996: 39). This is not meant to imply that all reflexivity involves the rational determination of the centred subject. Similarly, meaning construction involves the intersubjective.

In pursuing the goal of this chapter I will emphasise the importance of discourse for shared meaning and how the individual is transformed into the subject of discourse. The discursive operations position subjects and objects such that, as the subject of discourse, the individual is locked into specific relationships with other subjects and a plethora of objects. The effects of discourse set constraints on what can be said, while also opening up possibilities. This allows me to consider the role of reflexivity in the intersubjective process and how it influences meaning construction. On the other hand, the elaboration of shared meaning involves operations that vary across languages, and offers clues about the potential creativity of working multilingually.

Discourse

One of the difficulties associated with conceptualising discursive practice is that the importance of tacit knowledge runs counter to how the notion of the centred, rational, human subject is so important for the orthodox understanding of the nature of discourse and natural language. On the other hand, given that the focus is on shared meaning, the question arises of how to operationalise interaction without placing the emphasis exclusively on rationalism. It involves a shift from an overriding concern with the form of language as an object to viewing language as a tool that involves individuals in the construction of the social. That is, the social is itself constructed through the focus on shared meaning.

This is not to imply that linguistics and discourse involve the same approach by reference to the play of language. Linguistics pertains to the organisation or structure of any particular language and is studied by reference to different models that treat the same linguistic phenomena differently, often focusing upon specific elements or processes. Discourse, on the other hand, involves the subjective and social play of *enonciation* or statement. That is, discourse is a consideration of the *enonce* from the standpoint of the discursive mechanism that conditions it. It is important to note here that the focus is on the production of a statement. Thus Foucault's (1969) reference to 'enonciative modalities' does not refer to a propositional content, but to the status and institutional setting of a statement. Discourse does not pertain to the same properties of language as those that are of relevance to the linguist.

The emphasis on the play of meaning within decentred structures that are devoid of a fully constituted subject leads directly to this concern with discourse. Nietzsche referred to the perspectival character of knowledge in claiming that knowledge is '... always a certain strategic relation in which man finds himself placed'. Foucault (1994, vol. 2: 551) drew on this in stating:

> The perspectival character of knowledge does not derive from human nature, but always from the polemical and strategic character of knowledge. One can speak of the perspectival character of knowledge because there is a battle, and knowledge is the effect of this battle.

This reference to 'effect' is evident in how he understood that discourse did not simply express or reproduce already constituted social relations:

> Discourse battle and not discourse reflection... Discourse – the mere fact of speaking, of employing words, of using the words of others (even if it means returning them), words that the others understand and accept (and possibly, return from their side) – this is in itself a force. Discourse is, with respect to the relations of force, not merely a surface of inscription, but something that brings about effects. (Foucault, 1994, vol. 3: 124)

The struggle which Foucault refers to involves how a truth 'functions as a weapon' and how truth is always contestable and circumscribed. It is a manifestation of the essential ambiguity of meaning. He also sees the social as the effects of discourse. This contradicts much orthodox sociolinguistics which understands discourse as the effects of the social.

Narrative is that which involves the production of linked statements that incorporate subjects and objects, and which lead to accounts of events. They also incorporate previous events and accounts in the form of traces. Any statement is conditioned by prior discourse which influences the meaning that this statement is capable of achieving. Similarly, it can fix the meaning of particular subjects and objects. We draw on the past in how we use language, and we draw upon notions that not only derive from the past, but which carry structured relationships to other notions, subjects and objects. This allows us to recognise narrative as how people use language to accomplish their work. As such it is ubiquitous, effective and often tacit. It is also the basis whereby identity is negotiated. What is involved here is the role of narrative in the expression and transmission of social knowledge as a kind of tacit knowledge. It bridges the tacit and the explicit in that it is the basis whereby tacit knowledge can be demonstrated and learnt in an informal manner.

There is a sense of fixity and permanence in some of the preceding discussion. At the global level, the relationship between objects are stabilised within discourse, to the extent that they become institutionalised as the taken for granted for any given population. This involves a stabilisation without which the social is not possible. However, this stabilisation informs the normative order, and is always contestable in that the normative creates the deviant. On the other hand, discourse is very much a dynamic entity. Bakhtin's (1981) notion of dialogism insists that every use of a word in a different *enonce* involves a semblance of meaning difference. Yet we learn language already dialogised. Stabilisation is always relative.

Different discourses articulate into a relatively unified whole known as the discursive formation. Thus the discursive formation consists of statements that refer to one and the same object within a dispersion of statements. Relations are established between discursive formations, and such discursive relations are 'at the limits of discourse' and 'determine the group of relations that discourse must establish in order to speak of this or that object' (Foucault, 1969: 63). The statements of a discursive formation condition what can be said, and even what must be said, from a given place. This is because they organise the objects of the discourse. Furthermore, the internal organising force of a discursive formation conditions the production of meaning such that objects achieve the same meaning in relation to the same subjects within any discursive formation. Place does not conform with any sense of subjectivity since the *enonciateurs* are substitutable.

The unity constituted out of a dispersion of statements that make up a discursive formation derives from the common conditions and rules that govern dispersion. The different levels involve objects, modes of *enonciation*, concepts and strategies, and all entail restrictions on each other. The rules of discourse are constituted by the interrelationship of these elements, together with their own conditions of existence.

Discourses relate to social practice, understood as patterned behaviour within stable forms of social life. However, discourses also have effects on social practice. Thus the discourse associated with the notion of communities of practice, or alternative forms of managerial discourse, can have an impact on the operation of work. Similarly, the discourse of neo-liberalism is claimed to influence the processes and institutions of globalisation. Such discourses carry the historical nature of language but often they change meanings. Furthermore, they incorporate notions that establish how things should be done, and once they are operationalised, they influence organisational practices and their implementation. The shift from Taylorist working practices to team working and the associated interaction involves a shift in discourse that redefines not only working practices, but also the social construction of the worker. In this sense, discourses are manifestations of specific philosophies or narratives that are represented in and through discourse, philosophies that are grounded in specific theoretical discourses. How discourse flows across populations implies a level of shared understanding and, in this respect, it can be argued that the process of globalisation constitutes a flow of specific forms of representation and discourse that are shared across the globe. Evidently, discourse applies both to discourse as a feature of social life and as ways of representing the world.

Above I have made reference to the effects of discourse by which I mean that social practice or action is elaborated in and through discourse. It also involves how discourses play a role in constructing subjects and objects and the configuration between them. Evidently narrative has a central role in this respect. There is a division between those who claim that human agency is also the effect of discourse and those who afford human agency a role independent of discourse. Those such as Giddens involve the effects of discourse in how they understand the role and nature of agency. Thus he refers to how structure constrains agency without determining it, while structures are both produced and reproduced through agency and are capable of being transformed by agency. They refer to the non-discursive effects of discourse in the sense that the objects referred to in discourse are imaginary systems, but which are constituted in and through discourse. In contrast, those who reject the reference to system argue that the only 'reality' that exists is simply the effects of discourse, with subjects and objects being constructed and constituted in and through discourse without recourse to any sense of independent human agency.

This distinction between idealism and realism is central to the discussion of the discursive construction of the social. Realism asserts the existence of world external to thought, while idealism claims that all objects are given their meaning by virtue of discourse. An object will certainly have a material existence in the world, but the designation of the nature of that object is a consequence of discourse. The essentialisation of an object reduces the subject to a passive recipient of an already established meaning. Similarly, the essentialisation of the subject reduces the object to an object of thought.

Enonciative Linguistics[1]

A major development in recent years has been the rejection of the notion of a linguistic system as a closed and centred totality. This, in turn, has generated a renewed interest in discourse, or how the thread of language involves a series of signifying sequences which, when taken together, constitute a more or less coherent framework that conditions what can be said. As noted above, this notion of discourse breaks with the distinction between thought and reality of orthodox linguistics and most sociolinguistics. In this respect, it also negates the distinction between language and the social, making the linguistic co-extensive with the social.

Given the refutation of the rational subject as being fully in control of meaning, the focus is on how the infinite possibilities of language are transposed into meaning as the effects of discourse. The focus is on the social construction of meaning without recourse to the rationality of the centred subject in the explanation of that construction. Thus discourse is referred to by Benveniste (1966) as involving:

> ... the phrase, an indefinite creation, variety without limit, it is the life of language in action ... with the phrase, one leaves the domain of language as a system of signs, and one enters another universe, that of language as instrument of *enonciation*, where the expression is discourse.

Discourse does not pertain to the same properties of language as those that are of relevance to the orthodox linguist.

The predominant exponent of enonciative linguistics[2] is Culioli who, in contrast to the behavioural formalists, seeks to understand language through the diversity of natural languages. Where most linguists have used a metalanguage of universal scope in striving to create a universal grammar, he uses a theoretical and formal process to reconstruct the features that generate grammatical categories specific to each language. The key to this involves the discovery of that which founds and regulates language activity for different languages. He understands language as a representational activity which is only accessible through texts, or rather, through the patterns of markers which are themselves traces of underlying operations. The focus on language markers implies the existence of a form, which is the result of operations. The relationship between these operations and the language markers is simulated by means of a metalinguistic construction.

Wittgenstein's (1958: 241) reference to 'forms of life' relied heavily upon natural language:

> So you are saying that human agreement decides what is true and what is false. It is what human beings say that is true and false; and they agree in the language they use. That is not agreement in opinions but in forms of life.

Meaning did not involve what Frege (1892) referred to as 'sense' or 'reference'. That is, it bears little relationship to the link between predication and local truth conditions, nor to any denoted object. Meaning is neither subjective nor objective, but becomes intersubjective. As such it relates to the rules governing natural language use, rules that define how expressions or statements are used. Intersubjective meaning relies on the interlocuteurs recognising the rules that they are using. Knowing the rules is essential for understanding the language game or form of life, while understanding the form of life is necessary in order to grasp the rule. The focus shifts from 'knowing that' to 'knowing how', from information to knowledge. These are the very principles that relate culture, language and meaning.

The system is self-regulated through the subjects' conscious and unconscious reflection on their own language activity, giving a continuous transforming and deforming process. Furthermore, intersubjective regulation consists of adjusting frames of reference and representations, and in validating an utterance by reference to a state of affairs, or class of states of affairs. The systems of representation tend to be stable, innovative and adaptive, and make it possible for a subject to produce meanings that are recognised by another subject as interpretable.

However, Culioli emphasises that sentences or phrases must not be confused with 'utterances' (*enonces*). Also, a lexis is not an utterance, since it is neither asserted nor unasserted in that it is not located within an *enonciative* space defined by a referential network. This referential space involves intersubjective coordinates, a referential space and localisable linguistic objects. Similarly, logico-philosophical problems of reference involving truth values, external reference, the ontological status of individuals, etc. must not be confused with the construction of referential values assigned to utterances through the production and recognition of form by the interlocuteurs.

To produce or to recognise an utterance is to reconstruct patterns of markers viewed as the traces of operations to which we have no access. In this sense, the markers are representative of the inaccessible operations. These are encoded through metalinguistic representation. This raises the question of how one can construct a theory of operations when the intellectual tools take the form of a black box. This, in turn, raises the further question of the autonomy of the linguist who strives to metalinguistically represent the activity of subjects. Culioli responds by distinguishing between three levels. The objective involves reconstructing patterns of markers that are the traces of operations to which we have no access. These inaccessible operations constitute level 1, while level 2 constitutes the patterns of markers that are the representatives of operations at level 1. Level 3 then involves constructing operations at this level through a system of metalinguistic representation, that is, as representatives of representatives.

Table 6.1 Levels of metalinguistic representation

Level 1	*Level 2*	*Level 3*
operations	markers	Metalinguistic representations
	Representatives 1	Representatives 2
M	O	C

Source: Auroux, 1992, p. 42.

The object of psychology corresponds to level 1; that which is observable – the linguistic forms, O, to level 2; and the linguistic theory (C), to level 3. Since the latter is the representation of 2 that is, in turn, the representation of 1, in admitting that representations are composed as applications, one concludes that it is a representation of 1. One is tempted to suggest that level 3 is a knowledge of level 1, that is, as a kind of psychology. However, Culioli refutes this, claiming that the psychological is something that is not accessible to the linguist, whose work he refers to as involving the metalinguistic representation of the activity of subjects. He also states '... we simulate the operation-marker relation thanks to a metalinguistic construction' (Culioli, 1989: 2). Thus, if level 3 implies a knowledge of level 1, it does not constitute any kind of psychology. A psychology would be a representation of level 2 and not of level 3, its theoretical terms referring directly to level 1. Such theoretical terms are absent in the work of Culioli. One does not find a dualism where the representations of mental operations are connected to the other side, which consists of linguistic elements. Always, the reference is to the metalinguistic, that is, to the representation of language.

Culioli's work, therefore, involves an attempt to deal with the patterning of language markers as a kind of form. This form is the result of operations, which means that he is obliged to simulate the relationship between these operations and the language markers in question by resorting to a metalinguistic construction. As a consequence:

> The point therefore is not to reduce syntax to an arbitrarily restricted nucleus, but to treat everything which belongs to a methodologically homogeneous field or to locally homogeneous fields which can be connected to each other. I claim that we can provide a unified theory which will integrate phenomena that at present are treated separately in different sectors. (Culioli, 1990: 73)

This is quite different from how the practitioners of generative and transformational linguistics consider that the observable syntactic forms ought to be allowed to be inscribed within the inventory of forms obtained by the rules of syntagmatic grammar. Such hypotheses are, in principle, extrinsic to the laws that govern their object – the laws of syntax in action, in transformational grammar, are the transformations which, from a formal point of view, have nothing in common with syntagmatic rules. Milner (1992: 37) claims that enonciative linguistics is not disposed to such a hypothesis since the *enonciative* operations are constrained by a principle which does not lend itself to such processes. He refers to Culioli's work by reference to a science of language as projecting certain *enonciative* representations within a non-*enonciative* doctrinal space (Milner, 1992: 20). Wittgenstein (1988: 5.22) referred to operations as '... the expression of a relationship between the structures of its result and those of its base'. Any definition of an operation depends upon the two initial collections, of the collections of arrival and how one constructs the application. Any operation can be conceived of independently of that on which it operates. Further-more, in any statement of causality the operations can be characterised by the formal properties – communicativity, transitivity, symmetry, etc. However, all operations imply that there are terms on which they operate. This presents a delicate ontological issue involving what status should be accorded to these terms. To the extent that the linguistic forms are the markers of operations and not the operations themselves, it is unlikely that these forms could be the terms of operations.

Enonciation is the individual act of language use, whereas the *enonce* is the linguistic object that results from that use. In this respect, *enonciation* is that which makes the *enonce* possible, being essential, but unrecognised, behind the *enonce*. Thus, it is only the *enonce* that is capable of being stud-ied. Nonetheless, it is recognised that there is a form to *enonciation*. *La langue* as an abstract system is operationalised in discourse, but with a number of specific operations intervening. Therefore, the description of the functioning of *la langue* implies the setting to work of that system that makes the production of *enonces* possible, that is, the conversion of *la langue* into discourse by the *enonciateur*. Thus, using the term 'discourse' within the framework of theories of *enonciation* is not to relegate it to some unity greater than the phrase, nor to consider *enonces* from the point of view of their conditions of socio-historic production, but rather, to relate the *enonce* to the act of *enonciation* which supports it.

As the act of stating an *enonce*, *enonciation* is an event that is constructed in terms of time and space. This serves to create a sense of stability for the content of the *enonce*. Whatever the occurrence of an *enonce*, it does not have an existence independent of its *enonciation*. That is, one is not simply concerned with that which is stated, but also with the act of saying it, that is, with the *enonciation*, and it is this that is reflected in the *enonce*. One can-not understand the meaning of an *enonce* without reference to the context of the *enonciation*, that is, by integrating certain aspects of its *enonciative* context. These elements are an integral part of the meaning of the *enonce* and are referred to as shifters that cannot be interpreted except in relation to the act of *enonciation* that has produced the *enonce*, and which supports it. It is not that shifters are devoid of meaning, but that their interpreta-tion insists on knowing the context of their *enonciation*. That is, shifters are simultaneously both linguistic signs and things or concrete facts inscribed by their occurrence in a determined list of spatial and temporal coordi-nates. They allow converting *la langue*, as a system of potential signs, into discourse whereby the *enonciateur* and the *allocutaire* confront what they say in the world.

The linguistic phenomenon taken in charge by the theories of *enoncia-tion* involves much more than the shifters. If we reject the idea of allocating to language the role of a 'neutral' instrument, destined only to transmit information laid down as an activity between two protagonists, then the *enonciateur* and the *allocutaire* are involved in activity across which the *enonciateur* is situated in relation to the *allocutaire*, to the *enonciation* itself, to the *enonce* of that *enonciation*, to the world, as well as to earlier and later *enonces*. All such activity leaves traces in the *enonce*, and it is these traces that the linguistic seeks to systematise. Consequently, language is not a simple intermediary between an object and its representation.

Deixis

Above it was claimed that, for meaning to be conferred, the referent has to be located within an *enonciative* space defined by a referential network. This space involves intersubjective coordinates, a referential space and localisable linguistic objects. It is here that deictics become relevant. *Enonciation*, the fact of stating an *enonce*, is constituted in terms of time and space, and it is the deictic markers which fix subjects and objects and the relationships between them by reference to time and space.

Enonciative linguistics rejects the equation of the *enonciateur/enonciataire* with *locuteur/locataire* (speaker/hearer). This allows the problem of the centred subject to be limited. Language displaces these relationships and expresses interaction as a feature constructed into language, rather than in an innate, preformed way. As a consequence, it embodies three inter-related components – the *enonciateur, enonciataire* and what is referred to as the one-person (I, you, it; me, her; here, there, elsewhere; self, other, foreigner; etc.). This social deixis, involving time, person and place, is the means whereby discourse is able to operate in social reality.

These dimensions are integrated into a zero point of origin for its *enonciation* – 'I-here-now'. They inscribe the statements in place and time in relation to the *enonciateur* who is constituted as a reference point. It makes disassociating person from deictics impossible. This serves as a point of reference for other kinds of operations – one which designates an alternative place of *enonciation* ('you-there-then'), and others that operate alternative spatial points of designation that lie outside the existing field (she/he/it, elsewhere, once upon a time). These are the marks of discourse that designate the nature of the interaction. The other relevant dimensions of discourse are the modalities which involve situating what is said, in that every text is inhabited by the presence of a subject who situates what s/he says in relation to the certain, the possible, the probable, etc., or in relation to judgements of value. These various markers operate with the *enonciateur*'s and *locuteur*'s knowledge of normative practice in operating the 'free' part of the discourse, or that part of the discourse that does not carry relevant deictic markers, nor any modalities. Analytic work on the 'free' part involves incorporating the assistance of the native speaker.

It is through language that humankind constitutes itself as subject since it is only language that establishes the concept of ego. Each speaker establishes herself as subject by referring to herself as 'I' while, simultaneously, positing another subject totally external to the 'I' or 'me'. This 'other' is referred to as 'you' and also refers to 'me' as 'you'. These are the fundamentals of language, of which communication is a consequence. All linguistic acts that contain a signification, or a meaning capable of communication, are supported by a transcendental ego. Within an individual act of *enonciation* that they support, the 'I' and/or 'you' are the operators that convert language into discourse. That is, it is necessary to consider the act of *enonciation* in interpreting an *enonce* that contains 'I' and/or 'you'. It is not possible to know the referent of either independently of their use in individual acts of *enonciation*. In every exchange, every 'I' is a 'you' and every 'you' is an 'I', the positions inverting in the play of dialogue. *Enonciation* is supported, not by the isolated features of the *enonciateur*, but by the 'I-you' couple – Culioli's *co-enonciateur* – of an activity. It is customary to think of 'we' and 'you' (plural) as the 'plural' of 'I-you', but they are not plural in the sense that 'horses' is the plural of 'horse'. Rather, it should be understood as 'an extension of person'. In many respects, 'we' and 'you' are ambiguous in that 'we' can be 'I and I' or 'I and you' or 'you and you'. Structurally 'we' can designate several groups of people: *locuteur* + *locuteur*, single *locuteur*; *locuteur* + *allocataire*; *locuteur* + third person(s); *locuteur* + *allocataire* + third person(s).

As shifters, the deictics function to inscribe the occurrence of *enonces* in space and time in relation to the marker as a reference point that constitutes the *enonciateur*. In this respect, it is not possible to disassociate person from deictics. Similarly, if the person plays a dominant role, the triad I/you-here-now is inseparable and constitutes the key to all discursive activity. The point of recovery of spatial deictics involves the point occupied by the body of the *enonciateur* in the act of *enonciation*. While the spatial deictic is less rich and less complicated than the temporal deictic, it does contribute to the organisation of the temporal. The marker of the temporal indication is the moment when the *enonciateur* speaks – the moment of *enonciation*. It lies in relation to the real act of *enonciation* that the *locuteur* orders the chronology of her *enonce*, and imposes it on the *allocutaire*. There can be a difference between when the *enonce* is produced and that to which its deictics refer.

In describing semantic operations in discourse it is necessary to consider how the basic position generated by this model is either neutralised or involves oppositions. When 'we' in any discourse involves a meaning that includes both 'I' and 'you', it marks a reference that neutralises the opposition between 'I' and 'you'. In treating the zero position as origin it follows that if there are no marks, then the enunciating position includes at least all of the zero values of person, location, tense and modalities. The statement 'It is raining' includes the I-here-now and a non-determinative space. It will normally include 'you', and presupposes that 'raining' is not fixed in terms of time and space. On the other hand, the statement 'It is raining' made over the phone activates the opposition 'I-you', the face-to-face neutralisation not operating. The statement 'you see, it is raining' involves 'I' being aware that it is raining, but that 'you' is not aware that it is raining. The presence of the word 'you' prevents the position of 'you' being the same as that of 'I'. This leads to an awareness that in a speech event, both the *locuteur* and the *allocutaire* must use the marks in the text and must also use their knowledge to operate on the 'free' part of the interpretation. This free part operates by reference to the relevant socio-cultural context.[3] Thus, there is a distinction between *enonciative* places defined by the abstract *enonciative* space on which the discourse is operating and the practical places in the social and psychological space of the speaker and the hearer. The problem of mapping these two space – the *enonciateur* with speaker, *co-enonciateur* with addressee, etc. – involves what is referred to as 'taking in charge' (for the participants) and of interpretation (for the analyst).

Interpolation and Taking in Charge

Having briefly considered how discourse operates in the elaboration of shared meaning I would now like to consider how the individual is transformed into the subject of discourse. This involves how the individual is locked into discourse and how the effects of discourse operate on the individual.

Taking in charge involves how the subject of *enonciation* is '. . . supposed to take responsibility for the contents posed' or becomes '. . . the subject who takes up a position' (Pecheux, 1982: 156). The central thrust of the process involves how the individual is constituted as a subject. This occurs through the relationship between interpolation, signification and the taking in charge of discourse. This, in turn, implies an overlap between a language act that is supported by the construction of meaning and the *enonciateur* who takes the discourse in charge. The taking in charge derives from the marks in discourse and involves the various deictic markers referred to above which set out the range of a field with specific boundaries. When the individual identity changes, so also does signification. However, signification in itself is not akin to meaning, but must be accompanied by the effects of discourse. Thus the act and the event involve the relationship between signification and the real effect, involving how the *enonciateur* is transformed into the *locuteur*, occupying a real social place. The formal apparatus of *enonciation* operates when *locuteurs* are taken in charge, implying a social interaction premised upon shared meaning, and the implications of a relationship between the *enonce* and the situation. The individual becomes the subject of discourse.

The subject place opens up for the individual to take in charge or to refuse to take in charge. It is here that we do recognise the space for rationalism and conscious choice. This relationship between the *enonciateur* (formal) and the *locuteur* (real social place) involves the unwinding of the *enonciation* internal to discourse, and to social actions, of which discourse is the support. These social actions are either carried by the *enonce* or can run aground when taking in charge does not occur. If the statement 'hey, Taff' is made and I respond to that statement, I take in charge the subject place associated with 'Taff'.

In taking in charge a preconstructed the individuals who are interpolated as subjects accept, either partially or totally, both the social places which relevant linguistic marks construct and the point of departure that they presuppose. Any social actor can render account of his/her behaviour, and such accounts can be formulated by reference to presuppositions and implicits that delimit that which is thinkable, and thereby the space of choice. Nonetheless, between the linguistic level and the reasoning of the rational individual, there are other kinds of presuppositions which interject, and which constitute the discursive organisation. That is, there exists a materiality that is imposed on the *locuteur* and on the interpretative apparatus that organises the effects of position and disposition.

When the individual takes in charge the discourse, that individual is interpolated as the subject of that discourse. This subject is related to other subjects and various objects in such a way that it conditions what can and must be said from the subject place. The discursive activity puts the conventions that regulate the relations between subjects to work, attributing a status to each one. The *enonciateur* is obliged to suppose that the *co-enonciateur* shares all the presuppositions with her, in a kind of tacit contract. The notion of place implies that in taking in charge, the individual assumes a subject place, the place of *enonciation*, but simultaneously assigns a complementary place to the 'other', or the *co-enonciateur*. These places support the discourse. Foucault (1969: 126) expressed this as: 'To describe a formulation while the *enonce* does not consist of analysing the relations between the author and that which he has said (or wanted to say, or said without wanting to); but to determine what is the position which all individuals can and should occupy in being the subject.'

In a sense, the taking in charge of a discourse confirms an identity, in that the individual is interpolated into a subject position that is confirmed and contextualised by reference to other related subjects and objects. Each one accedes to his identity beginning from, and at the interior of, a system of places. In this respect, it is important to recognise that the theory of discourse is not a theory of the subject in advance of its constitutions through *enonciation*, but rather, a theory of the instance of *enonciation* which is, intrinsically and simultaneously, an effect of the *enonce*. Social identities are constructed within the relationship system of a particular language.

To recapitulate, the taking in charge of discourse not only transforms the individual into the subject of discourse but also anchors the subject in relationship to other subjects, and to a range of objects within the discourse. This has profound implications for what can be said as well as for the legitimacy of what is said. It involves Foucault's notion of *enonciative* modalities as a type of discursive activity that carries its own subject position. In relating *enonciative* modalities to how statements are made, he was emphasising how discourse is a practice. Social practice is conceived of in terms of discourse relations. The normative now becomes the modality of the object that affords truth value to particular objects.

Reflexivity

Questions of reflexivity are raised once the relationship between language and the world is not simply one of direct representation. Furthermore, reflexivity as a form of self-awareness is problematised once one maintains that the individual only becomes a subject in and through discourse. These two observations condition how reflexivity is reassessed in relation to tacit knowledge. If an actor cannot be fully in charge of any discourse, rationality is not only clearly limited but also reflexive. When we consider reflexivity as the interpretive capacity of the producers of meaning we are, somehow, able to create distinctive forms of meaning for language objects. The essential ambiguity of meaning, and how meaning is manifested in the discursive formation and the materiality of language, is the key to reflexivity. The relation signifier–referent only exists within and through discourse. The discursive formation affords an order or a form.

The problem is succinctly put by Authier (1995: 803) who claims that once one accepts that the process of *enonciation* is not transparent to the *enonciateur*, one has ceased to 'believe in taking the *enonciateurs* at their word'. That is, it is not possible to consider the images involved in a statement as expressing a faithful mirror, giving direct access to the object. In order to comprehend the status of these forms of auto-representation in the *enonciative* process where they operate, it is again necessary to explore beyond that which they represent. They represent traces of a 'negotiation', inherent to the *enonciation*, but which is also something that is unrepresentable.

The limitation that is placed on reflexivity by the tacit nature of natural language obliges a discussion about metalanguage, the metalinguistic and metadiscourse, and the relationship between them. Such a discussion was initiated by Jakobson and Benveniste. Metalanguage, as language, is a semantic system that presents formal characters. In this respect, it constitutes a system where the elements are the signs, while the units constructed are phrases. The meta pertains to how a natural meta language signifies the language. In this respect, all languages are a natural metalanguage. As a system of signs, a metalanguage of a language describes that language and is an integral part of it. Jakobson (1963) maintained that metalinguistic reflexivity involved '... the faculty to speak a language', which implies 'that one can speak of that language', and as such, it constitutes 'an aspect of our spontaneous verbal behaviour'. This is something that we practice 'without calculating the metalinguistic character of the metalinguistics of our operations, and plays an important role in our everyday language'.

The tacit nature of our reflexive activity was also exemplified by Jakobson (1963: 127): 'We practice meta language without giving an explanation of the metalinguistic character of our operations. Each time that the *destinateur* and/ or the *destinataire* judge it necessary to verify that they use the same code, discourse is central to that code, it serves a meta linguistic function (or a gloss).' A distinction is made between formalised metalanguage and natural metalanguage. The former is treated as the consequences of the construction of artificial languages, while natural metalanguage lies at the interior of natural language, which serves to speak of the world, and of the signs in which one speaks.

There are several forms of linguistic knowledge, or knowledges of language. In speaking we all claim to 'know' the language we use in one way or another. We always tend to relate knowledge to the conscious and the reflexive – in order to know, it is necessary that one knows what one knows! Culioli refers to the unconscious knowledge of language, and of the nature of language which all speakers of a language have, as epilinguistic. A central question by reference to reflexivity is how it is possible to use a language to reflect on that same language as an object. In response Culioli (1968: 40) claimed that '... language is an activity that itself supposes a perpetual epilinguistic activity (defined as "non-conscious linguistic activity").' It is an activity that is in no way controlled. This means that the unconscious nature of epilinguistic knowledge is not presented by the speaker in representation. This non-conscious nature of epilinguistic knowledge merely corresponds to the claim that it is not represented, or that it is not evident in representation. In this respect, we do not possess the means, that is, the metalanguage or the system of notation, in order to speak the language. Therefore, linguistic knowledge – the metalinguistic – is represented, constructed and manipulated in the aid of a metalanguage. The subject's reflexion on her own language activity, according to Culioli, varies by culture, and involves differences conditioned by language. Culture, as well as the social, is incorporated into language use as social practice. Thus reflexive activity is something that varies across languages. He outlines the relationship between properties of language and the reflexive process.

A central point here pertains to the difference between meta*langue* and metadiscourse. This issue was raised by Benveniste (1966) when he placed language and discourse in different, but articulable, universes. Beyond linguistics, in which he took an interest in terms of 'language as a repertoire of signs and systems and their combinations' (1966: 257), he referred to another linguistics which took as its object the 'manifestation of language in living communication' – the description of marks and discursive functioning, and their placing in relation to the empirical subjects within different institutional and situational contexts. This was 'discourse'. Similarly Lacan's claim that 'there is no meta language,' derived from distinguishing between meta language, meta *langue* and metadiscourse, and conforms to the orthodox references to language, *langue* and discourse, or, in Himslevean terms, to the semiotic, the system and the process. The language that Lacan referred to was not the language constructed by the linguists, but rather the language '. . . as that which is structured by the unconscious'. The central difference was captured by Benveniste:

> The language of grammar, which describes the use of the forms of the language, is a metalinguistics (*metalangue*). All the vocabulary of the meta linguistics are only applied within the language. That meta linguistics can in turn be described as a 'formalised' language in logical symbols posing the relationships of implication between this or that linguistic category. (Benveniste, 1974: 159)

In this sense, the language that is described in linguistic terms and concepts is an artificial language.

In some respects, there is an overlap between these arguments and the later work of Wittgenstein. For Wittgenstein there existed an internal relationship of representation between language and the world. The logic of that representation was not a theory, but assumed a transcendental nature. The internal properties of language were constitutive of themselves; it is impossible to think, that is, of representing the facts in the language without implicitly founding them on the properties of itself. To designate or describe these said properties it would be necessary to use a language that is not possessed, which is impossible. Thus a correct metalanguage is inconceivable.

Furthermore, Wittgenstein's work on the meaning of the word similarly denies the orthodox relationship between meaning and the intuition of the centred subject. It was a denial of how linguistics focuses on form. Where language is a signifying form, it is far removed from being an interpretive orientation. Wittgenstein treats solipsism as the product of interpretive and judgemental work that presupposes the existence of 'background expectancies'. What he seeks to do is bring to light the interpretive work, assumptions and expectations through which ontological claims are constructed. This involves a peculiar, esoteric conceptual and linguistic practice that focuses on the construction of a new 'notation'. Furthermore, it is a practice that has a deeply problematic relation with orthodox linguistics, and conceptual practices (Pleasants, 1999: 145–146).

The individual believes that she speaks, that speech crosses the individual, this being the central feature of Foucault's concept of episteme. That is, the knowledge on which the individual operates is extremely constrained, both in terms of the effects of prior knowledges that the individual cannot be aware of and in terms of the constraints that are placed on what can be said from a given place. Furthermore, the constant shifting between form and meaning has its effect such that meaning is never truly fixed. Thus social practice is constantly modifying the meaning of objects that are constructed and reconstructed.

It also bears relevance to the work of Bakhtin who maintained that we always learn language already dialogised. That is, a central tenet of his work was that in interaction 'understanding' is anticipated by the *enonciateur*, while it is also a response to prior *enonces*, and, thereby, enters into a dialogical relationship with the *locuteur*. The *enonciateur/locuteur* relationship is not one of interpreting an *enonce* after it has been made, but involves the *enonce* being shaped as it is made. *Enonces* thereby belong to at least both these subjects.

This 'non-controlled' metalinguistic activity, which is treated as a constitutive trait of language practice, being conceived of as a mark of internal distance and not as a behavioural automation, is manifested explicitly, especially in the 'glosses' whereby the *enonciateurs* 'comment' on a preceding statement in a spontaneous way, or in response to a request. Culioli (Culioli & Descles, 1976) states '. . . language is an activity which supposes itself as a perpetual epilinguistic activity.' There is a concern here with an implicit 'theorisation', as well as with how speaking subjects are involved in relation to a 'reflection organiser on the language'. It is something that constantly appears in how the foreign language learner suspends reference to theory in accessing conceptions related to the acquisition of the mother tongue.

The existence of elements of metalinguistic representation places a threshold between that which is epilinguistic and that which is metalinguistic, the relationship between the two constituting a continuum. The first does not cease with the appearance of the second; the metalinguistic does not automatically bring a new content. Without entering into the metalinguistic one can elaborate the codified procedures (control of correction, play of languages, etc.) in order to manifest that which can be possibly referred to as 'an epilinguistic consciousness'. The epilinguistic consciousness is not unconscious epilinguistic knowledge made conscious, but is simply a conscious relationship with certain contents of epilinguistic knowledge which, for all that, is always unconscious, that is, non-represented as such. It is thereby that we sense that a phrase is correct or not, it is not without power in explaining why, or when, in certain competencies one can decline all of a paradigm to children. The epilinguistic consciousness corresponds to that which certain linguists call 'the consciousness of the language'.

Meaning is never posed in relation to a non-language exterior; it builds across the mechanism of the archive where it manifests the materiality of the language. This rejection of any force outside of language playing a role in reflexivity is an explicit denial of the relevance of linguistics as a theoretical concern that can be employed to analyse natural language, and its relationship to the meta*enonciative*. Furthermore, the reference to 'archive' confirms the existence of form in that each mechanism of the archive establishes its proper place in the order. This means that while we may believe that reflexivity is a conscious process, we are not aware either of the tools that we use or of the processes wherein those tools operate. The epilinguistic manifestations that Culioli refers to differ from, but are essential for, the 'metalinguistic constructions' which he presents as '...[constituting] in their way...a system of representation internal to *la langue*, i.e. a meta language not totally controllable...', and representing a '...precious source of linguistic pieces of information' of which one is rarely aware (Culioli & Descles, 1976: 227). In this respect, reflexivity is itself a tacit exercise.

While the preceding discussion denies a determinant role for rationalism, this does not mean that the individual is relegated to some kind of automaton. Emphasising an active conception of knowledge leads to rational behaviour or judgements of truth involving the results of reflexive work on a prior base (Achard, 1994). Within any statement there is a need to distinguish between an assertion, or the act of pronouncement, and its modalisation – the semantic operators that allocate a status to it, and the linguistic marks of these operations. Those assertions which can be defined as those *enonces* which reveal the category of truth or falsity, or those which do not carry a modal mark, do not always function as such if one views them as acts. That is, truth is treated not as a property but as a constructed modalisation that assumes that a discursive environment exists that can accept that such a 'truth' makes sense. There is no guarantee that the conditions which permit a proposition to function in terms of the modalities of truth for a *locuteur* are also in force for the *interlocuteur*. The rationality of a behaviour implies a reflexive activity. There is no suggestion that the social actors are in control and determine the thread of discourse in its entirety. It is clearly impossible for any actor to be fully in charge of any discourse, as a consequence of which rationality is not only clearly limited, but is also reflexive. In taking in charge a preconstructed the individuals who are interpolated as subjects accept, either partially or totally, both the social places which the relevant linguistic markers construct and the point of departure which they presuppose.

Language is always a reflexive exercise involving the *enonciateur* in relationship to language, and an intuitive representation of subjective mechanisms adjacent to observable forms of meta-*enonciative* reflexivity. Authier (1995) refers to the heterogeneity of modalities whereby the *enonciateur* is linked with an exterior in the sense that a meta-*enonciative* 'position' of 'distance', 'externality', etc. by reference to words taken as objects reveals an attempt to intuitively represent a subjective mechanism related to meta-*enonciative* reflexivity. She proceeds to express this heterogeneity in terms of a reflexivity that is a measure of how the *enonciateur* comments on her statement. This implies a non-linguistic theoretical conception concerning the relationship between the subject and her language. Considering the relevance of discourse with a focus on ambiguity inevitably leads to a consideration of the relationship between the subject and the production of meaning as something that is produced in interaction.

Creativity and Multilingual Interaction

The implication in the preceding account is that, in referring to discourse as language use as social practice, reflexivity is not a conscious, rational process. Certainly, reflexivity in this context does not draw upon a formalised metalanguage. However, Beck has made the point that there are two kinds of reflexivity. One involves 'reflection' and the other is more akin to 'reflex'. In referring to his understanding of reflexive modernisation, Giddens (1994) relates it to '. . . knowledge (reflection) on foundations, consequences and problems of modernisation processes . . .' (Beck, 1998: 840). This involves an awareness of being involved in a reflexive process, replete with a clear understanding of the knowledge that one is reflecting upon. On the other hand, reference to reflexivity as 'reflex' involves an absence of any awareness of the reflexive process. It is in this second context that most of the preceding discussion proceeds.

This distinction between two kinds of reflexivity allows me to explore the nature of reflexivity within bilingual or multilingual contexts. Within such contexts, especially when the participants are insufficiently fluent in the relevant languages, or are insufficiently familiar with the associated culture to be able to proceed with language use as a social practice that does not require thinking about the content of one's speech, or when the nature of the interaction explicitly calls for reflection, the nature of reflexivity involves both kinds of reflexivity referred to above. Furthermore, the reflexive process involves recourse to both a metalanguage and a metadiscourse. Additionally, each language has its own metalanguage. It is these differences that can serve as the basis for the creative use of language.

Within multilingual interaction there is a constant process of translation and interpretation that interrupts the flow of language use as social practice. The reflex nature of reflexivity that is characteristic of language use as social practice is suspended. There is a search for shared meaning within a conscious and unconscious reflexivity. The individual is not merely translating language but also discourse, in the sense that she is comparing the constitutions of meanings in the respective languages, and this involves the conscious drawing upon both language and discourse. In a sense, there is a double play of language.

The individual is constantly interpolated as the subject of two different kinds of discourses, each with a different kind of discursive materiality. The identity of the subject is constantly shifting, as is the nature of signification. Beyond this, identity also relates to how the subject is constructed within the relationship system of a particular language. This occurs in relation to the same individual within different subject positions, involving a different subject position for each language. The translation process between the relevant languages involves the interchange between the individual and the subject on a constant basis. Furthermore, it often involves a form of 'talking with oneself' such that the individual is both the *locuteur* and the *allocutaire* of the discourse. Since the socio-cultural is an essential feature of how meaning is constituted in and through interaction, it seems clear that there is a complexity of reflexive practices involved. The symbolic variation in signification in relation to how objects are constituted, signified and symbolised within different cultures adds a further dimension.

Not only is there an involvement with different kinds of reflexive practices, if we follow Culioli in accepting that the socio-cultural is an essential feature of how meaning is constituted in and through interaction, we also recognise the existence of distinctive reflexive processes for each language. Herein lies the value of linguistic diversity for the generation of knowledge. The reflexivity partly relates to the relation between language components and signification, something that is subject to considerable variation. This involves an awareness of how translating language is relatively easy, whereas the translation of meaning is of quite a different order. Meaning must be constantly contextualised, and when this occurs across languages, the nature of reflexivity is intensified. The shift from one kind of reflexivity to the other, and the discursive processes associated with comparison in the search for shared meaning, serves as the basis for the construction of novel conceptions that achieve materiality.

The Social Construction of Meaning

It is in Wittgenstein's language play, and in his insistence that language games are a form of life, that we encounter the shift from the linguistic, which sets constraints on form, to the social, which involves meaning. Wittgenstein referred to the signification of a word as its use in language. It is in what Milner (1978) refers to as the 'real of language', where a language has a material existence, imposing its ambiguity on speaking subjects, their consciousness and their experience, that the social is most evident. We are obliged to focus upon Milner's difference between signification (linguistic) and meaning (the real effects and pragmatic understanding). Signification involves a systematic structure of places in relationship to the formal dimensions of person, place and time, or of diverse modalities which, in connecting with effective situations, allow language to perform the role of operator of interaction, in situating the discourse in relation to a series of places of *enonciateurs*, where the taking in charge of the discourse by the *locuteurs* has the effect of carrying the effect of the system along. That is, signification is put in play by the relationship between the notional functioning and deictics. Social interaction occurs where the *locuteurs*, in taking the *enonces* in charge, establish a relationship between the *enonces* that conform with those relationships which the formal apparatus of *enonciation* implicates between the *enonciateurs*. Social life is premised on form. Between the signification, which interpolates the *enonciateur*, and meaning, which constitutes the real of the *allocutaire*, is the act and the event, which are constructed by the internal structure of the *enonces*. In this respect, the 'putting in discourse' is coterminous with the 'putting in action'.

What is at stake here is how the language act takes its signification in the subject. It outlines how the specificity of the linguistic system produces interactions, it focuses upon the surface marks and their agencies and it explores the dialogical space where they are being enonced. This leads to exploring the dynamic between the 'selves' and understanding their interrelationships. Evidently, the insistence on the materiality of language, and the integration of linguistic form and their functioning in social interaction, is the cornerstone of the social construction of meaning.

Treating sociology *à la* Durkheim within an epistemological context as the description of a system of places defined by their mutual relationship, leading to a description of social processes that are not reducible to the psychological orientations of the individuals occupying those places, inevitably leads to the assumption that the system that it describes constitutes a materiality. On the other hand, this same materiality is conceived as a dialectic between two types of simultaneous and complementary inscriptions – that in the physical environment which is fashioned by the social processes, and that in the language (discursive materiality) which, despite its abstract nature, is no less material. Discourse is viewed both as a language process and as a social process such that the social/language distinction does not exist. Thus, language production not only puts the social structure in play, but also the elements of the individual personality that occupies that social structure. Thus, one is obliged to seek the effect of discursive materiality in the social production of meaning of discourse, and not in the production of discourse. This social construction of meaning of discourse has a consequence for the physical environment, as well as for the effects of discourse relations. That is, there is a rejection of the reduction of the material to the physical world. This means that language, rather than carrying a symptomatic value, assumes a central and active role in sociology (Achard, 1989).

It is in the discursive materiality, and not in the analytic metadiscourse of a sociology that is external to its object, that the social places are defined. However, to assume that one can retrieve all of the relations of places of any society in the form of lexical items is to fall into the trap of assuming the conscious mastering of the subject over the social. Sociology cannot be of that order.

For Achard institution refers to the stable structure of types of acts and the places with which they are associated. The individual cannot be drawn into these places other than through signification, and this interpolation of actor-speakers into the categorised places is a performative act. Language becomes a system of referenced forms directly, but not mechanically, linked to social acts. In taking in charge of the constructed or preconstructed, the subjects who are interpolated as actors accept, either partially or totally, the social places that are constructively marked, as well as the presupposed situation of origin. Thus, in discursive interaction any *enonce* only has virtual meaning, but this virtuality is presupposed and taken in charge by all the participants in the processes in a non-marked way. Not taking in charge is viewed as an explicit process of refusal. The explicit process (marked) can be actualised in the form of language acts (*enonciation*), or non-language acts (non-cooperation in the act). That is, the sociological concept of institution and the associated concept of institutionalisation are treated in terms of the relationship between the places that relate to the stable structuring of action and how individuals are interpolated into these places. In effect, what Achard confirms is that the institution, viewed as a stability of structure, is the main object of sociology as a discipline.

However, discursive materiality rests upon the functioning of language. By reference to the social, discursive formation is conceived of as the structuring of social space by the differentiation of discourse. Evidently, what we have is the discursive formation differentiating discourse, and thereby structuring localities, on the basis of regularities.

These regularities are akin to legitimisation, involving unmarked dis-course. From the point of view of signification there can be no difference between the language act and its *enonciateur*; the legitimacy is presup-posed. Whether or not the *locuteur* takes the discourse in charge, the place of *enonciateur* is external to signification and is a mater of meaning. In speaking, the *locuteur*, on the other hand, operates an act of pretension to legitimacy, and this is carried in the traces of the operation. The *allocutaires* who are in a non-marked position accept the legitimacy of the *locuteur* in so far as it is not put in question. The absence of mark in the taking in charge implies that the signification is the material face of an effectively accomplished language act.

It should now become clear how the concept of institutionalisation or the 'taken for granted' relates to genre and markedness/non-markedness. It should be equally clear how Achard refers to institution by reference to stabilisation, or the embedding of discourse, and the associated interpola-tion which is formalised as a specific origin of the locution of a register. The relevance of interpolation, where the individual is converted into subject via the taking in charge, places the operating force firmly in the independent form of a structured discourse.

Institution, or patterned or ruled behaviour, is conceptualised by invoking discursive structure, rather than the normative context of ortho-dox sociology in which the individual is socialised in relation to pre-established norms and value systems. The discursive materiality imposes itself on the *locuteur* in organising the effects of position and dispo-sition. The concept of interpolation is pivotal, but assumes a social rather than a psychological connotation. The above account also incor-porates the concept of social groups, in that the places that the indi-vidual is interpolated into are not merely individual places, but also pertain to social groups. Thus, a discourse on social differentiation may well open up places that pertain to gender, social class or language groups.

A 'fact' is social only when it is put in meaning, directly or indirectly in the speech act. An act becomes a social act through social signification, linked to its stability in the ruled system of social relations. However, it is equally evident that the social is defined by a certain type of stability – it is the shared meaning between the *locuteur* and others, a meaning which is manifested in analogous acts. However, in this respect, since there will be those who do not share this agreement, it is much closer to norm. 'Social actors' relate to the institutionalisation of behaviour or action and, in this respect, conform with the non-marked nature of the subject in dis-course. A language act creates institutional places, replete with subject places into which the individual is interpolated, taking in charge the dis-course in relation to the place that the discourse assigns them. The subject clearly lies at the intersection of form and meaning. This requires a fixity or embedding of discursive forms and, in a sense, the social boils down to shared meanings constructed around similar subject positions.

The relationship between institutionalisation and legitimacy is accommodated by reference to the relationship between markedness and legitimacy referred to above. There ensues stable relationships between forms and social practices. Yet this seems suspiciously like linguistic forms, except that it is premised on the deictic grammar rather than the syntactic. This suspicion is resolved by the recognition that discursive materiality is imposed on the *locuteur* in so far as the interpretive apparatus organises the effects of position. Signification becomes the key element in the embedding process, and the multiplicity of possible meanings links to signification, with each *enonce* having the linguistic attribute of signification. Enonciative linguistics builds on the relationship between *enonciation*, signification and the world, without seeking to have this relationship entirely mediated by the centred subject or a predetermined social form.

There remains the issue of social interaction. This is dealt with by reference to Bakhtin's dialogism, and the claim that an *enonciation* does not have any meaning in itself, in an already complete signification, since it consists of a multiplicity of plays of language. Evidently, it also draws upon deictics, and the notion of language act. This is not a reference to speech act theory. Speech act theory involves the linguistic act in a properly constructed language. An expression is not a signification, but an action. As such it is not to be understood via the meaning of the object it signifies but, like all other actions, through the rule that it is following. However, it does not refer to the natural language of dialogism and language play.

In Wittgenstein's 'forms of life' language is a natural language, a practical medium through which individuals participate in the world. Meaning is neither subjective nor objective, but intersubjective, and linked to the rules that govern natural language use. This intersubjective meaning involves participants recognising the rule in use. It involves 'knowing how' and not 'knowing that'. The rules are entirely external to the subject and involve finding their function in a form of life.

Bakhtin underlined the paucity of the communicative functions of language within linguistics while also underlining the importance of how texts and *enonciations* respond to earlier texts or *enonciations* that they respond to, and subsequent ones that they anticipate. In this respect, he anticipates the notion of the thread of discourse and how prior statements exist as traces. The resultant intertextuality contributes to the constitution of any statement. It is a conception that is reiterated in Foucault's (1969) work. On the other hand, Bakhtin simultaneously emphasised how each statement is novel, even if it does rework the historical. It is in the reworking that we encounter the centrality of change. However, it is a change that is mediated by relations of power.

Authier (1995) distinguished between manifest and constitutive forms of intertextuality, with the constitutive form incorporating discursive conventions into the interdiscursive. She emphasised how the intertextual involves a degree of ambivalence as a consequence of how different meanings coexist within the interdiscursive, or how it may involve difficulties associated with the determination of a meaning which may remain suspended. Such notions emphasise the relative stability of any discourse while emphasising the ongoing processes of destabilisation and change. The social is made evident in how Bakhtin underlined the importance of the notion of genre for his understanding of language use as social practice. He related genres to a particular 'compositional structure' (Bakhtin, 1986: 60) as a feature of the form of discourse. Here he was referring to the set of socially constituted subject positions and the associated linguistic style. The essential point is in how changes in social practice are paralleled by changes in the system of genres. Here he underlined how a system of genres involved a particular configuration of genres that was characteristic of a specific community of practice.

The relationship between dialogism and language play involves a constant moving from the linguistic, which sets constraints on forms, and the social, which involves meaning. It is this constant movement that is the essence of Wittgenstein's language games, and how they are a form of life. The play of language is seen as a practice of interpretation, being a practical relationship between the *locuteur* and the *enonce*. As a practice of interpretation it is impossible to ascertain to which play an *enonce* pertains from its external form. From the sociological perspective each sector of social life can be seen as a play of language. Furthermore, if the social actors are involved in a variety of activities that can be seen as plays of language, the same *enonce* can be placed within different plays of language. Bakhtin's dialogism maintains that an enonciation does not have meaning in itself, but that meaning is created out of a multitudinal plays of language. Furthermore, the play of language indicates that language acts are structured in domains that relate to genres of life. Consequently, meaning is not pre-given, but is the result of a practical meeting of social groups within societies and cultures, and language play is the product of open options at the heart of a discursive organisation.

Conclusion

The purpose of this chapter has been to focus upon the social construction of meaning. In this respect, it contributes to the discussion about how communities of practice operate, and to the role of language in the reflexive process that is so central to reflexive learning and knowledge generation. It has discussed how subjects are constructed in and through discourse and how individuals become the subjects of discourse. The interaction between *interlocuteurs* within this process relies on a series of operations that leave markers as traces. This allows for a degree of analysis of the process.

A central assumption involves how these processes rely on a form of reflexivity that involves the use of a metadiscourse as its basis. This metadiscourse is tacit in nature and implies a constant process of referencing on the part of the individual as the subject of discourse. The issue discussed here raises the question that if knowledge is tacit, and yet involves the use of language or the semiotic, what is the nature of that use of language? This leads to a discussion of natural language as opposed to the ideal language of grammar and linguistics. It should be evident that all formalist linguistics revolves around a paradigm of analysis that is of little value to the kinds of processes and analyses referred to above.

The argument is made that the reflexive process is enhanced by operating across more than one language. This is because of how, as Culioli argues, each language and each culture has specific operations associated with the epilinguistic process. If this is indeed correct, then it would appear that the value of working within communities of practice which operate across languages would be far more productive by reference to the generation of both knowledge and innovation than operating within monolingual contexts. Thus, rather than pragmatically seeking to stimulate the flow of operations by insisting on the use of a common *lingua franca*, firms would be much better off if they facilitated linguistic diversity in their operations.

This is not unrelated to how Nonaka (1994) refers to the development of a model of 'organisational model creation'. He argues that if knowledge-based organisations wish to transform individual implicit knowledge into explicit knowledge, they must pursue intensive communication processes such as 'rounds of meaningful dialogues', or the use of metaphors, which may give individuals an insight into their implicit knowledge (Nonaka, 1994). His model of knowledge conversion (Nonaka & Takeuchi, 1995) involves the following stages:

(1) socialisation, involving how individual tacit or implicit knowledge is transferred into collective tacit knowledge. This builds on sharing practical examples, common experiences and physical proximity;
(2) externalisation, which transforms this collective tacit or implicit knowledge into collective explicit knowledge (from embedded to encoded knowledge). This is essential in developing a common basis for sharing tacit knowledge;
(3) combination, which, in converting knowledge, generates individual explicit knowledge out of collective explicit knowledge. The already explicitly expressed components of (collective) knowledge

are systematically transformed into a new combination, thus producing a new form of knowledge;

(4) internalisation, as the final stage of knowledge creation, transforms individual explicit knowledge into individual tacit knowledge. It involves personal interaction, applying the new knowledge in practice-oriented situations and a high level of involvement.

Evidently, if these processes involve the use of more than one language there will be an enhanced reflective process in operation, a process which involves not merely metaphors but also the entire range of linguistic functions which involves signification and the symbolic, as they relate to the construction of the relationships between subjects and objects. These are the essential ingredients of a shared meaning that transcends both language and culture.

Research on knowledge sharing and innovation culture tends to emphasise a learning by doing which involves iterative, trial-and-error interactive feedback from experimentation by actors striving to survive and prosper economically. The greater the variety, the greater the opportunity for innovation arising from interactions with other actors. Opportunities for the swiftest innovation occur in conditions of proximate and related variety (Boschma, 2005). This is the essence of the notion of communities of practice, and operating such systems across language and culture promotes the kind of reflexive learning that is essential for knowledge generation.

Notes

1. In the following, the 'speaking subject' is the empirical being who is physically the author of the discourse; the *audiateurs* are constituted by the effective entourage in which the discourse takes place; the *locuteur* is the person present in the *enonce* as responsible for the *enonciation; allocutaire* is the person presented as those to whom the *enonce* is addressed; *enonciateur* and *destinataire* are respectively the person to whom the responsibility of an illocutary act is attributed and those whom that act is considered to be addressing.
2. To an extent, enonciative linguistics builds on Foucault's discussion of statement and the *enonciative* function in the *Archaeology of Knowledge* (Foucault, 1969).
3. This is why Culioli rejected the all-encompassing thrust of universal grammar in favour of an approach that emphasises language activity within language diversity.

Chapter 7

The Cultural Economy[1]

Introduction

One of the most prevalent features of the New Economy, one which has not been discussed thus far, is the new technology. For some it is the crux of the New Economy. It certainly plays an important role in the organisation of economic space. We saw in Chapter 2 how it allows the integration of global economic networks and how it permits the instantaneous flow of capital across vast space. Significantly, it is also instrumental in redefining economic activities, merging the different activities of the industrial age economy into entirely new activities. It opens up new possibilities.

In Chapter 4 it was claimed that there are different routes into the knowledge economy, and that for some regions this will involve what is referred to as path dependency. That is, pre-existing economic activities will be reformulated in accommodating the New Economy. It is a process that is characteristic of changes from one variety of capitalism to another. This does not necessarily imply any evolutionary continuum, but rather that the evolution of a system depends upon its history and its context. The historical dimension pertains to how technologies and socioeconomic systems can get 'locked in' to relatively constrained paths of development. It is an argument against the thesis of equilibrium.

The convergence of forms of media into multimedia lends itself to the exploitation of materials which, hitherto, were not considered as economically exploitable. Furthermore, it affords a range of different ways in which these materials can be exploited. Many regions have their broadcasting production and distribution institutions. They also often have their heritage archives in the form of museums, galleries and related institutions, where various aspects of the region's material culture are housed. These have tended to be treated as public assets that often absorb considerable sums of money in their retention and expansion. They also sometimes are treated as valuable educational resources. They tend not to be thought of as valuable commercial assets, capable of being exploited as a feature of the regional economy. This is rapidly changing as the potential of merging the skills of the new media with these cultural resources becomes apparent.

The commodification of culture implies that something that pertains to the public domain has been bounded, redefined and incorporated into the private spheres of commerce. This, in turn, implies working on pre-existing forms in the development of new works. These observations have particular resonances for how culture is commodified. When considered in a broader historical context, the term 'public domain' has a specific set of denotative and connotative meanings that constitute the artistic, intellectual and informational public domain as a geographically separate place, portions of which are presumptively eligible for privatisation. Yet, in another sense, viewing culture from a different perspective leads to the conclusion that it is its distributed nature across social space that determines its specificity. On the other hand, the context within which creativity occurs is what generates commonality. This context has a time depth, where already existing cultural forms are constantly recycled.

These observations have a particular relevance for the current emphasis on the commodification of regional culture and its exploitation. There are concerns that this process involves the use of intellectual property rights to privatise what are the resource properties of members of the regional culture. Simultaneously, there are arguments which claim that this can serve as the basis for a reorientation of regional economies. This chapter outlines how this process is developing by reference to the potential for the development of a regional content industry that exploits regional cultural resources.

The preceding chapters have also emphasised how the new structure of enterprises and work demand a total reorientation of relationships. This takes two forms. Firstly, the relationship between institutions and enterprises changes, leading to new networks and relationships. To a certain extent, it involves each institution or enterprise relinquishing the kind of autonomy they held within the industrial age economy. The subsequent changes require considerable work. The new context also involves restructuring and reorganising the entire work process in order to take advantage of the potential for knowledge generation. New workflows are developed. These workflows not only integrate the disparate features that merge within the new convergence of activities and institutions but also strive to meet the need for integrating work and knowledge generation. The workflows should operate around new ways of working, involving new relationship structures, and new learning environments.

It should be evident that the emergence of new varieties of capitalism will involve fundamental changes in various aspects of economic behaviour. This is the context for a discussion of resistance. Resistance is not referred to as the product of a rational mental process, whereby individuals developing a conscious opposition to any development. Rather, it is understood as how practices which derive from earlier or prior varieties continue to exert an influence on how the new varieties are operationalised. In this respect, it is a feature of the 'lock in' referred to above. It has been established that the introduction of new technology without organisational changes will only lead to productivity loss (Powell & Snellman, 2004: 208). The focus is on a new articulation of capitalism, media and technology. However, this development is by no means coherently established, and remains a project in development.

Convergence and the Digital Value Chain

A significant consequence of the new technology is how it leads to the redefinition and the reordering of substantial areas of economic activity. This is nowhere more evident than in how the convergence of the web and broadcasting is transforming the media sector into a plethora of multimedia activites. Economic activities are redefined (Figure 7.1):

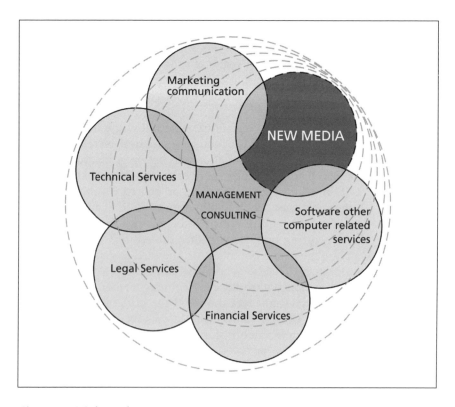

Figure 7.1 Multimedia activities
(*Source*: Toivonen, 2001: 75 Modified by Kentz)

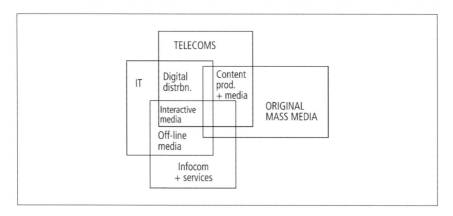

Figure 7.2 The Infocom sector

The convergence of ICT and media breaks down the barriers which have separated the world of broadcasting, publishing, communication and IT. New partnerships are required. The Infocom sector uses digital communication to create a content industry which uses hardware and software to distribute digitised information (Figure 7.2).

The synthesis of many fields of expertise links with IT capabilities and stimulates content and services production. This provides considerable opportunity for economic growth. There are already oportunities for the creation of new systems of entertainment which can reach a global market at relatively low cost. The key involves the link between product and process innovation (Williams & Kentz, 2003).

This content industry involves new processes in the development of contents as products. This includes the commodification of assets which hitherto were regarded as of limited value. Thus museum materials can now be digitsed; the rushes of film or television productions receive the same treatment. Together, these materials constitute the assets of large multimedia archives which serve as the resources for the development of new content. This recycling can have numerous functions. Thus a film company located in Wales wishing to film a drama on the Welsh in Patagonia can use the digital resources as backdrop for a set created in Wales, making the need to locate in Patagonia entirely unnecessary. Similarly, an archive of television film on Patagonia can be trawled for the cue 'guanacos', allowing the resultant materials to be recylced for an entirely different purpose than was originaly the case. The potential of such materials for certain regional economies is significant.

The European Community (EC) has consistently argued that the knowledge economy is such that it transforms the relationship between economy and culture. This involves the 'economisation of culture', the 'culturalisation of economy' and the transformation of the production-oriented economy into a consumption-oriented economy. This means that culture becomes increasingly commercial, while cultural content increasingly shapes commodity production. The EC's argument is that culture has economic value within the knowledge economy, being capable of serving as the basis for a culture industry. It is even more appealing when they claim, optimistically perhaps, that the content industry could be worth as much as 5% of EC GDP and could be responsible for employing 4 million workers. Its growth rate could be up to 20%, creating up to a million new jobs between 2000 and 2005 (European Commission, 2000b). One estimate (MKW, 2001) is that in 2001 there were 7.2 million content production workers in the EU, the annual employment growth between 1995 and 1999 having been 2.1%, mainly where the demand for content was greatest. There is a suggestion of 50% growth in the culture industries in Spain between 2002 and 2005 (Fundacion Tomillo, 2000: 210). Most of the existing workforce is employed in very small companies and include a disproportionate number of freelancers. The suggestion is that employment growth is likely to be more pronounced for content provision than for marketing and sales. ICT will be the driving force of the labour demand trends (MKW, 2001: 32).

The Digital Value Chain

One notion that is gaining considerable currency in the discussion of the knowledge economy is that of the value chain. Porter (1985) introduced the value chain concept as an elaboration of the more general principles of value-added partnerships in order to focus upon business activities, rather than on functional structures. His focus was on the individual company, but included the supply chain within which the firm operated. The exercise was simple in seeking to measure the value a company creates against the costs associated with creating that value. However, supply chains invariably tend to be linear in their conception. In this respect, the entire notion of value chains is not far removed from the processes associated with Taylorism. New business models do not operate on these principles. Yet the concept has heuristic value and we may wish to retain that value.

Value-added partnerships insist upon two components: the constant flow of information across the partnership, and a strong sense of mutual respect and confidence. It also replaces vertical integration. Thus, it does not place an essential emphasis upon spatial proximity. The value-added chain involves the various steps a good or service goes through, from raw material to final consumption. Economics customarily envisaged the transactions between links in the chain as being arm's length relationships, or hierarchies of common ownership. Value-added partnerships are an alternative to these two types of relationship. There is a heavy onus on partnerships within which each player in the value-added chain has a stake in the other's success. In this respect, there is a strong argument for focusing knowledge economy developments on such a concept.

The digital value chain (DVC) is understood as the links between the various stages in the production process of digital content. It involves a series of processes which integrate in the elaboration of a production process using resources created out of non-digital raw materials. That is, they link the creator of information with the user of that information. The only fixed points in the value chain are the creator and the user, and even this may be difficult to sustain as we move into collaborative features of content creation. All the other players must provide value which someone else – usually the end user – must recognise and pay for.

Evidently, the changes discussed above oblige a convergence, not only of technologies or even different stakeholders, but also of different facets of work. In putting together the value chain we need to consider the different steps or stages in the process of production. There is no certainty that regional DVCs constructed around content production will develop. It is as likely that global value chains which do not align themselves with any regionaly based assets, nor with the associated institutional arrangements, will emerge. Similarly, within each region it is possible that each institution which has the possibility of creating digital archives will restict themselves to developing in-house systems. In the absence of fully fledged regional chains there is the danger that the region's assets or primary resources will be exploited outside of the region, with the value-added dimension of content production accruing elsewhere. On the other hand, in historic regions located in the periphery, it is one of the most obvious forms of entry into the knowledge economy.

The DVC consists of a series of linked activities, beginning with the digitalisation of raw materials, and ending with the marketing procedures. This is presented in simplified form in Figure 7.3. It involves the following processes:

- The digitalisation of resources, whether this involves the transformation of analogue audio visual materials, the photographing of historical documents or other materials.
- The storage of these resources under the right conditions for their preservation.
- The development of multi media rights clearance (MMRC) issues which will allow owners of the resources to work together to develop a warehouse, or a Distributed Archive of digital materials which are available under use agreements that cover the entire holdings.

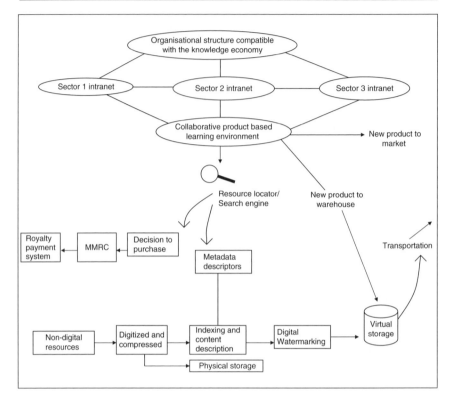

Figure 7.3 The digital value chain

- The watermarking of these resources so that they can be transported, viewed and purchased.
- The development of resource locators which can search, find and identify the resources, and which can also identify the conditions under which they can be used.
- The development of an appropriate transportation system, whether this involves the web or satellite.
- The development of an appropriate payment method.
- The transformation of these commodified resources into new marketable products.

This sequence of activities is what is necessary in developing the knowledge economy through:

- The use of these products in transforming the regional economy.
- The structuring of online learning in relation to the ability to exploit these resources.
- The marketing of these products via the internet.

Each of the above points has its own value chain, and there is a need to analyse these in order to uncover the 'digital steps' that must be taken within each region to enable entry into the entire value chain. What is implied in this conception is that this aspect of the knowledge economy depends upon the products and services generated by digitisation. The activities of the knowledge economy may well be the same as those of the industrial age economy, but how it conducts those activities will be drastically different. The consequence for companies operating in the knowledge economy is that they enter a global market, and they speed up all of their transactions. However, to take advantage of these circumstances, firms in the knowledge economy are obliged to develop new organisational structures. Some of the products of digitisation such as library images which previously gathered dust assume a new value within the knowledge economy.

As with any raw materials within the traditional industrial age economy, resources have value within the knowledge economy once they are transformed into digital resources. Thus, the first step of the value chain involves the commodification of resources through digitalisation. The import system responsible for digitisation also involves compression and pre-documentation, leading to a full documentation processes. These resources become raw materials that can then be sold across and within regions. However, for that value to accrue, the means whereby they can be transported and sold must exist.

The goal is the amalgamation of the different digital resources into a digital warehouse, or Distributed Audio-Visual Archive, readily accessible online to anyone. This means that a series of processes are necessary before such an objective can be achieved. The first of these processes pertains to developing MMRC. This means that the various holders of digital resources, be it the regional libraries, the regional museums or regional broadcasters, must come to agreement about the terms on which they are willing to allow their resources to become part of the archive, and the terms on which they will make these resources available for different uses. This, in turn, involves compiling a register of these resources as a basis for indexing. That is, content without information about it is worthless or, even worse, simply accumulates storage and management costs without realising any return. In a sense, we are discussing the creation of a massive Regional Digital Archive, one that, in time, will articulate with similar regional archives within an all-inclusive European archive. The content only becomes an asset when it is linked with copyright clearance. Clearly, this is one of the aspects that demands co-option which covers the triangular value relationship between media, data and rights, which lies at the heart of effective digital asset management. There must also be inter-operability between media formats and systems, and the potential of automatic exchange of metadata across archives.

The indexing of digital materials and the associated documentation system support advanced material analysis, and the interpretation of analysis results. The metadata which represents the information that is gathered must be capable of delivering information about individual segments, as well as about trains of materials such as video sequences. It must also contain the relevant MMRC information. Most importantly, it must conform with the emerging standards that will allow different archives to link with one another, and for different users to articulate with materials from diverse archives. The sharing of metadata standards is the *sine qua non* of a successful archive. The template manager provides templates for different formats – newscast edition, cinema magazine, fictional series, historical documentation, etc. It involves segmenting programmes at various levels to strict rules that are incorporated in the metadata which must describe content at various levels of annotation by embedding descriptive and identifying information in the video, audio or textual file as electronic metadata. It provides the link between business information and media technology by reference to user needs.

Retrieval and browsing pertain to how the end user is able to obtain access to the materials, to scrutinise them and decide on their use or rejection. Such intuitive browsing is available over high-speed networks and the internet. Users must be capable of using complex or standard keyword queries based on image, audio or video features. Advanced graphical user interfaces allow the documentor to validate or correct in producing the final annotation of the material.

The combination of intellectual property and media data provides everything required for the delivery and recycling of the media asset. What is further required is the means of distribution, and the online automated royalty payment procedures. There is little doubt that, as the technology improves, and becomes universally available to the extent that high resolution is widely available, the means of distribution will focus upon high-speed distribution via the Internet, and other high-speed wide area connections, including digital subscriber loops, broadband fibre optics, cable television networks and next generation wireless networks. Watermarking not only protects copyright but also facilitates the transition to online payment in line with the more orthodox developments of e-commerce. Speed is of the essence in all of these developments and associated transactions.

Finally, there is the need to transform this vision of media asset management and the development of a DVC into concrete business and technical strategies. This must encompass the value of the various resources as regional resources, without excluding regional enterprises from using these resources on cost effective terms. This, in turn, must consider the divergent scalable use of the commodities, both geographically and also by reference to different use sectors, such as education or the regional media/multimedia sector. Such issues will derive from the MMRC work. There is little doubt that the development of the value chain will lead to efficiency savings, better cost control of rights, added value to the viewer and listener and support for commercial transactions as appropriate.

This outline of an emerging potential for the exploitation of regional cultural resources by a media sector which transforms itself into multimedia activites has the strength of allowing specific regions to enter the knowledge economy by exploiting that region's raw materials. However, such developments have pronounced implications for a number of related activities, all of which must be put in place in developing the apppropriate infrastructure.

Partnership Formation

The most obvious of these implications involves how the restructuring of the media sector into a multimedia sector obliges the creation of new regional partnerships. It should be evident that the different links in the value chain involve institutions which, hitherto, have existed as separate entities, some of which may have had only a marginal relationship to the productive activities of the media sector. It involves new relationships between firms, both in the public and the private sector. It also involves a need to develop partnerships across the various agencies responsible for striving to promote and develop the regional economy. This is partly the reason for the emphasis on new partnerships such as those involved in the Triple Helix, involving higher education (HE) establishments, public sector institutions and private firms.

It is useful to distinguish between networks and partnerships, the former referring to structures of relationships, and the latter to the qualitative relationships that emanate from a particular setting. Thus partnerships involve a number of crucial developments which allow them to operate as cohesive elements in exploiting coherent strategies. Such strategies will result in an outcome that is different from that which would be the result of each member of the partnership operating independently within a network.

The apparently simple process of partnership formation is significantly compromised by the demands of the knowledge economy. How the notion of the DVC derives from the principles of value-added partnerships has already been emphasised. The centrality of the flow of information, and the importance of mutual respect across the partnership, implies a strong sense of trust, but also a strong sense of leadership. This will involve stakeholders who have a vested interest in their own status within the enterprise or the institution and, consequently, in their status within society. The stakeholder will attain this status through her involvement with the relevant institution and may be reluctant to significantly interfere with the autonomy of that institution.

The disparity of sectoral involvement of the players in the Triple Helix implies the existence of quite different goals for the respective establishments and also quite different conceptions of how to operate – what some would refer to as the organisational culture or sub-culture. Perhaps the most surprising aspect of these differences is how universities systematically fail to be learning organisations. The sense of inertia within them involves numerous factors. They tend to be vertical organisations, involving very rigid hierarchies, and an associated flat structure with a limited sense of internal mobility. The organisational structures rely heavily on a form of internal democracy which sits side by side with the hierarchical authority, obliging a reluctance to devolve responsibility, and accountability. The limited levels of authority involve a lack of sensitivity to rank, with the result that those in authority have difficulty in asserting that authority. This is linked with a totally nebulous reporting structure.

Such factors contribute to the need for frequent committees. Many of these cut across the internal organisational boundaries, giving rise not only to the need for ever more committees, but also to raising doubts about the effectiveness of decisions. The consequence is that not only is there a limited degree of flexibility, but also that decision making takes an inordinate amount of time.

These circumstances derive, not merely from the autonomous history of universities, but also from how this history has involved what Furnham (2005) calls 'managerial amateurism'. He claims that most academics regard management as involving common sense, or as something that can be picked up in a relatively short period of time. Scientists, it would seem, play an inordinate role in university management. Their academic work peaks early, and they look to administrative roles for career and salary enhancement. They lack management training and tend to be sceptical of such training. Consequently, there tends to be little change in the managerial organisation and implementation, allowing problems to persist.

Universities also assert powerful central control, and also tend to be highly secretive in how they manage resources. Resources are moved around in accordance with the success or otherwise of disciplines and departments in recruiting students whose decisions are made on the basis of limited information or knowledge. The autonomy of the individual department means that the resources are carefully protected, and the activities conducted with little outside consultation. Yet the same resources can be rechanneled, with no associated means of redress. Outsiders are often bemused about how the limited degree of individual or departmental engagement in regional development partnerships not only omits some who are better placed to play a role in such partnerships, but also appears to claim the involvement of the entire university, most members of which know nothing about the associated activities and involvements. This autonomous departmental action also leads to internal jealousies, and even to a tendency to be critical of the involvement of peers and colleagues. The knowledge economy demands, not merely highly educated personnel, but people who have been educated in a particular way that focuses upon the importance of reflexivity. Yet the extent of this understanding within the academic community is limited (*THES*, 27.7.06).

This does not sit well with a knowledge economy that insists on a high degree of flexibility, and an associated rapid process of decision making. It would seem that while universities may well be drawn into networks, it is quite another matter for them to enter partnerships. What they can do is to assume responsibility for developing the specific knowledge which complement the tacit knowledge generated in partnerships.

Different problems are involved by reference to the regional development agencies. The expertise that exists in the universities tends to be missing within the regional agency, where the role of the developer tends to be seen in terms of enabling and empowering. As the servants of democratically elected government they have both the political legitimacy and the funds to drive the partnership. It is not that their knowledge is entirely missing, but that it tends to be piecemeal. Thus, for example, they may have a certain knowledge of clusters, and will locate media firms in close proximity to one another. However, they do not follow this up with any action, and may well leave the firms to their own devices. The transformation of the networks which are meant to derive from relocation receive little assistance by reference to their transformation into partnerships, nor into communities of practice.

The arm's length relationship with the regional developer generates other problems. Thus, regional developers may well fail to recognise that, often, for the media companies 'the idea' is everything, to the extent that any networking across firms will stop short of sharing 'the idea'. Yet within the peripheral regions, in the absence of large technological firms such as IBM, Nokia or Ericsson, the regional development agencies are called upon to play the lead role within the partnership. Within the knowledge economy, making choices is more important than making things, so that the capacity for decision making must be central to the planning environment. Also, e-commerce, telecommunications and the Internet, together, increase the speed and flow of economic activity, demanding the ability for rapid decision making close to the 'problem'. What tends to be missing in many regions is a clear and profound understanding of that 'problem'.

On the other hand, there is a sense in which the leading role is determined by the specific nature of the project. The development of the potential for a regional content industry derives as much as anything from the 2002 eEurope initiative, which directed all European member states to digitise their cultural resources. This was interpreted as involving the memory institutions, whose primary role pertained to producing the digital resources that could serve the tourist industry. This interpretation has served as a legitimation of a rather narrow conception of archiving as involving the retro-digitisation of existing archives held by the memory institutions. It has also meant that much of the initiative has focused on the actions of the memory institutions which have tended to develop plans that have been promoted in relationship with the regional authorities.

This has particular implications for the DVC. As a production and marketing chain the end point is the development of new content for the global market. However, the memory institutions tend to interpret their activities as being restricted to providing services, free at the point of contact. This interpretation cuts short the value chain that, consequently, does not extend to making the various assets in the archives available for multimedia companies to exploit in the development of commercial content. This has implications for the membership of any partnership. In effect, while there is a concern about process innovation, there is little attempt to come to terms with commercial product innovation. However, a recent report from the European Commission concluded '. . . diverse needs of citizens and users for such products and services demands entrepreneurial and publishing skills that are more evident in the private sector. The market needs are best serviced by commercial exploitation of PSI' (European Commission, 2000a). Making the case for allowing commercial exploitation of this data, the European Commission study goes on to estimate that the value to the economy, should the UK follow a more open publishing regime, is somewhere in the region of €11.2 billion.

The other players in the equation – the media companies, commissioners and producers, the memory institutions and the private technology firms – all tend to operate according to their own organisation arrangements, and their own autonomous existence. They may well put a partnership in place, but this will rarely extend beyond regular meetings where key decisions are taken. The relative infrequency of these meetings often means that those attending often have to begin from scratch at each meeting by reference to their understanding of what is at stake. There is usually no attempt to consider the integration of the respective workforces with the initiative.

Yet the very notion of a value chain depends upon the integration of the different facets of the workflow associated with the entire structure. This means merging the various organisations, it means developing integrated work teams which can work collaboratively within communities of practice. In effect, it means dismantling existing organisations and constructing an entirely new enterprise with organisational structures, workflows and working arrangements that are compatible with the principles of production within the knowledge economy. While the focus is on partnership collaboration using shared resources, this is not easy across a range of different agencies.

There is one further factor that requires attention. There is a significant difference in how the DVC develops that is determined by the nature of the various European regions. The historic regions tend to implement the development of their own regional value chains, placing considerable emphasis on the relationship between regional archive development and the regional culture. In contrast, the newer regions, which have been created at the NUTS II level, lack this level of regional initiative. The archives and partnerships tend to be developed in the state capital, and any reference to regions involves the incorporation of regional references in the metadata.

Ultimately, of course, the objective is the creation of interoperable archives using standard metadata. The member states have already adopted an open method of benchmarking digitisation policies as a basis for good practice awareness, and the improvement of practices, coordination and investment at the state level. Furthermore, they will share national experiences and create a common platform for cooperation and coordination of state-level activities across the states. This should allow the regions to integrate with this structure.

Furthermore, the diversity of cultural contexts where the knowledge economy emerges and evolves does not preclude the existence of a common matrix of organisational forms in the process of production, consumption and distribution. Without such organisational arrangements, technical change, state policies and the strategies of firms would be able to come together in new economic systems. While the rise of the knowledge economy is characterised by the development of a new organisational logic that is related to the current process of technical change, this organisational logic manifests itself under different forms in various cultural and institutional contexts. In many respects, the problem of corporate governance assumes a different meaning in high- and medium-tech sectors. A major feature of any project must address the role of the region in economic transformation, while also mapping the spatial configuration across regions. Information is, above all, a 'relationship' that develops structures in the form of networks and interdependencies, as much between firms as between these firms and their distinctive cultural and socio-cultural environments. Production becomes a feature of collective activities that attain a particular function which flows over into the strictly defined economic field.

Transregional Systems

The predicted growth rate of the content industry is estimated at 20% per year. This content will draw upon specific resources that require digitisation and it will be exploited by reference to service provision, entertainment, interactive and orthodox broadcasting, stand-alone entertainment products, etc. That is, it involves contexts and platforms that currently lack integration. Central to this production are cultural resources. Yet no single region has sufficient diversity of cultural resources to go it alone, and online working across language and culture is desirable, even if not essential, in order to overcome this limitation. These simple observations condition the nature of the DVC that extends from the digitisation of non-digital resources and their amalgamation into digital archives to the other end of the chain which involves using such resources for content production and marketing. The resource end of the value chain is fairly coherent, in that it incorporates a range of projects that have developed coherent Digital Asset Management Systems. Indeed, there are systems already in existence that enable end-to-end content flow. However, there are developments which are essential, involving metadata capture at the point of digitisation, and the further integration of the separate steps of the management system, automated image analysis, collaborative tools that can integrate the metadata and digital resources with the working environment, and the more general integration of knowledge technologies with the basic resources of the digital economy. This is less true of the other end of the value chain where it is only the larger enterprises that develop in-house DVCs that are integrating digital resources with production. However, the range of products in even these larger enterprises is limited. If development is left to these larger in-house activities associated with large enterprises, then that component of the path dependency argument that focuses upon SMEs will be excluded from such essential developments.

Broadband services cover a range of activities, including video on-demand, video web casting, interactive television, e-learning, public services, communications, entertainment, news, B2B, B2C, B2E, multichannel television and even multiple dwelling units. It involves a broadband-integrated service management system that will link with the Digital Asset Management System and broadband-enabled devices. Associated with these components are the working platforms and architectures that allow online working. This must accommodate a system that incorporates the semantic web, and some form of technologies such as XML and RDF that enable the potential of the semantic web to be exploited. It must incorporate the human language technology that allows online working to operate across languages. The current limitations of human language technology (HLT) involve its development from the formal, syntactical basis of formal linguistics, rather than a semantic basis such as enonciative linguistics. Its relevance for online working across cultural differences is limited. This will hinder the role which tacit skills that are closely integrated with language and the social construction of meaning have in integrating the reflexive aspect of working as it relates to developing communities of practitioners. It is conceivable that markets for many of the various digital products will be structured by language, with different language versions of the same product being produced side by side with products that have a particular language-related market in mind. If markets will be increasingly structured by language rather than regulation, there is a clear need to develop the capacity for linguistic and cultural customisation. The HLT must be capable of integrating the entire range of languages within the EU, not merely those which it currently serves. Again the notion of the digital divide is relevant.

Such an integrative approach dovetails with the conception of enterprise development for a knowledge economy. In some respects, the technological aspect is the easy part. There is a clear need to build on what has already been achieved by reference to computational modelling, and the middleware that can handle distributed virtual archives and computing resources within the context of security and reliability. It extends to new collaborative tools, customised for specific work environments and delivery platforms that involve a high degree of interoperability of applications that transcend visual and data contexts. Digital resources must be linked with terrestrial and satellite-based mobile and wireless systems that can facilitate collaboration using shared resources and integrated platforms. There must be an extension to incorporate the potential of Internet narrowcasting as the basis for lifestyle entertainment of both real time and stored assets. This includes access to cross-media service platforms and networks that exploit convergent contexts. Wherever practical, these should involve customisation capacities. The work achieved within the context of creating digital asset management systems must be expanded and made more robust. They should be developed by reference to both marketing potential and a collaboration potential that facilitate knowledge sharing and creative interpretation that accommodates linguistic and cultural diversity. The end vision is of a system that can access digital cultural resources, transform them and deliver new products within multilingual and multicultural formats by the various distribution systems that range from next generation telephony, broadband and satellite television, as well as the other delivery contexts. This should result in ubiquitous systems for personalised broadcasting and entertainment on-demand.

Workflows

The most obvious reason for developing new workflows within the multimedia sector pertains to how the new activities merge with previously disparate activities. Thus, for example, broadcasting activities must merge with those of publication or music production, as well as with a range of other, related, activities. Similarly, the end product will be different, and will require new marketing strategies. However, there are other, equally compelling reasons for rethinking workflows.

Workflow pertains to how different tasks or features of the work process are organised in such a way that the production process is efficient and adequately managed. As we have seen within industrial age economy, work was organised, automated and managed from a functional context in order to maximise efficiency. This is replaced in the knowledge economy by the organisation of collaborative teams responsible for end-to-end process completion so that product-related and process-related knowledge flow across functional boundaries. This awareness obliges the shift from thinking in terms of the division of labour to conceptualising production teams, and from information hoarding to collaboration.

There is a sense in which the goal of trying to coordinate and structure the different components of workflows undermines the need for flexibility. Thus, how software aims to codify and store business rules as the operational process changes, how process knowledge is modelled and integrated into software programmes or how the knowledge base is codified and developed into shared knowledge must all allow space for flexibility, experimentation and innovation. Companies that are organised by process are few and far between. Given the uniqueness of all knowledge-generating processes, it is difficult to see how this can become a customised solution.

Nonetheless, it is futile to consider a knowledge economy based upon workflow that does not fully exploit the potential of ICT. Tools exist that allow the workflow process to be defined uniformally in the workflow computer system. Such programmes assign the work, pass it on and track its progress. There are numerous advantages that derive from this – work is not misplaced, it leads to labour saving, work is performed precisely by the best person, and with specified priority, and two or more tasks can be performed concurrently with efficiency.

It is sometimes claimed that the introduction of a Digital Asset Management System within a broadcast organisation is not expected to lead to fundamental changes in workflow, even if significant changes in detail will occur. However, this is a narrow view, both of work and of the multimedia sector. It ignores the principles of working within the knowledge economy and how it promotes the generation of knowledge. It also operates with a narrow understanding of how broadcasting changes within the context of convergence. It is a statement that focuses far too narrowly on the impact of technology. Unfortunately, there are many broadcasters who have failed to recognise the new possibilities of convergence and proceed to produce digital content with exactly the same methods and conceptions as they did for analogue broadcasting.

The obvious advantage of online systems is that data can be accessed from anywhere at any time. It is possible to open this access, or to restrict it. This means that key information can be extracted to move with the workflow. An integrated Digital Asset Management System can allow users to access assets and metadata created during any production, from anywhere, any time. It is this that facilitates online collaborative working, using shared resources. While this is an immense advantage, as we shall see, it does create problems by reference to the relevance of such work in the knowledge economy.

Any gains in the efficiency associated with distributed working groups can derive from eliminating redundant work processes, and from the improvement of the integrity of the collective information database. This only becomes possible if the Digital Asset Management System is integrated with the whole production workflow. It is tempting for the kinds of partnerships of museums, libraries, broadcasters, etc. that are being developed in order to harness regional cultural content archives to think of their own Digital Asset Management System merely as the end of the story. This may well be the case in so far as how their public sector role defines actions in terms of the provision of a public service that is free at the point of contact. It does little if the archive assets are to become the bases of regional content production economies.

If any newly created content and the associated metadata have to be fed into the archive and Digital Asset Management System at the point of creation, then the workflow has to be optimised in such a way that the metadata introduced into the system need only be written once within a continuing process of asset augmentation. This does involve paying attention to considerable detail, and also to 'imagining' where the event leads in terms of metadata.

The main issue that is claimed to hold up the transformation of asset management into the management of commercially exploitable assets is intellectual property rights (Withers, 2006). Current thinking involves moving from 'copyright' to 'copy left', in the sense that if the game is to move into its next phase, 'owners' must become 'sharers'. This is in line with what we have already said about sharing within the knowledge economy. In theory, the new content should be worth considerably more than the individual assets used to create it, and if content production is to be a team process, it is from content sales that the profit from assets will accrue. Implementing this principle is much easier said than done.

Nonetheless, the intellectual property right is one of the three essential components of the Digital Asset Management System:

- The asset management system linked to;
- a machine control system that can synchronously transfer assets between the archive, production and transmission, and
- the administration of intellectual property rights.

Together, they constitute the core component with which the elements of the working process will interact.

The content creation process begins in the orthodox way with the planning of the programme content. This is compatible with the convention of developing story lines, except that the entire work team should now be involved in the process. Furthermore, programme content now has to be rethought in the sense that it involves far more in multimedia than in the production of a television or radio programme for transmission. This is combined with the scheduled assembly of all elements in acquisition, post-production, transmission, online publishing and associated discussions spaces. It is at this stage that the first metadata is created. It will, subsequently, be continuously enriched in the course of the actual content production process.

Any materials acquired from external production, external feeds or in-house productions are ingested into the system, being associated either with new objects or with already existing objects. The first annotation of the materials can be generated. Extraction tools now exist that allow this to operate automatically. It is sufficient to support basic query and, thereby, the selection of suitable material. The editors access the entire Digital Asset Management System through metadata and the use of a structured search and query operation. At the same time, the cataloguing department will work on the detailed description of content selected for long-term archiving. They will also check the quality of annotations created by automatic tools and, if necessary, they will correct them. The main task here involves searching for the intellectual property rights in order to update the intellectual property rights status of the stored content. This might be undertaken by a separate licence department.

In post-production the assembled content is transformed into the end product, whether this involves a programmes for transmission, a multimedia editorial or some other product. The outputs of the work must be reintroduced into the Digital Asset Management System and the archive, allowing anyone to reuse the materials in future work. For broadcasting production, the transmission logs will be added by transmission control.

To a great extent the existing technical infrastructure within a broadcasting organisation will constitute the decisive component for the definition of workflows since it defines how assets and metadata will be generated and transported through the production chain. It is essential to rethink this infrastructure by reference to the goals of the knowledge economy, and especially those goals associated with team working and operating as a community of practice. This does not mean that the same elements of the architecture will not reappear. Thus, for example, the assets will be digitised in full resolution by a suitable encoder and will be recorded on a server. Similarly, production quality assets, key frames and preview copies are stored permanently in near online mass data storage, for example, a tape robot. The web server provides the graphical user interface to all the workstations connected through the local area network.

The digitising process involves creating assets of different qualities – high-resolution copies are recorded on a video server, while low-resolution Internet copies are made for preview purposes. If resale is an objective, then the low-quality items will be offered for viewing, and the high-quality assets exported on payment. Special algorithms can automatically extract information about the assets – edit points, key frames, speakers, faces and key words. Also, intelligent tools based on semantic description standards allow augmenting information that has previously been extracted automatically. At this stage, manual logging is of particular importance, being the first manually generated information in the production process. It is here that the collaborative process is crucial. It requires in-depth knowledge of documentation and an intimate knowledge of the requirements of editors and teams that will work on the materials. Thus the editor, the cataloguers and archivists and any other asset users and manipulators should work as a team. In this sense, job descriptions change from those of analogue production.

This leads to a detailed search and query request that is usually submitted by the editor. Again it should be emphasised that this involves team work. Single hits are evaluated by accessing metadata, key frames and preview video and audio. Any selected materials are automatically transferred from the Digital Asset Management System to the editing station for final editing and programme conformation. This is followed by using technical, legal and contextual criteria for conforming the edit results, and the end result is routed to the play-out server for transmission, after which the programme is transferred back to the archive.

What is evident is that team work for multimedia is essential, and that new job profiles are required. This derives partly from the need to create a closed loop for metadata generation along the production chain, together with the possibility of transferring content automatically from system to system on the one hand, and on account of the advantages that derive from knowledge generation on the other. It does mean that specific jobs give way to multi-skilling, and that responsibility and accountability become team functions. In a sense, all workers must also be 'media managers', carrying the main responsibility for insuring that specific content required in different phases of production are reliably available, whenever and wherever needed.

Marketing

The other end of the process involves marketing. Where, in the industrial age economy, there was a tendency for the production process to be driven by the manufacturer or creator who mysteriously sought to gauge the market, within the knowledge economy, the market drives production. Furthermore, that market is global, and must be seen as global. Business within the knowledge economy differs from industrial age economy on at least two counts. Firstly, the technology that is available drastically alters the basis whereby business is undertaken. This involves far more than marketing, and how deregulation, and the ability to use technology, expands the reach of industrial age markets. It involves new conceptions of the producer/consumer relationship. Furthermore, if, as is sometimes implied, the theoretical basis on which the knowledge economy exists is fundamentally different from that associated with the industrial age economy, then both the process of production and the marketing principles of the knowledge economy should change.

Many of these ideas are beginning to structure the role of planners and the thinking that guide their practices. The DVC consists of primary links that directly add value and secondary links that add value indirectly by supporting the primary links. Several link types can be defined in determining different kinds of added value. In this respect, it is an orthodox business model, albeit that it is supported by the new technology. It remains very much a linear conception and retains a close affinity with Taylorism. Porter's (1985) original conception involved the individual company and its associated supply chain. This linear notion must be transformed into one that involves the articulation of the new technology with the principles of the knowledge economy. The global digital economy structure makes it self-evident that knowledge economy business plans and models must be significantly different from those of industrial age economy. Knowledge-intensive New Economy is competence-sensitive. Thus, companies exploit one another's resources and competences – that is, they search for the best possible partner for a given situation. Work becomes project-based and the idea of co-optition comes into operation. Bovet and Marta (2000: 18) argue that, associated with the change from the value chain to the value net conception are more demanding customers, globalisation, growing competitive pressures and the internet and digital technology. Of these, it is the internet and digital technology that create the business, seen as the interface for value aggregation.

Consequently, value chain networks have evolved into a digital economy business web (b-web), within which a large network of actors, whose traditional roles as primary and support activities become diffused, operates and competes. Partnership know-how and support activities are based on specialisation and on a high level of expertise. In other words, primary actors are more than ever dependent on support actors, and certain support actors (sub-contractors) may actually guide the process, especially where the necessary competence is scarce and substitutes for them do not exist. Such conditions are particularly prominent in peripheral labour markets. An ideal value net is customer-focused, open to co-operation, agile and scalable, sensitive to changes in customer and rival markets, digital and fast-flowing (c.f. Ojala, 2001). Figure 7.4 presents a simplified value net structure.

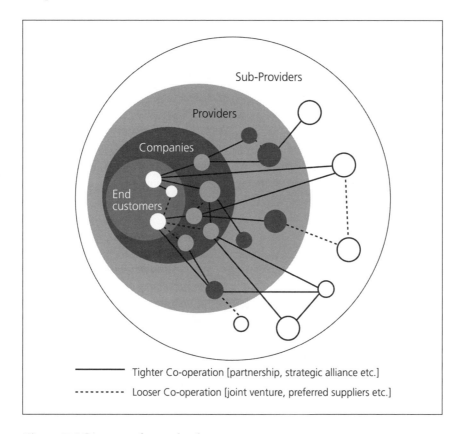

Figure 7.4 Customer-focused value net
(Modified from Bovet and Marta, 2000, 4; Reingold, 2001)

A value net (e.g. Tapscott *et al.*, 2000), in which the traditional roles of customers and regions are changing, gives peripheral regions new competitiveness and the opportunity to participate in the global economy. A business web is a distinctive system of suppliers, distributors, commercial service providers, infrastructure providers and customers that use the internet for their primary business communications and transactions (Tapscott *et al.*, 2000: 17). However, the role of these players differs significantly from how they are understood in industrial age economic systems. There is far more integration of roles, and some role redefinition. In other words, while the value chain model supports the exclusiveness of the global economic system, a value net offers peripheral regions new kinds of opportunities for participation. Furthermore, the value net model is well-suited to community of practice activities that drive company innovation in peripheral enterprises and organisations, through their own learning and the transfer of competence. A systematic value net that exploits regional competence resources is able to compete with other agglomerations and value nets outside the region.

The current interpretation implies that the dynamic and complex structure of a value net is more reactive and proactive in its relationship with customers. Indeed, the role of the customer changes from that of a passive recipient of commodities which meet that customer's needs or demand, to an interactive context within which the customer plays a central role in determining the nature and assembly of the product. The partnership involved in the system learns from the customer (Sandberg & Augustsson, 2002) who, to an extent, becomes an element of the system. Table 7.1 below highlights some of the differences between a value chain and a value network.

Table 7.1 Differences between a value chain and a value net

Value chain	*Value network*
• End value orientated	• End customer orientated
• Value is created in a linear order between different companies or business units	• Value is created dynamically in an efficient network
• Little/zero information sharing between enterprises	• Information is shared between enterprises who learn new 'knowledge' from the community of practitioners
• Customer not included in the processes	• Customer included in the processes
• Push strategy	• Pull strategy
• Fixed structure	• Agile and scalable structure
	• Digital, e-business exploitation

(TBRC, T. Reingold, 2001)

Value production models – chains, nets and infrastructures – demand a new way of thinking, new ways of regional political decision-making and financial resource allocation within regions. They also demand renovation of the educational sector to meet the needs of the regional value net. However, it is clear that, simultaneously, regional companies and workers must have the courage to organise themselves around new tasks and partnerships.

Conclusion

The global restructuring process extends to encompass the restructuring of value chains which tend to become extended and more complex as globalisation, outsourcing and the use of the new technology take hold. There is also a tendency for the vertical disintegration of activities. The structure of the value chain now extends across space and cuts across languages and cultures. The ownership of links increases in complexity and demands different scenarios of recomposition and integration. The relationship to both suppliers and customers changes.

There are substantial changes in the individual organisation, with divisions of work changing, and new workplace designs emerging. The division of work now stretches across the boundaries of work so that employment is managed across boundaries, often within multi-employer environments. Yet there is a tendency for global value chains also to exert pressure towards the centralisation of management, formalisation and control.

Firms place an increasing emphasis on flexibility. This tends to involve both the flexibility of work and the flexibility of employment, the former being imposed by the conditions necessary for the generation of knowledge, and the latter being a consequence of the reduction in worker's rights. The emphasis on project work will often involve the employer being employed merely for the duration of the project. This is often achieved through sub-contracting and short-term employment agreements. More flexibility is demanded of some categories of workers than of others. Flexibility takes different forms, from time arrangements to the assumption of multi-skilling that links with specific forms of learning arrangements. While this is meant to enhance the empowerment of the worker, there are questions concerning how this assumption derives from weaknesses in the neo-liberal argument.

The emphasis on team working within new workflows obliges a degree of multi-skilling, something that can blur the nature of the job or occupation description. This is accompanied by a growing subjectivity in work, with a much greater degree of worker autonomy. This, in turn, is accompanied by a heightened degree of worker responsibility, not as something that is monitored by reference to time and motion, or productivity, but in relationship to the rest of the team and the enterprise. This means that a high level of commitment is demanded, without this necessarily being rewarded. This high level of commitment on the part of the worker is accompanied by precariousness and insecurity by reference to both employment and income.

There is no reason why regional DVCs should emerge, and it requires a particular sensitivity to regional culture and the regional economy for them to emerge. It is much more probable that larger regional players will develop their own in-house systems. They will use these for their own local or regional interests, but may well integrate their archives with institutions of similar interests in other regions. The likelihood is that such institutions will only have an interest in a small part of the potential of regional cultural systems. The opening up of global markets structured around language and culture involves the various cultural diaspora which serve as the consumers of such products. On the other hand, there is little doubt that many regions will develop their own digital archives and associated management systems. However, the danger is that these will consist of part of a truncated regional digital value chain, and that the development of a regional content industry that will replace the existing media producers will be curtailed. If this does occur, then the transregional work will be restricted to developing the basis for an integrated archive that can be exploited by anyone, from anywhere.

Note

The work on which this chapter was based was undertaken as part of an EC IST Programme project titled 'Technology and Economic Development in the Periphery' undertaken between 2001 and 2003. The comparative study involved work in Finland, Austria, Ireland, Hungary and Wales.

Chapter 8
Social Theory and Language

Introduction

This book is ostensibly about the relationship between language, culture and the knowledge economy. However, it has thrown up a variety of issues that extend beyond this relationship. Among these issues are the relationship between economy and society, between society and governance and the relationship of language and culture to these three institutions. There is a pervasive claim that globalisation is leading to far-reaching social changes that have profound influences upon the institutions of society. In this context, the book has also considered the emergence of a new form of modernity. Thus far the discussion of the role of language in such changes has received limited attention. Yet it can be argued that the current emphasis on multilingualism derives from the breakdown in the authority of the state in the march of globalisation. This contributes to a need for a revaluation, and a new understanding of the relationship between language and society. In this concluding chapter I propose to stand back and consider these issues, drawing together the different threads of the preceding arguments and claims.

While the knowledge-based economy remains a capitalist economy, it has been argued that it constitutes a new variety of capitalism, significantly different from industrial age economy, one that is sometimes referred to as 'informational capitalism'. Industrialism and the industrial age economy tend to be aligned with modernity (Touraine, 1992). If, as is implied in much of the literature, there is a fundamental difference between the knowledge-based economy and industrial age economy, with the former replacing the latter, it raises the question of the extent to which modernity is also in demise. Given that the concept of industrial society, as expounded by St Simon, Comte and Durkheim, was understood as a feature of modernity, it also opens the debate about social change. This change has been a recurring theme among sociologists in recent years, involving the diverse claims for postmodernism, post-industrialism, a second modernity or reflexive modernity.

Such issues have tended to derive from treating particular kinds of society as characteristic of stages in human history. There is a link between periods of history that correspond with specific modes of development

that involve fundamental changes in the main factor of production associated with the generation of wealth. From the time of Bacon in the
17th century, the progressive development of knowledge was viewed
as natural and normal. In the following century this was linked with
the idea of progress as inevitable. It was set in the context of civilisation, involving culture as well as ideas and institutions. It constituted the
linking of progress with the notion of social complexity. In the work of
Kant, humankind proceeds through a steady and progressive evolution
towards a state of perfection. This led to social evolutionism, involving the search for a law of progress. Placed in a global context, it is the
progress of civilisation, involved in the evolution from one type of society
to another. Progress was associated with an increasing complexity, and the
eradication of earlier forms that hindered its development.

   This essentialist notion of unilinear social evolution has plagued the
social sciences since its inception. It is something that contemporary
thinkers are at pains to avoid. Consequently, discussions of contemporary social and economic change tend to treat knowledge as a factor of
production that is locked into periodic transitions. As agriculture, involving land as the primary factor of production, gave way to industrialism,
which had capital and manual labour as primary factors of production,
so 'informationalism', based on information, communication, technology
and intellectual labour, emerges as a new form. This escapes the tendency
to treat value as locked in the immanent, eternal qualities of things, by
emphasising the centrality of social relations in value creation.

   The past quarter century has witnessed various accounts of the
undoubted social change that we have witnessed, and how it has been
interpreted by reference to modernity. All of these accounts point to the
same forms of social change while providing different interpretations for
them. These changes have run parallel to at least three developments that
have had a profound impact upon the economy – the new technology,
the heightened emphasis on knowledge in economic activity and globalisation. The enhanced emphasis on knowledge generation can be viewed
as a positive development, since it presents new insights. Similarly, the
positive value of technology lies partly in how it changes the rules of
the economy. It influences the nature, pattern, organisation and context
of work, but, on the other hand, it cannot determine them on its own. As
has been emphasised, new technology without organisational change will
not have an impact upon productivity. Nonetheless, it does contribute to
increasing skill levels.

   On the other hand, globalisation is far more contentious. It is the consequence of a particular political philosophy – neo-liberalism – and it is
often interpreted as having quite negative consequences (Giddens, 2002).
It uses technology and relates to a form of politics that sanctions economic deregulation, and, according to some, an emphasis on a specific

form of democracy. This does not imply that capitalism carries the same form in all locations. It is claimed that a familial form operates in India, and a form which has substantial state involvement operates in Russia and China. Nonetheless, it is argued that globalisation does contribute to a heightened degree of global inequality (Giddens, 2002: 15–16). Within states, the demise of the labour movement is often accredited to forms of neo-liberal governance that leads to an enhanced degree of inequality. It is also argued that the current nature of international government is inadequate to resolve the problems that derive from the unconstrained degree of economic exploitation.

The concern of the debates about modernity is not with how such developments enhance productivity, nor how they fit with the modernisation project. Rather, it concerns the consequences of modernisation and questions whether what are categorised as the features of social change represent new forms of modernity. The relationship between increased complexity and knowledge intensity within socio-economic systems leads some to make claims for the existence of an information or knowledge society, distinct from industrial society.

The other element of change that demands attention involves the changing nature of the polity. The arguments surrounding the loosening of sovereignty associated with the demands of operating within a global context replete with risk have surfaced several times in the preceding chapters. It implies the emergence of a supra-state form of governance. Such a context applies to the European Union (EU) which appears to be moving towards a strengthening of its decision-making authority by reference to the constituent member states. This creates a dilemma for the EU in that it presents the message of 'unity in diversity' by reference to language and culture, while requiring an efficient operational system that involves the use of far fewer languages than has hitherto been the case. This is a contentious issue, not merely by reference to its implications for the sovereign state, but also by reference to how it becomes possible to sustain Europe's linguistic and cultural diversity within the new order. The tension between universalism and particularism is evident.

Modernity

The evolutionary theme tends to focus upon the changing nature of 'modernity'. Among the diverse ways in which modernity is understood, the idea of an evolving order is, perhaps, the most influential meaning. This involves, on the one hand, the historical realisation of Enlightenment's conception of a present that is different from the past and, on the other hand, a faith in the inevitability of progress (Habermas, 1987). That is, it represents the antithesis of 'tradition'. As the driver of progress, rationalism was to transform tradition. Similarly, the notion of progress involves justifying the present as something that heralds a future.

Modernity is also thought of as a kind of society, again by reference to stages within human history. More accurately it refers to kinds of society. Thus industrial society is understood as a model of the lifeworld within which various institutions are interlocked. Each state had its own form of industrial society. It is a differentiated society, with a pronounced division of labour. It is a society divided into social classes, with a family structure focusing on the nuclear family and the notion of the predominance of the male wage earner, and a strongly hierarchical technical organisation of work. 'The civil identity of the citizen is completely tied into and dominated by particularistic loyalties of gender, family, ethnic group, class and so forth. The contradictions that exist in identity structure between universalistic claims and particularistic reality of granted and denied rights to freedom are settled by and within the ontology of differences' (Beck, 1998: 73). Thus, rights of freedom of language use in public life for minority language speakers were denied. It involved a faith in language as a form that was capable of signification and representation. Languages were different as objects because of their distinctive forms. This conception derived partly from how science was the motor of change in how it informed the mastery over nature. Scientific reasoning was the desideratum of success.

On the other hand, modernity is also understood as a context of experience associated with this kind of society (Berman, 1983). This encompasses a view of modernity as a constantly changing and evolving condition. As such, it seeks to emphasise the prevailing ethos associated with a particular historical conjuncture, without fixing its nature. It involves conceptions of space and time, and of the self in relationship to others (Foucault, 1966). That is, it focuses upon the three dimensions of deixis – time, person and place which, together, allow a social conception to emerge through language. The particular configuration of these elements provides the basis for how we experience the world. It may also include the emphasis on rationalism which Weber identified as a predominant feature of modern society.

The transformation of a metaphysics which relied on the notion of divine intervention into a modernity which placed the onus for change on the individual and society involved fundamental changes in the perspective on the world (Foucault, 1966). The new perspective emphasised the efficacy of its immanent force and powers, while creating a distance between humankind and the world. The worldly surroundings served as a backdrop for what was known by humans, who were constructed as both subjects and objects of knowledge. Reducing this distance between humans and their worldly surroundings served as the basis for developing control over the natural and social environment. The biological and social sciences came into play. Freedom was seen as a measure of control over this environment. Social and political liberation became the bases for the achievement of freedom. It was a freedom that was vested in the notion of individual self-development. It is this that informs Berman's observation about how self-development confronts an unknown world where 'everything solid melts into air'.

Marx identified transformations in society as deriving from the laws of motion of specific socio-economic systems. Each mode of production, including capitalism, had its own dynamic and destabilising character. It was a view that again suffered from its expression of the inevitability of social progress, while also being criticised as being excessively imbued with economic determinism. Nonetheless, it does raise the question of whether it is capitalism or modernity that constitutes the best way of theorising the relationship between the Enlightenment conception of modernity and that of modernity as expression (Callinicos, 1999: 298). It raises the question of whether or not modernity has transcended capitalism, a view that is implicit in the work of Beck and Giddens that is discussed below.

Language and Modernity[1]

During the 19th century the theme of progress was linked with the idea of an evolving social complexity. It involved, not merely social organisation, but also cultural and linguistic forms. Among these traits were democracy, cohesion and harmony, all of which could be guaranteed by the state. Modernity, viewed as Enlightenment's conception of a present, involved language in how specific languages and cultures were categorised as capable of presenting reason. Domains of knowledge became independent and were viewed as structures or organic unities (Foucault, 1966). Life, labour and language became the new positive regions of knowledge. A new space opens up between philosophy and biology, economics and philology, allowing the appearance of the human sciences. Humankind is now subject to the laws of biology, of production and language.

The creation of the modern state rested on the merging of a population that resided within a specified territory and locating it within a single economy, with a single labour market. Access to that labour market insisted upon a knowledge of the state language. It was argued that only certain languages had the capacity for rational expression. As the custodian of the search for perfection through progress, the state constructed some languages as the languages of reason, leaving the other languages somehow outside of the realm of reason. They were vested in the world of a tradition that had to be overcome in achieving modernity. Rational society involved the extension of scientific and technical reason to encompass the government of humankind and the administration of things. Society and the state encompassed overlapping interests and were coterminous. It was inconceivable that anyone could lie outside of society or the state which, between them, were responsible for the construction and conservation of a creative social order conditioned by reason. There was a drive to create a uniform citizenry, united by language, culture and reason.

Languages designated as state languages were deployed for the activities that demanded a capacity to reason – administration, education and science. Other languages were excluded, and were deemed fit only for 'private' use in the home, and perhaps the community, as relevant only for the world of 'tradition'. A distinction emerges between logic and passion, between reason and emotion. It incorporates the classification of languages. Non-state languages were those which named the objects which strike the senses, in contrast to state languages which first of all names the subject, then the verb and finally the object (Calvet, 1974). Languages that are held to follow the order of sensation had a corrupt syntax, in contrast to those that respect the logical order and result in a clarity of expression. Through legislation, the state could eliminate any interference to progress, making progress inseparable from the polity. The state became the custodian of the search for perfection through progress. Linguistic diversity became the obstacle to development. Expurging the world of tradition involved eliminating the languages that conveyed and expressed this world. This was achieved through an education that was practised entirely through the language of reason. It left members of non-acceptable language groups devoid of the capacity, and the means, to resist their denigration and categorisation.

The social sciences derived from similar principles. Sociology began as an explicitly political endeavour. It involved a search for an understanding of the order that was implicit in the concept of society, and for the dynamic that fuelled its development. Many of the concepts that remain fundamental to the social sciences began as expressions of the modern order. Each state had a single society, served by a single culture and a single economy. Linguistics follows a similar path (Williams, 2005). It became the tool for standardisation, imposing form on a speech which some claim held far less unity than was implied by syntacticians (Auroux, 1994). The focus shifts to a homogeneity of language, with variation construed as deviation from a norm. It led the comparativists to conceive of an original language that becomes fragmented. Language and representation becomes a general relation, inferring the unconscious from the fact of representation as in Durkheim's social facts, Marx's account of ideology or Saussure's account of language. Human sciences could now reveal the unknown of representation.

Languages become objects that are analysed according to an internal structure. In some respects, a judgement about the capacity of this structure remains in how languages are labelled as 'modern', without marking their 'Other'. Yet languages marked the border between states and peoples, being characteristic of the distinction between 'us' and 'them'. They were incorporated into a kinship of languages that separated polities while also uniting them in a common European cause. What is, and is not, a language is very much a political, rather than a linguistic issue.

Late Modernity

Habermas (1985) makes the point that modernity is 'an incomplete project'. For several years there has been a discussion about the nature of change in the nature of modernity. This has involved postmodernity, late modernity and reflexive modernity. Where the first of these approaches argues for a new stage associated with the demise of modernity, the other two concepts refer to shifts in the constitution of modernity. The distinction is important because of how it relates to evolutionary arguments. The most influential authors associated with this rejection of postmodernism are Giddens, Beck and Habermas.

Giddens offers an account of change in modernity. It is an account that sustains much of the argument about modernity, while adapting his understanding of society and its operations. In developing his account he contributed to revising much of sociology, and how it portrayed and explained the operations of society. Firstly, his theory of structuration, discussed in Chapter 5, responds to the problems associated with the equilibrium model of society and how it fails to accommodate an adequate account of the dynamic nature of society. This development shifts the focus from a concern with how structure determines action to how action is structured as everyday life, and how structured action, or social practice, is reproduced. In many respects, this overlaps with the concern with normative social practice. It relates structuration with social reproduction.

Social action involves a discussion of an emphasis on the importance of a social practice that relates to tacit knowledge. It can be argued that any theory of history presupposes an account of the relationship between social structure and human agency. Giddens's notion of social structure does not view it as a negative form that sets limits to action, but rather, as something that enables as well as constrains. This means that historical agency is no longer restricted to involving different combinations of contractuality and domination, or as an inexplicable leap beyond the existing 'formative context' (Callinicos, 1995: 151). He resolves the structure–agency dilemma by constructing the individual as a knowledgeable, autonomous agent who is active in formulating her action. At the heart of this theoretical concern is the human subject who carries and

embodies tacit knowledge. This form of knowledge is presented as a privileged form of knowledge in that it is that which drives economic growth
through its capacity for stimulating innovation. The behaviour that relates
to this tacit knowledge derives from a specific form of social organisation
(Pleasants, 1999: 92).

The focus on the human subject has been contentious for several years.
The Cartesian subject, viewed as a logical being, allows separating the
intelligible and the emotional, sense and non-sense, the rational and the
mad, while also excluding women, children, the 'primitive', etc. The Eurocentric notion of the subject constructs her as sovereign and autonomous,
in control of her world. Such a view was assumed into the sociological
study of industrial society, but with the subject disappearing behind the
study of systems and structures which were held to determine the nature
of the subject. However, of late, it would appear that the link between
society and the subject is under threat, presenting a threat to this notion.
It is increasingly recognised that the notion of the free and autonomous
human subject is a social construction. The elaboration of this view culminates in Foucault's *Mots et les Choses,* and Wittgenstein's notion of the play
of language.

Touraine (2007) has been among the most vocal in demanding a focus
on the subject in the study of society. To an extent this has occurred
through the focus on social practice. It is often claimed that the focus
on the subject is a prerequisite for the analysis of what are referred
to as new social movements. This is because of how it requires the
analysis of how actors are formed, and the role that they play in transforming rules and institutions through their involvement in new social
movements. It is argued that the discourse of the official institutions
repress specific forms of social practice, to the extent that the practice of the actor does not correspond with the social system. On the
other hand, there has also been a reconsideration of the earlier understanding of the relationship between the actor and the social system or
social structure, an understanding that reduced the actor to a passive
observer.

If, as Giddens implies, agency is a creative force that enables as well
as constrains, the problem that this creates is how to operationalise this
notion of creativity if knowledge is tacit, and thereby beyond the reach of
the rational human subject. It is here that the notion of reflexivity plays
a part. While not all action is claimed to be goal-oriented, it is monitored by a reflexive process wherein actors reflect on what they are doing,
how others react to their action and the circumstances in which it takes
place. Actors are able to explain why they act as they do, and can also
provide rational reasons in explaining their action. While motivation may
be unconscious, Giddens's notion of 'practical consciousness' sounds very
much like tacit knowledge, in that he claims that it is known without being

articulated as such. Nonetheless, it is capable of being made explicit, and can be incorporated into what he calls 'discursive consciousness'.

It is here that we encounter reflections on Saussure's distinction between *langue* and *parole*. Giddens makes the point that language use is central to social life, and that '. . . in some basic respects it can be treated as exemplifying social processes in general' (Giddens, 1976: 127). Importantly, he is at pains to retain the distinction between language and society! Drawing upon the distinction between *langue* and *parole*, he proceeds to argue that the distinction between language as an object and how subjects are always present in speech implies a distinction between the specific and the general. That is, while speech involves the deictics of time, person (subject) and place, language as an object is 'virtual and outside of time', while also being devoid of a subject in the sense that it is not the product of any single subject. He then makes an analogous distinction between interaction and structure, claiming that structure consists of 'rules and resources' that are drawn upon in interaction. That is, he claims that there is a social metadiscourse that informs social practice. This he refers to as '. . . systems of generative rules and resources', again drawing upon the model of linguistics.

He continues with the link to linguistics by referring to these rules and resources as 'modalities'. Indeed, there is a close resemblance between the linguistic and sociological concept, in that modalities are conceptualised as the lines of mediation between interaction and structure. It represents an 'interpretive schema', between communication and signification. That is, in referring to the communication of meaning within interaction, he claims that the subject draws upon interpretive schemas that are capable of analysis as 'semantic rules'. In applying sanctions that imply legitimation within interaction, subjects draw upon norms that, at the level of structure, are capable of analysis as 'moral rules'. He also refers to this as 'normative sanctions'. Thus, it would appear that he conceives of structure by reference to the normative. Clearly, in focusing on meaning he is making statements, not only about the social, but also about semantics. The construction of meaning is social in nature.

From such an understanding of the social, Giddens develops an account of the transformation of modernism and its implications for society. A question that emerges involves the relationship between capitalism and modernity. Some suggest that modernity is the consequence of capitalism, whereas others claim that capitalism is merely one dimension of modernity. Giddens subscribes to the second of these views, arguing that none of the 'four institutional' dimensions of modernity – capitalism, industrialism, surveillance and war – are reducible to the others, which means that capitalism cannot be responsible for the features of modernity. The implication is that both capitalism and modernity arose together without any necessary causal relationship. Modernity is characterised not so much by an individual reflexivity, but by 'institutional reflexivity', involving how people constantly and dynamically adjust their social practice to changing information and circumstances. It involves the relation of individuals to bodies of 'expert knowledge'. In this respect, there is a relationship between them, and access to expert knowledge depends upon the know-how of practical consciousness. Institutional reflection is held to be why modernity has vast capabilities, while it is also threatening the autonomy of its functional systems and destabilising its institutional foundations.

At the heart of the argument about the prevalence of reflexivity in social practice is the argument that pre-modern life was determined by tradition, whereas in late modernity it is transformed. Globalisation leads to a 'cosmopolitan world' within which actors from quite different 'traditions' are in contact. This obliges drawing upon rationality in justifying traditional praxis within a 'detraditionalising society'. As tradition retreats, so life involves a more open and reflective quality (Giddens, 2002: 36–50). It is interpreted as a 'freedom from the constraints of the past'. Yet there is little doubt that the past continues to play a fundamental role in how subjects are constituted, while 'tradition' can be understood as the product of the modernist discourse, rather than as a form that, somehow, lies outside of modernity.

This, in turn, leads to the question of whether modernity has transcended capitalism. A positive answer to this question is inherent in the claims made for a 'high' or 'late' modernity. The conflation of tacit knowledge with custom and tradition was, according to Giddens, characteristic of simple modernity, where people were submerged in tradition. Knowledge had an external, regulative relation to social behaviour. It is being replaced by late modernity. This involves a social order that is permeated by globalisation, and a way of life stripped bare of tradition.

Giddens distinguishes between different types of knowledge and ways of knowing, while relating what he refers to as 'late modern society' to types of knowledge and reflection. Giddens's ontological view of the individual as a knowledgeable, autonomous, agent, actively involved in developing her social practice, links with the relationship between tacit knowledge and social organisation. The human subject embodies tacit knowledge, but the associated behaviour derives from the form of social organisation. While maintaining a link between tacit knowledge and economic behaviour, he refutes economic determinism, and the static nature of society. He also denies structural causality associated with the human subject, claiming that the social subject contributes to society. This lies behind his claim that modernity is characterised by an institutional reflexivity. That is, reflexive modernity is an institutional rather than an individual phenomenon. On the other hand, it is dependent on individual reflexivity. Social actors do not merely react reflexively to systemic

processes but constantly adjust their social practices. The associated constitution and reconstitution of social life is fed by knowledge, and the
relationship of individuals to bodies of 'expert knowledge' that condition their action. The distinction between 'simple modernity' and 'late
modernity' pertains to how, in the former, knowledge had a regulative
role vis-à-vis social behaviour, whereas in the latter, knowledge becomes
an integral feature of how social life is constantly reshaped.

Beck (1998: 84–102) argues that Giddens's understanding of reflexivity involves polarising different modes and types of knowledge, and that
he relates claims about late or reflexive modernity to specific forms of
knowledge and reflection. By institutional reflexivity he means how scientific and expert knowledge 'disembeds' and 're-embeds', resulting in
changing structures and forms of social action. Space and time are differentiated, thereby exposing everyone to global systems and dynamics. This
globalisation of modernity involves the global interlinking of economic,
political and cultural processes that are linked to crises and conflicts at
the institutional level. This includes the capitalist mode of production,
how industry transforms nature and forms of social surveillance. As the
'reflexive appropriation of knowledge' proceeds, control over the global
interconnections becomes more difficult, despite the enhanced tendency
for global fusing.

Such a schema obliges Giddens to clarify the relationship between the
inherent systemic dynamism and how actors influence this structure. This
he does by reference to the notion of 'trust'. In contrast to the role of tradition in earlier modernity, where standardised rules of behaviour and
action provide an 'ontological security', he argues that members of modern society can merely hope that functional systems fulfil expectations.
Meanwhile, their awareness of risk, uncertainty and insecurity merely
expands through the reflexive dynamisation of modernity. Risk emerges
through a future orientation, and a focus on change. It involves confronting a future that we have never known, particularly when the order
that we have constructed for society and nature is under threat. As such
it reorders the relationship between time and space. Trust and risk are
less controllable within a global interconnectedness, where the state is
increasingly emaciated (Zolo, 1992). The deference which previously prevailed in much political activity has been replaced by scepticism, and a
mistrust of politics and politicians. Political power based on authoritari-
anism is incompatible with the flexibility and dynamism required of the
knowledge economy within a global context. This becomes evident within
a society where the voter, through the internet, has as much information
and knowledge as the elected. However, everyday social practice is locked
into this world, and it is the socialisation process that re-embeds the social
in global interdependency. The focus shifts to an 'active trust', a trust that
must be won. It relates to his notion of the 'reflexive citizen' and how

individual autonomy and responsibility fit with the understanding of the possibilities of social action.

Reflexive Modernisation

In pursuing these issues Beck refers to his theory of reflexive modernisation. In developing his argument he leans heavily on the overcoming – how modernity transcends tradition. He argues that industrial society was only a semi-modern society in that it retained feudal characteristics that were not mere traditional survivals, but were the product and foundation of industrial society. These forms include how labour and capital divided society into classes, the nuclear family, the sexual division of labour and the existence of large-scale public and private bureaucratic organisations. They arise from the modernisation process itself as a consequence of '...a contradiction between the universal principles of modernity – civil rights, equality, functional differentiation, methods of argumentation and scepticism – and the exclusive structures of institutions, in which these principles can only be realised as a particular, sectoral and exclusive basis' (Beck, 1992: 118). What this implies is that modernisation incorporates a democratising force which allows institutions to be transformed.

He views modernisation as an ongoing, dynamic process that feeds on itself, thereby undermining the structures of industrial society. The consequence is the appearance of another form of modernisation. Class culture and consciousness, gender and family roles dissolve. Since the social and political organisations and institutions in industrial society relied on these forms of collective consciousness, they also are dissolved. This he regards as a form of detraditionalisation that is accompanied by a 'social surge of individualisation'. On the other hand, the relations of inequality are stabilised. Class commitments and the associated solidarity are replaced by individual trajectories of social mobility. This individualisation serves to break down class identities which lead to class-based inequality becoming a problem that confronts the individual. It is a process that Touraine (1997: 24–26) discusses by reference to how the state, as the mainstay of belief and justice, of regulation and integration, is attacked by the globalisation of the economy and the fragmentation of cultural identity.

Another feature of modernisation identified by Beck is a questioning and problematisation of the natural sciences. The very force that was held to liberate humankind from dependency on nature is now brought into account for the errors that it produces. The positive transforming role of industrial society is undermined. He suggests that when a global perspective is invoked in the criticism of science as the basis of progress, it can lead to workers siding with management against protesters in order to save their own jobs. Science becomes the perceived cause of catastrophes that derive from the human exploitation of the physical world. Simultaneously, science is locked into an institutionalised internal dynamic, divorced from its use as the basis of instrumental goals, while nature has been absorbed as something for the industrial world to work upon.

Such an analysis lies behind Beck's emphasis on risk. He stresses the degree of uncertainty and risk, and how we have tended to rely on the institutional structure to safeguard us from them. He claims that as the modernisation process proceeds, and the bases of industrial society dissolve and transform, or even self-destruct, it leads to a different type of society. The directing organs – parties, trade unions, etc. – become impotent. Similarly, an ultra-liberal conception that reduces society to a market, and the social actors into competitors, can fragment collective action, leading to what Beck calls 'sub-politics' (Touraine, 1997: 121). Certainty and confidence are replaced by doubt, and order by risk which, between them, undermine trust. Such contexts may lead to a reflexive attitude within industrial society, or it may not, thereby resulting in a catastrophe engendered by its own functioning. Such an extreme form of defiance of the consideration of modern society, the rejection of the Enlightenment Utopia and of the dream of a society that is increasingly rational and conscious of itself can lead to detachment from the hopes of industrial society. It requires an enhanced reflection in order to avoid what Beck refers to as the unconscious and non-intentional reflexivity (Touraine, 1997: 46–47).

The emerging of industrial society as a 'tradition' to itself, with its necessities, functional principles and concepts being undermined, fractured and demystified, leads to a collapse in the faith in the role of modernity in human progress. The ground for conflict shifts. It now focuses on those directly involved in primary modernisation, and on those striving to relativise the project of modernity. The state is no longer the focus of conflict. Rather, how industrial modernity destroys the world becomes the concern of everyone. The Western model of development appears to be suicidal, and generates demands for its subversion in the name of the common good. The damage it causes extends beyond the ecological to engulf the welfare state, wage labour, transportation, health and pensions.

One feature of Beck's thesis is the claim that in the future conflict will be between states, regions and social groups involved in primary modernisation and those that are attempting to self-critically relativise, and reform the modernity project as a consequence of their own experience of it. These two forms of modernity become the sight of a struggle over the compatibility of survival and human rights on a global basis. It is the outcome of how Castells implies that regions and groups which fail to engage with the knowledge economy will become the source of displaced labour for that economy. It predicts a global scenario of profound inequality.

Postmodernity

There appears to be general agreement that the nature of modernity has changed in recent decades, and there also seems to be a degree of agreement that current society represents something other than simple or early modernity, even though there are disagreements about how to refer to the current form. Observers point to a variety of symptom of this change – a reduced faith in science as that which drives progress through its mastery of nature, fundamental changes in the family, heightened individualism, increased tendency of risk and uncertainty, etc. If there has been a shift in the nature of modernity, how are we to understand the nature of this change?

One highly popular account of shifts in modernity focuses on post-modernism. Postmodernism involves a questioning of the main features of modernity. In this respect, it builds on Nietzsche's rejection of modernism (Touraine, 1992: 149) and how he focused his critique on the idea of the subject. In some respects, the work of the postmodernists seizes upon how the various disciplines were conditioned by the historical conjuncture within which they were formed. Postmodernism treats the disciplines, and the account that they develop as 'grand narratives' that provide comprehensive interpretations of human history, rather than as the means of achieving truth and reality. In this respect, it challenges the entire edifice of modernity. Meta-narratives or grand narratives are totalising cultural narrative schema that order and explain knowledge and experience. That is, they are the means whereby meaning is ascribed. The critique that emerges includes the argument that the different meta-narratives of progress were incapable of achieving progress.

Among the grand narratives that are rejected is the Enlightenment account of society and history. This leads to the claim that modernity has been transgressed, and that society rejects modern ideals, replacing them with what are claimed to be reactions to their limitations. As a consequence, recent technological and economic changes involve new types of thinking. Perhaps the most significant contribution of postmodernism lies in the critique of existing theories. This allows us to recognise how there is a conflict between essentialism and anti-foundationalism, between universalism and relativism, and how the former are characteristic of modernism, and the latter are taken to be characteristic of postmodernism.

Jameson points to specific characteristics of postmodern society, identifying what he calls a 'new kind of superficiality' where Cartesian models used to explain people and objects by reference to an 'inside' and an 'outside' are rejected. The 'Utopian gesture' whereby misery is transformed through art into beauty, and that emotion is disengaged from the subject, disappears. Central to his argument is that distance 'has been abolished in the new space of postmodern[ity]' giving rise to a 'new global space'. Furthermore, '... the prodigious new expansion of multinational capital ends up penetrating and colonizing those very pre-capitalist enclaves (Nature and the Unconscious) which offered extraterritorial and the Archimedean footholds for critical effectivity' (Jameson, 1993: 54). This view of postmodernity as a condition claims that it derives from the enhanced speed of transportation, broader communication and how it becomes possible to retreat from the standardisation of mass production. This leads to a system which places greater value than hitherto on a wider range of capital, this value accommodating a broader variety of forms.

There are parallel claims that, on account of the scepticism about the relationship between economic growth and progress, there is a greater resistance to the notion of making sacrifices in the name of progress. This is encompassed in environmentalism, and in movements that oppose conflict. This is linked with the claim that economic and technological conditions have led to a decentralised, media-dominated society that lacks a stable or objective source for communication and meaning. This form of life is driven by globalisation, creating a global society devoid of any single source of power, communication and intellectual production. Objective knowledge is replaced by intersubjective knowledge, and the ready availability of knowledge on a global basis fundamentally changes the relationship between the producer and the consumer.[2]

The central claim revolves around the collapse of the 'grand narratives' that sustained capitalism and modernity, offering particular interpretations of history. As such it places faith in a critique that is devoid of theory. This is inherent in Luhmann's claims that postmodernism is merely a self-description, in that it lacks a principle of operation (Rasch, 2000: 196). This is unsettling for many social scientists. In many respects, it involves revisiting the work of earlier critical social scientists, especially Nietzsche and Heidegger. The postmodern condition is characterised by what Lyotard (1984: xxiii) refers to as 'incredulity towards meta narratives' that sought legitimacy in one or other grand theory. Much can be said in favour of the rejection of attempts to portray history as the theatre of some theoretical thrust. The past is a discursive construct that is constituted in the writings of historians, and remote from any sense of reality that exists independent of this discourse. Nonetheless, each subject draws on the past in interpreting the present, and to this extent each of us has her 'history'. Yet, this is not to imply that there are no continuities among such individual, subject-centred, histories. If such was the case, the possibility of sharing meaning, and thereby of engaging with the social, would be impossible.

Given its long historical heritage from Spinoza, through Nietzsche and Heidegger, it is futile to think of postmodernism as a new form of critique. Neither should postmodernity be viewed as a transformation of modernity, since this would merely involve acceptance of modern historiography and the unwinding story that it tells. Rather, postmodernism should be understood as a movement which offers a critique of the principles that support modernity, presenting it as merely one of alternative ways of accounting for the conditions of being, and as the guide to a desirable future. As such it questions its ontological status.

It is important to distinguish post-structuralism from postmodernism. Post-structuralism rejects the notion of the autonomous subject and thereby fits into the camp of anti-humanism. As such it does not develop a theory of the subject. Rather, the subject is treated as the effect of discourse. Similarly, discourses are 'practices that systematically form the objects of which they speak' (Foucault, 1969: 49). Power is understood as a multiplicity of highly specific relationships relevant at the local level and which, together, constitute the social body. A range of local tactics unintentionally combine to function by reference to an apparatus of knowledge-power. The power relation correlates with the constitution of a field of knowledge, while the knowledge simultaneously presupposes the power relations. However, there is a productive side to power, in that it transforms individuals into the subjects of discourse, and thereby positioning them within the social. In constituting the individual as the subject of discourse, power is thereby operationalised.

One of the outcomes of post-structuralism is an undermining of the objectivity of scientific rationality. This constitutes part of a critique of modernity. Yet this critique makes no pretence to either extending the notion of modernity or of replacing it.

Reflexive Communities

Lash takes a different position on the nature of change (Lash, 1999). He persists with how reflexive modernisation equates with a modernisation of knowledge. This involves how knowledge is circulated, consumed and enhanced, and how this relates to conflict. As a consequence of reflexive modernisation, the foundations of social life and action are questioned and restructured. On the other hand, he distinguishes between cognitive, moral and aesthetic reflection, claiming that the emotional features of 'aesthetic reflection' cannot be resolved emotionally, cognitively and morally but contribute to the formation of 'reflexive communities'. Such communities link global markets, mobility, forms of consumption, local symbolisms and ways of life. As such they also permit social, global and personal identities that are mobile, and interchangeable, without prohibiting their expression in a standardised way. It is an expression of the local–global duality.

In elaborating his case for a reflexive modernity he emphasises how reflexivity implies difference, and the existence of the singular subject. This subject bears a relationship to objects that are implicated in the reflexive process. Furthermore, reflexivity also implies ontology, an argument that appears similar to how Giddens draws upon modalities in his understanding of reflexivity. The central point that he develops is how positivism and the natural sciences operate, involving the construction of social things as the functions of theory, ultimately resulting in instrumental rationality. Furthermore, the subjects are caused, which means that they are not free, and determined, and, consequently, cannot be reflexive. It is an argument that is quite ingenious in how it develops an argument on the basis of the principles of post-structuralism. Reflexivity becomes the critique of determined reason, especially by reference to a freedom from social structure.

He also focuses upon how this new modernity generates inequality, arguing that access to information networks and unequally distributed information leads not only to the reorganisation of production, circulation, capital accumulation and consumption through knowledge but also to forms of inequality. Such inequality involves science and expert society, as well as information and communication society. It leads to new rules for inclusion and exclusion, for the 'us' and 'them' of society.

Within the same context, his work focuses on how community formation operates within conditions of advanced individualisation. As might be assumed from his discussion of the new form of modernisation, this no longer involves a consensus on religion, social class, etc. Evidently, he is discussing that which counters the trend towards individualisation. In pursuing this enterprise he counters the kind of social constructivism that discards collective identities as 'imagined communities'. He resorts to the concept of 'reflexive communities', which he claims must be communities of practice '... with an internalist orientation towards the practices and goods they involve' (Lash, 1999: 214). It is an alternative account of Castells's (1996) claim that these developments involve a new form of social organisation based on a networking logic.

The instrumental rationality of what Lash calls the 'first modernity' is avoided through the intersubjectivity of praxis. This leads him to claim that reflexivity is meaningless without how intersubjectivity is grounded in the 'sociality of community'. He emphasises that no ontology is possible without the situated intersubjectivity of praxis. Freeing both the subject and the object from instrumental reason results in the object 'open(ing) out onto ontology'. Reflexive judgement insists on a ground or a basis, such as that of community. This ground can assume a number of forms, including memory, tradition, sociality, situated intersubjectivity, etc.

While distinctive, it also runs parallel with Touraine's account of how the dislocation of the economy and cultures leads to the reduction of the actor to the logic of the global economy, and to the reconstruction of non-social identities founded on cultural appearances, rather than on social roles. It becomes more difficult to be defined as a citizen or a worker within that global society, inviting to be defined by ethnicity, religion, etc. understood as cultural communities. He emphasises that this new basis of identification derives from liberating cultural diversity from the '... iron cage of Enlightenment rationalism' (Touraine, 1997: 47).

Language and the New Modernity

The relationship between objects such as language, nation, the state or community are stabilised within discourse to the extent that they become institutionalised as the taken for granted, or as a form of normativity that is unquestioned. It is this relationship that has been destabilised as a consequence of globalisation and the new modernity. Languages are being reconstituted in relationship to new forms of boundary setting. The relationship between the state, the individuals and the institutions that are contained within it is being reconfigured, while the resetting of boundaries influences how the 'us' and 'them' of discourse are constituted. The state no longer regulates the constitution of social groups, including language groups, in the same way as it once did. Similarly, social groups are not defined and constituted by reference to belonging and identity in the same way as they were in industrial society.

It may well be conceivable that whatever will be said about any part of Europe will be applicable across Europe. On the other hand, the internal variations are given their distinctive contexts by the relationship between the local and the global. This tension between the local and the global exists because these objects are historical constructs within which this tension is manifest. They are not constructed by a closed history on a pre-existing community, but as a singular means of constructing human groups in interaction with others, within a dynamic where the relationship to others guarantees the originality of a specific comparison.

Some (Laplantine, 2007: 41) have questioned the Eurocentric notion of the subject and how it is challenged by the effects of globalisation. The focus on the white, heterosexual, in control of his values, he argues, constitutes an abstract universalism, simultaneously ahistorical, and meta-cultural. This heralds the breaking of the link between language and state, language and region, and the entire notion of autochthony. The language of the social changes; we no longer refer to 'primitive' or 'traditional' societies but, rather, to 'peripheral society', or to issues of peripheralism.

Given how identity is no longer tied to tradition and the associated institutions of industrial society means that language groups will no longer necessarily consist of individuals who have learnt the language through family or community membership. It involves opening the language group to anyone with sufficient interest to want to learn whichever language provides access to the language group. The motivation to do so may derive from a number of sources, the desire for employment and social mobility being among them. Decisions about such alignments are made autonomously and individually. It obliges the language group to display an openness towards the 'other', and to accommodate them in the relevant institutions and networks. It also involves reflexively accommodating external cultures in the relevant features of language use as social practice.

The limiting of institutions that support the learning of a language to education and the media will serve to promote linguistic change. What were standard forms for the traditional language group – mutations, personal forms, etc. – may well give way to new forms, often consisting of calques. A struggle may well arise over issues of language purity. On the other hand, there are other developments that preclude allegiance to other forms. Correctness of language use is relaxed which, in turn, has an influence upon the relevance of linguistics as the arbitrator of correctness. By the same token, the reduction in the salience of social class, and the enhanced social mobility, reduces the significance of class dialects and the judgement about their social, employment and political relevance. The enhanced openness of occupational recruitment will play a similar role in the re-evaluation of class dialects. Linguistic markers of difference and their relationship to issues of language purity will similarly recede.

There is an element of struggle involved with such issues. This is because of how social change is never uniform. Much of the knowledge economy will be accompanied by vestiges of the industrial economy (Williams, 2000). Consequently, modernity and late or reflexive modernity will coexist. As we have seen, Beck (1997) has referred to how the change from modernity to reflexive modernity involves a process of embedding, and re-embedding. Some actors will remain embedded in modernity, while others are re-embedded in late modernity. The different forms of discourse associated with each constitute an inter-discursive context, replete with different potential constructions of meaning. Struggle ensues, the outcome of which will depend upon how institutional structures afford priority and status to one or other forms of discourse.

Whereas globalisation involves a worldwide integration process that may well include a degree of cultural and linguistic dissemination, it also involves an interaction between local phenomenon and the deepening of new aspects of modernity. The devolution of governance to the regions of the different states plays a role in this respect. For the historic regions this will involve integrating a language and culture with a long history into the policies and practices of governance. It will involve exploiting and promoting this language and culture in order to promote the 'identity' of the region. This will engender the same divisions and hostilities as hitherto, but at the official level the tension between the state and the region will recede. For the new regions, the devolution process will require a coherent attempt at 'region building', a difficult process where the features of distinctiveness are neither physically nor discursively visible. Regional dialect may well become a potent symbol in such constructions.

The relationship between languages and language groups also changes. *Langue franche* are languages that have been disassociated from their territory of origin. This means that they exist in a context where the state originally identified with the particular language does not play a direct role in their reproduction. The transnational context gives such languages a purchase within a different context to most languages, although it is possible that they can be adopted as official languages in the adopted states. They become the basis for interaction between individuals who do not share the same native language. Such interaction tends to focus on specific activity contexts.

The economic basis of globalisation tends to focus on MNCs whose allegiance is to their shareholders, rather than to any national government or its population. This means that they are cut adrift from any direct link between both language and economic activity, and language and the labour force employed. Their link is with an international labour market that often involves personnel who have a high level of geographical mobility. They deploy whichever language is expedient, both for their personnel and for their different economic activities. Despite a flexible attitude towards language use in the social practices of work, there has been a convergence towards the use of English as a global *lingua franca*. This has far-reaching implications.

In Europe, individuals and states have assumed that the most valuable language within the global labour market is English, and have focused their educational aspirations and activities on this language. In recent years there has been a dramatic shift towards the teaching of English across Europe (Williams *et al.*, 2007). This has had a knock-on effect on the teaching of other *lingue franche*, most notably Russian, French and German. It appears that the relative decline in the teaching of Spanish is less pronounced, largely as a consequence of the perceived relevance of this language in the American markets This goes hand in hand with the liberalisation of education such that decisions concerning curricula are increasingly made at the regional, or even the local, level, with schools being obliged to conform with parental wishes. Increasingly, curricula policies are determined at the individual rather than the institutional level. As educational systems pamper to the wishes of the individual student, pupils increasingly avoid the study of language because it is 'too difficult', while languages increasingly compete with other, more prestigious, subjects. This has implications for teacher employment, with the teachers of languages other than English being displaced through the hegemony of English.

This emergence of English as a global *lingua franca* has generated a debate among linguists about the status of the different varieties of the language that appear in different locations globally. Are these varieties to be treated as varieties of English, or are they independent languages? If we recognise the traditional relationship between the state, language and culture, there are many contexts in which English is taught and learnt quite remote from either the state or the culture that it sustains. This implies that each form of English should be treated autonomously. It also suggests that the future may well lead to the emergence of an international English with its own normativity, allowing these different forms to operate as *lingue franche*.

This does have implications for the relative economic 'value' of the respective languages. Grin (2005) estimates that the English language industry is worth €17–18 billion to the UK economy annually. Given the purchase of English in higher education (HE) and the scientific community, it is a figure that is likely to increase in the future. He regards this as regrettable in that it detracts from the economy of competing states, while having a detrimental effect upon the scope of European multilingualism. Be that as it may, it remains that the vast majority of European states are realigning their education policies to accommodate the learning of English, usually at the expense of other European *lingue franche*.

As English expands as a global *lingua franca* in relationship to an economy that is increasingly globalised, so the relationship between language and different labour markets changes. The internal labour market of the state, often focusing on public sector activities, will continue to insist on a knowledge of the state language for employment, whereas the international labour market increasingly focuses on English. This generates a labour market segmentation wherein those who have a bilingual competence in English and the state language have access to more prestigious and more lucrative employment opportunities than those who only have competence in the state language. This serves as the motivation for further expanding the relevance of English in education.

What is not clear is the extent to which English is also becoming the language of social practice in areas of public life other than work. Given that the state language remains the universal language, it is unlikely that, despite its enhanced prestige, the use of English will replace the state language in public life. If it does, it is likely to achieve a degree of universality that will undermine its prestige value by reference to the state universe. James (2000) has argued that while English has tended to be discussed by reference to individual rather than societal bilingualism by reference to education and popular culture, the use of English is more societal in nature. He further makes the obvious observation that there has been a shift from elite bilingualism, through cultural bilingualism to popular bilingualism. What he is describing here is the process whereby the use of a *lingua franca* becomes legitimised through its incorporation into mass education, and how this involves a shift from a particular social group to society writ large. This links with how Halliday (2006) has emphasised that as a language extends its field of operation, the change is not simply institutional, but is also systemic. Yet it remains to be seen to what extent this involves the institutionalised use of the *lingua franca* as normative social practice. If such a process covered the range of life contexts within any society, the language would cease to be merely a *lingua franca*.

All of this has implications for language planning. Evidently, the outmoded approach of Reversing Language Shift (Fishman, 1992), based as it is on structural functionalism, is no longer adequate. The new understanding of society and the associated social processes must be integrated with policy objectives. There must also be a re-evaluation of the relationship between regional, state and *lingue franche* within language planning. In this respect, there must be a keen awareness of the relationship between different labour markets, language and education, as well as an awareness of the importance of labour market flexibility. A state or region can develop what it regards as coherent language planning objectives and public sector policies but, in the long run, it is the relevance of the private sector that is most influential in determining the future of languages. Thus, MNCs which have no allegiance to either a state or a region will have a stronger determining effect that may well unbalance the effects of any language planning.

Such language planning developments must encompass the emerging form of multilayered governance, together with an understanding of the relationship between both the public and private sector and the role that they each play at the different levels associated with governance. It is not inconceivable that the EC's favouring of 'mother tongue and two other languages' (EC, 2000d) becomes a necessity rather than a mere objective. This depends upon the relationship between local and multinational companies, between governance and language use. There will be a constantly shifting relationship between the use of language and their embedding as social practice within the different economic and political contexts. The essential flexibility of languages makes earlier concepts such as 'class varieties', or 'minority languages', increasingly outmoded.

It cannot be taken for granted that involvement in various language or culturally related institutions constitutes the diacritica of ethnicity. Thus there is no essential link between watching television or reading newspapers or literature in a particular language, or participation in culturally related institutions or activities, and one's ethnic or language group identity. The institutional basis that sustains the language group no longer depends upon traditional institutions, but increasingly focuses upon the relationship between individual alignments and the kind of community building referred to by Lash (1999). Activists within language movements will not be linked primarily to tradition, but will align with different bases of identity formation. This means that how the individual is transformed into the subject of discourse achieves an enhanced importance. The various discourses that structure the relationship between the individual as subject and languages as objects will be more diffused in that they relate to a range of other objects in structuring the range of personal identities.

Identity, State and Language

The relationship between objects such as language, nation or community is stabilised within discourse to the extent that they become institutionalised as the taken for granted, or as a form of normativity that goes unquestioned. This involves what is common to all discursive domains – constitution, stabilisation and the setting of boundaries. Thus, by reference to the political, there are two key elements – stabilisation involves the relationship between the state and the institutions and individuals which are contained within it, while the setting of boundaries pertains to the relationship between the group that is circumscribed and other groups. The issue of constitution can oscillate between these two elements. The setting of boundaries involves differentiating those on the interior of the boundary – 'us' – from the 'them' who are outside the boundary, even though they lie within an alternative boundary.

Within modernity, the legitimate member of the political community is the citizen, but the relationship between the citizen and the national dimension is never expressed directly, even if the space that articulates the political and the private sphere already predetermines the relationship between state and culture in such a way that the preconstruction of what is political and what is private inscribes the conditions of legitimacy. It is here that we encounter the state/civil society distinction that has been so central to radical politics. It is also the place where we encounter the relationship between the individual and the state, and how this relationship is legitimised through the social construction of the 'nation'.

The issue of stabilisation pertains to what Seriot (1997) calls *demos*, where the political involves social groups that are constituted around the regulating activity of the state. It is here that we recognise the linking of a normativity with universalism. The discursive structure is one in which the representation leads to formulating the problem in terms of the right of the collective to intervene in the individual or private space – the idea that what is not forbidden is permitted, or the distinction between the moral and the legal. This *demic* dynamic involves a progressive disengagement of the private sphere, by a distinction between morality and law, and by a limitation on the extent to which the private sphere crosses the political.

In contrast, *ethnos* refers to how the political constructs a group within the political dimension in contrast to a group of 'strangers'. The focus shifts from internal organisational problems and the content of the political, towards the group itself, and to the definition of the group. Where, in the *demic* dynamic, the specific project and legislative practice are at the heart of the organisation of discourse, in the ethnic dynamic, it is belonging and identity that dominate. In some respects, it is war and conflict that reinforce the ethnic dynamic, whereas economy and science prevail by reference to the *demic* dimension.

These two dimensions are not opposed but are co-present in the construction of contemporary politics, being the analytic notions that words such as 'people' convey. Both represent the field of legitimacy of political discourse. *Demos* presupposes the group without questioning it, while posing the question of the legitimate field of political activity. On the other hand, *ethnos* presupposes agreement on political activity, and poses the question of who belongs to the group. Whereas *demos* privileges the rights of the soil, natural frontiers and accepting the rules of citizenship, *ethnos* emphasises birth, faithfulness and 'cultural' modes of life – something which the *demic* conception relegates to the private sphere – and the impermeability of groups by reference to one another.

In this respect, it is conceivable that there is a sense of uniformity across Europe. However, there are internal variations, albeit that they are influenced by the shifting relationship between the local and the global, and how it modifies the meaning of relevant constructs. Thus the meaning of the notions of 'nation' or 'national minorities' varies considerably, even though the discourses that construct these notions appear 'natural' to different constituencies. Each state seeks to locally regulate the relationship between *demos* and *ethnos* as a feature of its normativity, and sense of social order, even if the nation constitutes a local compromise between *demos* and *ethnos*. It also relies upon its insertion within a global context. In a sense, the *demos/ethnos* relationship constitutes a dialogism, not only by reference to the play that focuses upon the local, where the 'we' of political practice pertains to the *a priori* legitimacy or non-legitimacy of specific actors, but also because these local relations link to the global as a particular actualisation of a common rule of legitimate power. It is this that constitutes the legitimacy of Europe.

Language emerges as a specific object within the discursive formation that links nation and state. It pertains to the institutional structure that can legitimise or de-legitimise discourses, and that has the right to speak about specific issues, and the role of language as an object in such 'speaking'. The issue of what is, and is not, a language is clearly a political issue, one that constructs speakers and non-speakers as political subjects. In this respect, it pertains directly to the setting of boundaries. The relationship between language and territory is established in the concept of autochthony, where the spatial boundary also becomes the boundary which distinguishes the 'us' of the language group from the 'them' of 'other speakers'. This does not mean that there will not be 'other speakers' within that territory, but that autochthony involves laying claim to the territory in the name of the language group. Where the autochthonous language is also the state language there is no tension; the citizen is also the subject that belongs to the language group that lays claim to the autochthonous territory. *Ethnos* and *demos* overlap. On the other hand, where the state lays claim, not only to the territory that defines the spatial extension of the state, but also to the territory within that space which is claimed as the autochthonous of a different language group, the resultant tension is not only over space, but also over the identity that accompanies it. *Ethnos* and *demos* may be in contradiction.

It is at particular historic conjunctures that the discursive conditions arise that allow certain things to be said, and limit other thing from being said. These conditions involve how objects and subjects are aligned so that certain things can and must be said in order to be the subject of specific discourses. This involves classes of objects with essentialist categorisation, with a discursive and performative order, involving individual *locuteurs* in identity and solidaristic groups. It is the discursive universe that assigns value to these objects. It is necessary to consider the different forms of discourse, for example, the political discourse that assigns value to notions such as 'nation', but only in relation to other objects such as the 'state'. In this sense, it pertains to a far broader register that we call 'modernity'. For those such as Foucault, history is a study of the relationship between discursive formations, subjects and objects across such wide registers. Nonetheless, it is in the specific of the discursive–practical register of politics that we encounter the production of meaning within the various national categorisations of each specific case.

If the case for the undermining of simple modernity, and the emergence of a high or reflexive modernity, is correct, then this raises question by reference to the relationship between *demos* and *ethnos*. Castells (2006) emphasises how the world is facing problems that are incapable of being managed within the national framework. The ensuing crisis of representation is claimed to derive from the failure of the state to engage with multiple sources of identity. The deregulation of the state in certain contexts, together with how devolution transfers aspects of the regulatory role to the regional level, begins to undermine the modern constitution of social groups. In political terms, the EU has established what Castells refers to as a 'network state', wherein national governments work together within institutions in sharing sovereignty. This links with the various international institutions. It involves a heightened and different relativisation of the self and society within the global (Friedman, 1992). The associated identity emphasises an undifferentiated humankind, perhaps threatened by the consequences of modernity's drive to harness nature. The individual is identified with humankind. Simultaneously, the fragmenting effect on national and international hegemony foments local and regional identities whose authenticity is linked to roots and place.

The states respond to what is viewed as a crisis of legitimacy by devolving power to the regions, focusing their activities on the international and global context. Consequently, states no longer play their traditional role, but serve as a single point in a supra-national network. They are obliged to cede sovereignty in order to survive and, in so doing, become somewhat more remote from their constituency. The relationship between the *demic* and *ethnos* changes. By reference to *demos*, the group is no longer presupposed, and the preconstructed that anchors the sense of place by reference to the state is brought into question. This raises the issue of the legitimacy of the field of political authority. The frontiers of territory are rearranged through redefinition, but without being changed. It is here that the historical attains a heightened significance. It constitutes a shift in the relationship between the global and the local.

Language and culture are heavily implicated in this process. The enhanced degree of geographical mobility raises questions about the relationship between language, culture and territory; between language, culture and the state as the source of legitimacy. There is a profound contradiction between globalisation as involving processes producing power, wealth and information on a global scale and how identities tend to draw on unique cultural and even local traits. The current separation of the state and the nation, partly expressed in the difference between how the values of the state focus on the instrumental, and on managing the globalisation processes and networks contradict how national values affirm identity. The values of the state are premised on the politics of fear, whereas those of the nation are based on trust, legitimation and incorporation.

The state assumes a specific role by reference to the relationship between certain core values and globalisation – the emphasis is now less on 'national culture' and the integrity of the state, and more on responsibilities within a global context. This parallels the devolution of responsibility and accountability from the state to the individual and the community. Simultaneously, the relationship between language, mobility and labour markets changes. The dichotomy of local and global labour markets, and of the relationship of labour markets to them, generates a new relationship between language and the economy. A tension emerges between the global economic role of a limited number of languages, and the specific economic role of local languages. Each has an influence on the other, and they cannot be understood in isolation. This involves the closing of space for multilingualism and multiculturalism in some contexts, and its opening in others. Identity is no longer confined to the parameters of the state, and how one performs within its class structures. In consequence of the demise of social class as a dimension of inequality, so the relationship between class, language and culture changes. Class varieties of language and popular culture become acceptable within the normative context. This also opens the space for minority languages and culture to be reassessed. The relationship between the time, person and place of language is in flux.

To an extent, self-identity becomes a reflexive project – an endeavour that we continuously work and reflect upon. While much of what we know is tacit in nature, it is also shared with others. It is the sharing that feeds the constitution of the social. It requires constant negotiation, especially self-negotiation through reflexivity. It involves constantly questioning who we are, and our relationship to how history leaves its traces in our discourse. We are constituted as the subjects of discourse in such a way that it determines our identity, but we are also free to develop and change its nature.

The New State?

The preceding discussion has underlined one of the most pervasive arguments concerning the effects of globalisation and the advent of a new form of society which claims that the sovereign state is being undermined. It rests on how states, on the one hand, are obliged to assume a greater involvement with international affairs on account of various existing and potential crises such as the current economic crisis, or the threat of global warming, and, on the other hand, the concurrent emergence of devolved governance. Globalisation has de-nationalised the normative space of society, and the state is losing its monopoly on power. This raises various questions about the nature of future forms of governance, and about associated principles such as the persistent debate between universalism and particularism. Given how closely the fate of languages has been tied to their constitution as 'national' and 'international' objects, this issue has a firm relevance for our analysis of language.

Among the effects of globalisation is how the EU has been transformed from an economic union into what increasingly appears like the early stages of state formation. States strive to retain their sovereignty by reference to the movement of people, yet their sovereignty is increasingly limited as regards the movement of capital, markets and information across frontiers. This raises numerous questions about the nature of such a hypothetical 'state' and the role of language within it. The EU has broadened its earlier ambitions so as to take into account the different cultures, languages and nations of its member states. It acknowledges that it is obliged to support multilingualism and cultural diversity, and defines some language rights in its own treaties, and in the Charter of Fundamental Rights. Yet, there is also a concern that the future will involve a pragmatic decision to administer by reference to a single language.

By reference to citizenship, globalisation has a contradictory effects. On the one hand, it opens up the circulation of people beyond frontiers, permitting individuals to transcend the representation of a univocality, entirely anchored in the territory of origin, in experimenting with forms of a plural identity realised on the ideal of flexible citizenship. In the global acumen there is room for a prevailing cosmopolitanism that may well be confronted by a restricted, enclosed, vision, based on the primacy of national sovereignty. The other face of globalisation involves the generalised circulation function, in a universe where historical, political and cultural realities are omnipresent. Frontiers are not a simple territorial artefact; they materialise from different conceptions of nation, of sovereignty. They are currently the site of a struggle to provide an element of permanence within the new modernity, involving a new normativity while acceding to the rights that confer the quality of political subjects. If one recognises that the contradiction between openness and frontiers, between cosmopoliteness and the primacy of the nation state, is an elementary given of globalisation, it obliges recognising that there is the danger of an entrenchment of political action around the traditional institutions of sovereignty. It involves collective actors confronting the new power of neo-liberal capitalism.

Globalisation has also adjusted the notion of time in the sense that the traditionally static notion of time wherein objects were viewed as relatively eternal is displaced by an emphasis on flexibility and continuous change.[3] Ost (1998) argues that this new sense of time, sometimes referred to as evolutionary time, is characteristic of what he calls virtual time. The transition to virtual time, in his view, involves the transition from writing to word processing, being the equivalent of the earlier transition from oral transition to writing (Derrida, 1978). Writing was historical, in the sense that documents were fixed, whereas word processing allows the continual rewriting of documents, involving the incorporation of recycling of what has previously been written. It can also involve the absence of a specific author as *enonciateur* and *locuteur* constantly change in online interaction.

The Enlightenment claims about the inevitability of progress was linked with the idea that the latent force inherent in nature's provision could be harnessed, but only through the role of the state in developing 'the capacities of mankind' (Kant, 1963: 11). Furthermore, a relationship between states was an added precondition to this end. Governance was the means whereby that which was latent in nature's provision for progress could be actualised in society. Order was to be the condition for progress, and the state was responsible for forming order by organising the existing moral and intellectual resources, while promoting 'the general mental advance of the community'. Consequently, the link between the state, reason, social order and progress was understood as a universal phenomenon which was applicable globally. It became a norm whereby all historical phenomena are to be understood.

Given how the Enlightenment was a discourse which argued for an equation between reason and a specific political order, while also adjudicating what was aligned with reason, and what was contradictory to reason, it is inevitable that the universalism was selective. It was not only feudalism that lay outside of reason, but also languages and cultures which did not constitute the diacritica of the state. The Kantian connection between emancipation and enlightenment, understood as the transcendence of immaturity, involved what Kant referred to as the inability to deploy 'one's own understanding without the guidance of another'. He claimed that this kind of enlightenment presupposed freedom.

Habermas has recently emphasised how the 'globalisation of risks' has resulted in a new emphasis on universalism in that it has 'objectively unified the world for a long time, making it an involuntary community based on the risks run by all' (Habermas, 1996a: 74). It is this thrust that constitutes the original *raison d'etre* of the EU. Given Beck's (1992) emphasis on how the world increasingly encounters the issue of risk, to the extent that its future survival is open to question, it would appear that such a universalism will persist. The question that is masked by the equation of globalisation with the economy involves not merely what has been referred to as 'the McDonaldisation of culture' (Ritzer, 1996), but the more real danger of a link between economic hegemony, global law and the imposition of 'universal values'. This threat can be interpreted in at least two ways – as a claim for the relevance of particularism, or as a claim for a universalism that avoids the imposition of the culture of a hegemonic order in favour of a sharing of common values.

Habermas's reference to an 'involuntary community' involves a perpetuation of the preoccupation with universalism even though he now resorts to what he calls a 'discourse theory of democracy' or 'deliberative model of politics'. These concepts rest on a decentred view of society. In many respects, this builds on his earlier concern with language in that the emphasis is on the intersubjectivity of communicative processes within the parliamentary bodies and the public sphere. The net result is the fomenting of 'rational opinion and will-formation' (Habermas, 1996b). It is an argument that emphasises deliberative democracy '...in terms of the institutionalisation of a public use of reason jointly exercised by autonomous citizens'. In pursuing this goal his emphasis is on moral questions of justice and instrumental questions of power and coercion. He is at pains to avoid collapsing issues of justice with those of the good life.

There is a parallel argument that the autonomy of the citizen should be safeguarded from its dominance by self-interested but powerful political parties within a decentred public sphere.

Universalism contrasts with how particularism has been understood. Particularism rests on the claim for the artificiality of the political, and the naturalness of people defined by language and culture. Unity is defined in familial rather than contractual terms, this unity having a spatial dimension. However, it is a different spatial dimension than that associated with the Kantian state. The relationship between the state, nation, the people, language and culture is quite different. The emphasis is on difference and how these differences are conditioned by history in addition to numerous political, cultural, religious, economic and social variations. It would lead to a claim that since there is no global collective memory, and since economic resources are not equal, rejecting this position in favour of universalism is tantamount to condoning a form of global imperialism.

This relationship between universalism and particularism has been resolved in modernity by maintaining the essential equation of the state with a form of universalism, while conceding its integrity by reference to its particular form. It is this that justified the equation of the uniqueness of the modern state with its role in promoting a citizenry rooted in the language and culture that was grounded in rationalism. It is this relationship that now serves as the basis for a reconsideration of new forms of political order. Giddens (1990) stresses how the simultaneity of the global and the local within globalisation implies a persistence with the relationship between universalism and particularism. It is a relationship that is challenged by the postmodernist attack on the Enlightenment discourse. The relativism of postmodernism, with its emphasis on constructivism, undermines universalism's notion of a truth to be explored. Its limitation lies in how it is able to analyse agency, but fails to invoke agency as a feature of moving beyond criticism to any theory of practice.

While there is no denying the relevance of the postmodernist critique, and the need to redress the injustices that it identifies, one always returns to 'system' as the effects of discourse, and that any redressing will be based on planning of one sort or another. The struggle is to avoid the basis of the injustice identified by postmodernism in elaborating planning parameters.

An attempt to balance universalism and particularism without privileging either is found among those who argue for diversity being balanced by features of commonality such that public deliberation leads to collective power promoting the interests of the collectivity (Wolin, 1996). Simultaneously, it is an argument against the legitimised nature of unequal powers and in favour of collective access to public resources. It is also an argument against the equation of democracy with a form of government. There is a sense in which it constitutes an argument against the equation of place and identity (Honig, 1996). Yet, it appears to remain an argument that favours universalism over particularism. It leaves open the question of the extent to which universal principles can serve as safeguards against the dangers of fascism, xenophobic nationalism and right-wing populism.

This leads to a discussion of the notion of distributive justice (Rawls, 1972). There is no doubting that globalisation produces a tension between sameness and differences, between the universal and the particular, between cultural homogenisation and cultural heterogenisation. In a global economy, diversity in terms of race, ethnicities and nationalities has to be managed for the market economy to function smoothly. In this respect, it can be claimed that multiculturalism aims at preserving different cultures without interfering with the smooth functioning of society. It is such issues that underlie the notion of distributive justice which argues that the wealthy have an obligation to assist the poor. This is a thorny issue when it is discussed by reference to any future global system, many making arguments about how globalisation is an impoverishing process supported by a proselytising force in the form of democracy (Benhabib, 2004; Delmas-Marty, 2003).

The notion of distributive justice has been taken up by reference to language in the work of Francois Grin (2005). His economic analysis focuses upon efficiency and fairness, the former pertaining to the allocation of resources, and the latter to the distribution of resources. By reference to efficiency, he strives to assess the net benefits of each policy option by comparing advantages, understood as benefits, and drawbacks, understood as costs. In so doing he includes symbolic benefits and costs. By reference to fairness he focuses upon how resources are distributed. Despite being a limited conception of justice, it does, nonetheless, have considerable analytic value. As such, this body of work does serve as a framework for comparing and evaluating policy alternatives.

Various models, involving different configurations of languages, have been proposed for the European Parliament (EP) – monolingualism; a reduce multilingualism involving the use of six languages; an asymmetrical system; a controlled multilingualism involving 20 languages, bi-active interpretation and the use of three pivot languages for translation purposes; full multilingualism. Only the last two guarantee intercommunication between MEPs. The cost of the different models varies from €108 million (at 2002 costs) or 9% of the EP budget for the first model to €992 million or 79% of the EP budget for the last option. The controlled multilingualism option would cost €427 million, or a third of the EP budget, and in contrast to the full multilingualism option is regarded as cost effective, at a cost of €0.9/European citizen. In terms of fairness, only the full multilingualism option is regarded as providing equality when the different languages of all Members of the European Parliament (MEPs) are treated equally, and when all MEPs are allowed to express themselves and receive communications in their language of choice. On the other hand, the controlled multilingualism is regarded as fair by reference to the second factor but not the first (Gazzola, 2006).

This is the same kind of analysis that Grin (2005) has undertaken by reference to language education. He explored the difference between three models – 'all in English', 'plurilingualism' and 'esperanto' – by reference to efficiency and equity. His analysis leads him to conclude that the UK benefits from the *de facto* priority of English to the tune of at least €10 billion, rising to as much as €18 billion when a multiplier effect is included. The plurilingual context would not be more efficient by reference to costs, but would be more equitable. On the other hand, the 'esperanto' option would benefit France to the tune of €5.4 billion annually, while all of Europe, including the UK and Ireland, would benefit to the tune of €25 billion annually. Such analyses again underline the difficulty of implementing public language policies when the forces responsible for the hegemony of specific languages lie in the private sector, and how the public understands the role of languages in the associated practices. Nonetheless, it does serve as a stimulating example of what can be achieved by reference to the question of the relationship between language and distributive justice. In focusing on a decentred public sphere and a pluralistic civil society it also opens the door to the contrast between Habermas's search for a form of democracy that seals itself against the forces of cultural life and a view of democracy as focusing on ethical and cultural questions. However, it can be argued that Grin's empiricist evaluation of efficiency and equity needs to be extended to accommodate a debate around the justification and foundations of forms of democracy.

One of the most evident international developments of recent years involves the enhanced commitment to multiculturalism. Multiculturalism derives from the breakdown of the authority inherent in the march of globalisation. It contributes to a need for a revaluation, and a new understanding of the relationship between language and society. Representations of citizenship vary from one state to another. This involves the articulation between the political community and national identity. It also involves the play between allegiance to the state, nationality and what Anderson (1991) calls 'nationess', or the sentiment of belonging to a collective defined in terms of culture, language and history which is not to be confused with nationality. The central question being presented in the face of the enhanced mobility of people is the relationship between migratory movements and the diversification of people within a territorial framework. To what extent is it possible to harmoniously combine the exercise of political citizenship and cultural difference? State governance is the product of a representation that is simultaneously universalist and individualist. The notion of individuals equal in the face of the law is characteristic of the subjectivisation that, according to Foucault, is indispensable for assuring the regulation of the population. Citizenship lies at the heart of the biopolitical project because it allows the organisation of the control of subjects by the sovereign in assuring their consent to the established order.

Is it possible to reduce the process of subjectivisation to its explicit juridical content? Citizen-making seems not to involve a dialogue between the individual and the state, but a model that involves state imposition. Ong (1999) uses the concept of cultural citizenship, defined as 'the right to be different (by reference to race, ethnicity or indigenous language, by reference to the norms of the dominant national community)', to refer to how this subjectivisation process is managed in practice. This right to difference becomes the precursor of democratic participation. However, the institutions and organisms in charge of the social politics instil the norms and the values of exclusion, and a neo-liberal conception of citizenship that exalts individualism and the spirit of enterprise that enables the citizen to construct her own human capital. It stimulates an assimilationist discourse that distinguishes those who display the dynamism and the autodiscipline of the successful native from those who do not display these values, but who resemble the underclass. It is against such injunctions that the individual is obliged to negotiate their identity.

Many such views derive from Rawls's (1972) notion of distributive justice. Of late this has pursued through various stages to encompass deliberative justice, communicative justice and discursive justice. The shift in emphasis from deliberative to communicative justice came about because of an awareness of the relevance of language for reaching the shared meaning that serves as the cornerstone of the notion of liberalist justice (Young, 1996). Nonetheless, the emphasis remained on rationalism which led to Mouffe drawing on the work of Wittgenstein in arguing that shared meaning relies upon an awareness of the relevance of language use as social practice. Students of language must have a great deal more to contribute to this debate.

In the absence of a global government that he deems unnecessary and impractical, Habermas's (1998) utopian vision designates a superior system distributed across the people of the EU. It appeals to the birth of a European, post-national identity based on an allegiance to a sovereign Europe that he refers to as a 'constitutional patriotism', involving European solidarity. This constitutional patriotism is balanced by a cosmopolitan solidarity which would be imposed on the elites by the European citizen, leading to a redistribution of responsibilities. While this may well provide an answer to the lack of faith in the present forms of governance among the European public, it leaves open the question of how the existing governance of the citizen can be changed. How will the transition from a solidarity based on the nation-state to a post-national solidarity to be effected? For Habermas it involves changing the consciousness of citizens in order to promote a 'cosmopolitan solidarity', this being more important for the citizen than for the elites, if the former are to impose the new order on the latter. The notion of a cosmopolitan solidarity is for Habermas the *sine qua non* for a 'redistribution of responsibilities'. However, he also acknowledges that the current condition by reference to European unity is insufficient to generate this cosmopolitan solidarity.

Barbier (2008: 251) argues that Habermas's vision requires attention to language and culture, claiming that the language of a real political democracy that authorises the inclusion of all citizens must be diverse, and must overcome the pragmatic functionalism of using either international English or a language without history. In this respect, it is interesting to consider the position of Bourdieu (2001), who is one of the few sociologists to have made considerable reference to language. By reference to Europe he has argued for a multilingual scientific exchange, while simultaneously presenting a contradictory argument in expressing the belief that 'English dominates'. On the other hand, he 'accept(s) the use of English without being exposed to being anglicised in the mental structures, without having the brain washed by the linguistic routines'. It is for a political reason, involving the strategic use of language, that he has this reservation. English seems to him to involve 'more of a semantic universe rather than an ethico-political problematic', and involves 'a neoliberal vision of the world'. Unlike sociolinguists his focus is on function, and how it relates to individual needs, rather than on signification. The three 'needs' he identifies involve an 'identity' function, a 'national' function and an 'international vehicular function'. In contrast, Barbier (2008: 251) argues that the language of a real political democracy that authorises the inclusion of all citizens must be diverse, and must overcome the functionalism of using international English or a language without history.

It would appear that by reference to Europe as well as the nation-state it is within frontiers that the future citizen is realised. On the basis of the principle of inclusion and exclusion, the generation of community and otherness, it is the state that delimits the conditions of appearance and non-appearance. The most potent force in sustaining this trend is claimed to involve the monopoly that the state has by reference to social protection (Barbier, 2008).[4] It involves a form of closure exerted by reference to state boundaries, while also promoting a sense of solidarity in the community within these boundaries. On the other hand, it is precisely social protectionism that is the central feature of the current debate about forms of justice within democracy (Habermas, 1996b; Rawls, 1972, 1996), which proclaims that justice and social morality can only relate to the 'abstract rules' of social life that are capable of meeting the Kantian criterion of 'universalisation' – the priority of the right over the good (Pleasants, 1999: 84).

There remains a strong sense of Eurocentrism in these pronouncements on the future of Europe. In this respect, they contrast with how others place the emphasis on deterritorialisation, enhanced migration and the opening of citizenship. Emerging international laws based on universal principles of human rights make a growing impact on state sovereignty, weakening the ability of the state to satisfy the needs of its citizens (Apter, 2001). The deterritorialisation of law makes it necessary, not merely to address the reconfiguration of sovereignty, but also the reconstitution of citizenship. It is a citizenship that engages and identifies with global issues and forms of transnational governance (Benhabib, 2004). It has been claimed (Castells, 2006) that globalisation leads to a crisis of political representation, influencing the restructuring and reconstitution of identities; this crisis is a result of the failure of the state to engage with multiple sources of identity. The deregulation of the state in certain contexts, together with the devolution of aspects of the regulatory role to the regional level, while executive functions are increasingly privatised, begins to undermine the modern constitution of social groups (Sassen, 2006). As a result, the relationship between territory, authority and rights is changing.

Confronted with these conditions sociologists have rediscovered the notion of cosmopoliteness (Beck, 2007). It involves an evaluation of diversity in conceiving of new democratic forms of political authority that extend beyond the nation-state. It is argued that the break with tradition implicit in the concept allows a distinctive social approach to cultural diversity (Beck, 2006). Rather than relating the notion to a spatial dimension as occurs in the distinction between local and global, or national and international, it is treated as a concept that is applicable in any location. As such it allows thinking of Europe by reference to a regional society in relation to global interdependence. It also involves a rejection of hierarchical subordination which serves to exclude social groups from identity and equality through their categorisation as 'others'. In this respect, it acknowledges the existence of universal norms that facilitate the justification and institutionalisation of the equal treatment of others. Cosmopoliteness emphasises the recognition of diversity as a maxim for reflection, social life and practice, by reference to both the interior and the exterior. The other is treated both as different and as equal. The stranger is no longer viewed as dangerous, non-integrative and divisive, but as enriching. Linked to this understanding of cosmopoliteness 'identity' and 'integration' designate the hegemony of the majority over the minority.

Such views lead to a view of a cosmopolitan, as opposed to a nationalist, Europe. It obliges the opening of the past, the present and the future of national societies and the relations that exist between them. This means not only integrating the different cultural and normative orders, but also counteracting the basis of difference associated with modernity. It also means disaggregating citizenship and opening it out to 'the stranger' (Benhabib, 2004). In this respect, it overturns how collective identities and cultural solidarity have been conceived as static entities, often rooted in a golden past, rather than as dynamic constructions. It is precisely such views that generate a concern about how the 'alien' constitutes a threat to the established linguistic and cultural order.

Conclusion

All of these accounts point to the same forms of social change – while providing different interpretations for them – a heightened sense of individualism, changes in family structure and organisation, emaciation of the state and a distrust of democratic institutions. This implies that these are the characteristics of the information society. However, it would be wrong to think that the information society simply consists of some reordered social structure. It involves a different form of rationality and a distinctive form of reflexivity. It is in this sense that Lash claims that whereas in the first modernity thought was based on cognition and is epistemological, in the second modernity it focuses on experience and becomes ontological. It involves a questioning of, if not a disdain of, science, and a quest to find alternative bases for knowledge and 'explanation'. It questions viewing the world as a systematic totality, arguing for its replacement with a plurality of different orders, each with its own set of practices which can only be understood from within. In this respect, it involves a heightened role for culture, while the institutional structure has to be adjusted or changed in order to operate within the new context. Equally important is how the division of labour is organised on the basis of knowledge, with the social division of labour being facilitated by the new technology.

The emphasis on human capital within the knowledge economy places a new emphasis on language and culture. The distinction between economy as a feature of rationalism and of culture as the domain of emotion dissolves. The new integration affords a new understanding of the relationship between language, culture and society.

Simultaneously, structural change on a global level carries its contradictions. There is a contradiction between the various attributes that are claimed to be essential in engendering a successful knowledge economy, and how globalisation is claimed to undermine many of these attributes. The sense of mutual trust and cooperation that facilitate the generation and sharing of knowledge are claimed to be in retreat. The heightened individualism and the loss of state hegemony, authority and power in confronting crises undermine citizenship, and its relationship to culture and language. The globalisation process seems to be driving a need to simplify economic activity by focusing on particular *lingue franche*. At the same time, the role of languages and linguistic diversity in the reflexive process can make a profound contribution to the knowledge economy. Yet, many languages and cultures remain locked in 'tradition', waiting to be reinterpreted. This reinterpretation will involve a concern with discourse and meaning, thereby allowing freedom from categorisation based on form. As such, its role in reflexivity is revealed. Language will be free from the politics of syntax. Perhaps the reconciliation involves a shift in the objects associated with these attributes – away from the nation-state towards decentralised governance, from a focus on monolingualism towards linguistic diversity and from monoculturalism to a multiculturalism that is based on sharing and mutual comprehension.

What is evident is that the changes we are witnessing and striving to analyse are not only far-reaching, but are threatening the principles whereby modern states have been governed for the past 200 years. The stability of modern systems is being undermined to the extent that we are obliged to consider alternatives. The thrust of change is such that there is a sense of irreversibility about these developments. Undoubtedly, whatever emerges from how the emerging order achieves a sense of stability will rely on many of the principles of modernity, but it will also involve substantial realignments in how we understand society, the economy and the polity. With such developments will come significant changes in how we understand language, as well as how it will be analysed.

Notes

1. Among the various accounts of gender and modernity is Fraser's (1996) work. It leads to emphasising how modernity constructs not only language groups but groups based on other dimensions of inequality which should be analysed in tandem.
2. Such arguments treat power as some kind of entity outside of that which is influenced by it, rather than as the effects of discourse in the sense of being constitutive of identities and relationships. Thus objectivity is understood as a political force dependent on the categorisation of difference and otherness.
3. It is important here to distinguish between globalisation and universalism. Where the former pertains to a worldwide movement, objects such as the car are both global and universal. On the other hand, when it comes to values, the two notions diverge. Thus globalisation refers to the spatial distribution of objects, whereas universality implies a shared meaning.
4. On the other hand, Fraser (1996) argues that the current privatisation of welfarism represents the demise of state welfare systems.

Bibliography

Achard, P. (1989) Quelques propositions en sociologie du langage. *Courants Sociolinguistique*. INALF, 39–53.

Achard, P. (1994) Sociologie du langage et analyse d'enquêtes: De l'hypothèse de la rationalité de réponses. *Societes Contemporaine* 18/19, 67–100.

Adler, P.S. and Kwon, S.W. (2000) Social capital: The good, the bad and the ugly. In E. Lesser (ed.) *Knowledge and Social Capital: Foundations and Applications* (pp. 89–115). Boston, MA: Butterworth-Heinemann.

Adler, P.S. and Kwon, S.W. (2002) Social capital: Prospects for a new concept. *Academy of Management Review* 27, 17–40.

Amin, A. (1999) Industrial districts. In E. Sheppard and T. Barnes (eds) *A Companion to Economic Geography*. Oxford: Blackwell.

Amin, A. and Thrift, N. (eds) (2004) *The Blackwell Cultural Economy Reader*. Oxford: Blackwell.

Ammon, U. (1991) *Die Internationale Stellung Der Deutschen Sprache*. Berlin & New York: Walter de Gruyter.

Ammon, U. (1995) To what extent is German an international language? In P. Stevenson (ed.) *The German Language and the Real World*. Oxford: Clarendon.

Andersen, H. and Rasmussen, E. (2004) The role of language skills in corporate communication. *Corporate Communications* 9 (3), 231–242.

Anderson, B. (1991) *Imagined Communities: Reflections on the Spread of Nationalism*. New York: Verso.

Angwin, D.N. (2001) Mergers and acquisitions across European borders: National perspectives on pre-acquisition due diligence and the use of professional advisers. *Journal of World Business* 36 (1), 32–57.

Apter, D.E. (2001) Structure, contingency and choice: A comparison of trends and tendencies in political science. In D. Keates and J.W. Scott (eds) *Schools of Thought: Twenty Five Years of Interpretive Social Science* (pp. 252–281). Princeton, NJ: Princeton University Press.

Asheim, B. (1996) Industrial districts as 'learning regions': A condition for prosperity. *European Planning Studies* 4, 379–400.

Auroux, S. (1992) La philosophie linguistique d'Antoine Culioli. In n.a. *La Théorie D'Antoine Culioli* (pp. 39–61). Paris: Ophrys.

Auroux, S. (1994) *La revolution technologique de la grammatiation*. Paris: Mardaga.

Authier-Revuz, J. (1995) *Ces Mots qui ne vont pas de soi*. Paris: Larousse, Vols 1 and 2.

Aydalot, P. and Keeble, D. (eds) (1988) *High Technology Industry and Innovative Environments: The European Experience*. London: Routledge.

Bahktin, M. (1981) *The Dialogical Imagination*. Austin: University of Texas Press.

Bakhtin, M. (1986) *Speech Genres and Other Late Essays*. Austin: University of Texas Press.

Barbier, J-C. (2008) *La longue marche vers l'Europe Sociale*. Paris: PUF.

Beck, U. (1992) *Risk Society*. Cambridge: Polity

Beck, U. (1997) *The Reinvention of Politics*. Oxford: Polity.

Beck, U. (1998) *Democracy Without Enemies*. Cambridge: Polity.

Beck, U. (2006) *Qu'est-ce que le cosmopolitisme*. Paris: Aubier.

Beck, U. (2007) La condition cosmopolite et le piège du nationalisme méthodologique. In M. Wieviorka (ed.) *Les Sciences Sociales en Mutation* (pp. 223–237). Paris: Éditions Sciences Sociales.

Benhabib, S. (2004) *The Rights of Others: Aliens, Residents, Citizens*. Cambridge: Cambridge University Press.

Benhabib, S. (2007) Crépusule de la soverainté ou émergence de normes cosmopolites? Repenser la cityonneté en des temps volatiles. In M. Wieviorka (ed.) *Les Sciences Sociales en Mutation* (pp. 183–205). Paris: Éditions Sciences Humaines.

Benveniste, E. (1966) *Problemès de linguistique générale I*. Paris: Gallimard.

Benvensite, E. (1974) *Problemès de linguistique générale II*. Paris: Gallimard.

Berman, M. (1983) *All That Is Solid Melts into Air*. Chicago: University of Chicago Press.

Blinder, A.S. (2006) Offshoring: The next industrial revolution. *Foreign Affairs*. March/April.

Boschma, R.A. (2005) Proximity and innovation: A critical assessment. *Regional Studies* 39 (1), 61–74.

Bourdieu, P. (1972) *Outline of a Theory of Practice*. Cambridge: Cambridge University Press.

Bourdieu, P. (1979) *La Distinction*. Paris: Minuit.

Bourdieu, P. (1980) *Le Sens Pratique*. Paris: Minuit.

Bourdieu, P. (1982) *Ce que parler veut dire*. Paris: Fayard.

Bourdieu, P. (1987) *Choses Dites*. Paris: Minuit.

Bourdieu, P. (1991) *Language and Symbolic Power*. Cambridge: Polity.

Bourdieu, P. (2001) Quelles langues pour une Europe democratique? *Raisons Pratique* 2, 41–64.

Bovet, D. and Marta, J. (2000) *Value Nets: Breaking the Supply Chain to Unlock Hidden Profits*. London: Wiley.

Braczyk, H.J. and Schienstock, G. (eds) (1996) *Kurswechsel in der Industrie: Lean production in Baden-Württemberg*. Stuttgart: Kohlhammer.

Braczyk, H-J. and Heidenreich, M. (1998) Regional governance structures in a globalized world. In H-J. Braczyk, P. Cooke and M. Heidenreich (eds) *Regional Innovation Systems* (pp. 414–441). London: UCL.

Braverman, H. (1974) *Labor and Monopoly Capital: The Degradation of Work in the Twentieth Century*. New York: Monthly Review Press.

Breidenbach, J. and Zukrigl, I. (1998) *Tanz der Kulturen. Kulturelle Identität in einer globalisierten Welt*. München: Kunstmann.

British Chambers of Commerce (BCCLS) (2004) *The Impact of Foreign Languages on British Business*.

Cairncross, F. (1997) *The Death of Distance. How the Communication Revolution Will Change Our Lives*. Boston: Harvard Business School.

Callinicos, A. (1983) *Is There a future for Marxism?* London: Macmillan.

Callinicos, A. (1995) *Theories and Narratives: Reflections on the Philosophy of History*. Cambridge: Polity.

Callinicos, A. (1999) *Social Theory: A Historical Introduction*. Cambridge: Polity.

Calvet, L.J. (1974) *Linguistique et Colonialisme*. Paris: Payot.

Carter, R. (2004) *Language and Creativity*. London: Routledge.

Cartwright, S. and Cooper, C.I. (2000) *HR KnowHow in Mergers and Acquisitions*. London: IPD.

Castells M. (1996) *The Rise of the Network Society*. Oxford: Blackwell.

Castells, M. (1998) *The Information Age. Volume 3: End of the Millennium*. Oxford: Blackwell.

Castells, M. (2006) Globalisation and identity: A comparative perspective. *Journal of Contemporary Culture* 1, 56–66.

Chiswick, B.R. and Miller, P.W. (1998) The economic cost to native-born Americans of limited English language proficiency, Report to the Center for Equal Opportunity, available at http://www.ceousa.org/earnings.html. Accessed 2006.

Chiswick, B.R., Patrinos, H.A. and Hurst, M.E. (2000) Indigenous language skills and the labor market in a developing country: Bolivia. *Economic Development and Cultural Change* 48, 349–367.

Chomsky, N. (1965) *Aspects of the Theory of Syntax*. Cambridge: MIT Press.

Chomsky, N. (1972) *Studies on Semantics in Generative Grammar*. The Hague: Mouton.

Chomsky, N. (1986) *Knowledge of Language: Its Nature Origin, and Use*. New York: Praeger.

CILT (UK National Centre for Languages) (2006) *ELAN: Effects on the European Economy of Shortages of Foreign Language Skills in Enterprise*. EC, DGE&C.

Coleman, J. (1988) Social capital in the creation of human capital. *American Journal of Sociology* 94, Supplement S95–S120.

Cook, G. (2000) *Language Play, Language Learning*. Oxford: Oxford University Press.

Cooke, P.N. (1998) Origins of the concept. In H-J. Braczyk, P. Cooke and M. Heidenreich (eds) *Regional Innovation Systems* (pp. 2–25). London: UCL.

Cooke, P.N. (2001) *Strategies for Regional Innovation Systems: Learning Transfer and Applications*. New York: UNIDO World Industrial Development Report (WIDR).

Cooke, P.N. (2002) *Knowledge Economies: Clusters, Learning and Cooperative Advantage*. London: Routledge.

Cooke, P., Heidenreich, M. and Braczyk, H. (2004) *Regional Innovation Systems* (2nd edn). London: Routledge.

Crevoisier, O. (2001) Der Ansatz des kreativen Milieus. *Zeitschrift für Wirtschaftsgeographie* 45, 246–256.

Culioli, A. (1968) La formalisation en linguistique. *Cahiers pour l'analyse*. Vol. 9.

Culioli, A. (1989) Roles des representations metalinguistique en syntaxe. *Proceedings of the XIIIth Congress of Linguistics, Tokyo, 1982*.

Culioli, A. (1990) *Pour une Linguistique de l'énonciation: Operations et representations*. Tome 1. Paris: Ophrys.

Culioli, A. and Descles J.P. (1976) *Considerations sur un programme de traitement automatique des langes et du langage*. Pitfall no. 26, University of Paris 7.

Debaere, P. and Mostashari, S. (2005) *Do Tariffs Matter for an Extensive Margin of International Trade? An Empirical Analysis*. CEPR, DP 5260.

Delmas-Marty, M. (2003) *Global Law: A Triple Challenge*. Ardsley: Transnational.

Delmas-Marty, M. (2007) Mondalisation du droit et crise des pouvoirs. In M. Wieviroka (ed.) *Les Sciences Sociales en Mutation* (pp. 115–129). Paris: Éditions Sciences Humaines.

Denzau, A.T. and North, D.C. (1994) Shared mental models: Ideologies and institutions. *Kyklos* 47, 3–31.

Deloitte Research (2003) *The Cusp of a Revolution: How Offshore Trading will Transform the Financial Services Industry*. London: Deloitte Research.

Derrida, J. (1978) *Writing and Difference*. London: Routledge and Kegan Paul.

Dhir, K.S. and Goke-Pariola, A. (2002) The case for language policies in multinational corporations. *Corporate Communications* 7 (4), 241–251.

Dore R.P. (1973) *British Factory, Japanese Factory: The Origins of National Diversity in Industrial Relations*. Berkeley: University of California Press.

Dosi, G. (1988) The sources, procedures and microeconomic effect of innovation, *Journal of Economic Literature* 26 (3), 1120–1171.

DTI (1996) Competitiveness White paper. *Competitiveness Forging Ahead*. London: HMSO.

Dumont, J-C. and Lemaitre, G. (2005) Counting immigrants and expatriates in OECD countries: A new perspective. *OECD Social, Employment and Migration Working Papers* No. 25.

Durkheim, E. (1984) *The Division of Labor in Society*. New York: Free Press.

Eckert, P. (2000) *Linguistic Variation as Social Practice*. Oxford: Blackwell.

European Commission (EC) (2000a) *The Commercial Exploitation of Europe's Public Sector Information*. Pira International, University of East Anglia, KnowledgeView Ltd report for the European Commission. Brussels: European Commission.

European Commission (EC) (2000b) The new economy of the global information society: Implications for growth, work and employment. Luxembourg, IST Programme.

European Commission (EC) (2000c) Presentation of the Inauguration of the eContent Programme, Luxembourg.

European Commission (EC) (2001) *Eurobarometer 54 Special*. Brussels: EC.

European Commission (EC) (2006) *Europeans and Their Languages*. Special Eurobarometer Survey. Brussels.

Firth, A. (1996) 'Lingua Franca' English and Conversation Analysis. *Journal of Pragmatics* 26, April, 237–259.

Fishman, J.A. (1992) *Reversing Language Shift*. Clevedon: Multilingual Matters.

Florida, R. (2002) *The Rise of the Creative Class: And How It's Transforming Work, Leisure, Community and Everyday Life*. New York: Basic Books.

Follath, E. and Sprol, G. (2007) An inside look at Europe's coolest cities. *Der Spiegel*, 28/8/07.

Foucault, M. (1966) *Les Mots et les Chose*. Paris: Gallimard.

Foucault, M. (1969) *L'Archaeologie du savoir*. Paris: Gallimard.

Foucault, M. (1994) *Dits et ecrits*. Paris: Gallimard.

Fraser, N. (1996) Gender equity and the welfare state: A postindustrial thought experiment. In S. Benhabib (ed.) *Democracy and Difference: Contesting the Boundaries of the Political* (pp. 218–242). Princeton: Princeton University Press.

Freeman, C. (1987) *Technology and Economic Performance: Lessons from Japan*. London: Pinter.

Frege, G. (1892) Über Sinn und Bedeutung. *Zeitschrift für Philosophie und philosophische Kritik*, NF 100, S. 25–50.

Friedman, J. (1992) Narcissism, roots and postmodernity: The constitution of selfhood in the global crisis. In S. Lash and J. Friedman (eds) *Modernity and Identity* (pp. 331–367). Oxford: Blackwell.

Friedman, T.L. (2005) *The World Is Flat: Brief History of the Twenty-first Century*. New York: Farrar, Straus and Giroux.

Fukuyama, F. (1995) *Trust: The Social Virtues and the Creation of Prosperity*. New York: Hamish Hamilton.

Fundacion Tomillo (2000) *Posibilidades de Creacion de empleo en el sector servicios – bloque IV: Servicios culturales*. Madrid.

Furnham, A. (2005) *Management Mumbo-Jumbo*. London: Palgrave.

Gambetta, D. (ed.) (1988) *Trust: Making and Breaking Cooperative Relations*. Oxford: Blackwell.

Garofoli, G. (1991) Local networks, innovation and policy in Italian industrial districts. In E. Bergman, G. Maier and F. Tödtling (eds), *Regions Reconsidered: Economic Networks, Innovation, and Local Development in Industrialised Countries*. New York: Manell.

Gazzola, M. (2006) Managing multilingualism in the European Union: Language policy evaluation for the European Parliament. *Language Policy* 5 (4), 393–417.

Giddens, A. (1976) *New Rules of Sociological Method*. London: Hutchinson.

Giddens, A. (1979) *Central Problems in Social Theory*. London: Macmillan.

Giddens, A. (1984) *The Constitution of Society*. Cambridge: Polity.

Giddens, A. (1990) *The Consequences of Modernity*. Cambridge: Polity.

Giddens, A. (1991) *Modernity and Self-Identity*. Cambridge: Polity.

Giddens A. (1994) *Beyond Left and Right: The Future of Radical Politics*. Cambridge: Polity.

Giddens, A. (2002) *Runaway World: How Globalisation Is Reshaping Our Lives*. London: Profile Books.

Graddol, D. (2000) *The Future of English?* London: British Council.

Gramsci, A. (1971) *Selection from Prison Notebooks*. London: Lawrence & Weidenfeld.

Granovetter, M. (1985) Economic action and social structure: The problem of embeddedness. *American Journal of Sociology* 91 (3), 481–510.

Granovetter, M. (1992) Problems of explanation in economic sociology. In N. Nohria and R. Eccles (eds) *Networks & Organisations: Structure, Form & Action*. Boston: Harvard Business School Press.

Grin, Francois (2005) *L'Enseignement des langues étrangères comme politique publique*. Paris: Haut Conseil de l'évaluation de l'école, Rapport No. 19.

Grin, F. and Sfreddo, C. (1998) Language-based earnings differentials on the Swiss labour market: Is Italian a liability? *International Journal of Manpower* 19 (7), 520–532.

Gunnarsson, B-L. (2006) Multilingualism within transnational companies. An analysis of company policy on equality and integration. Paper presented at the 16th Sociolinguistic Symposium, Limerick.

Habermas, J. (1979) *Communication and the Evolution of Society*. New York: Beacon.

Habermas, J. (1985) Modernity – An incomplete project. In H. Foster (ed.) *Postmodern Culture*. New York: Pluto.

Habermas, J. (1987) *The Philosophical Discourse of Modernity*. Oxford: Polity.

Habermas, J. (1991) *The Structural Transformation of the Public Sphere: An Inquiry into a Category of Bourgeois Society*. Trans. Thomas Burger with Frederick Lawrence. Cambridge, MA: MIT Press.

Habermas, J. (1996a) La Paix perpetuelle, le bicentenaire d'une idée Kantienne. Paris: CERF.

Habermas, J. (1996b) Three normative models of democracy. In S. Benhabib (ed.) *Democracy and Difference: Contesting the Boundaries of the Political* (pp. 21–31). Princeton: Princeton University Press.

Habermas, J. (1998) The European nation-state: On the past and future of sovereignty and citizenship. In C. Cronin and P de Grief (eds) *The Inclusion of the Other: Studies in Political Theory*. Cambridge: MIT Press.

Hagen S. (ed.) (1993) *Languages in European Business: A Regional Survey of Small and Medium-sized Companies*. London: CILT.

Halliday, M.A.K. (2006) Written language, standard language, global language. In B.B. Kachru, Y. Kachru and C.L. Nelson (eds) *The Handbook of World Englishes* (pp. 349–366). Oxford: Blackwell.

Harris, R. and Cher Li, Q. (2005) *Review of the Literature: The Role of International Trade and Investment in Business Growth and Development*. Report to UK Dept. of Trade and Industry.

Harvey, D. (1996) Rethinking Marxism. *Journal of Economics, Culture & Society*, 8(4), 1–17.

Harvey, D. (2001) *Spaces of Capital*. Edinburgh: Edinburgh University Press.

Hayek, F.A. (1944) *The Road to Serfdom*. London: Routledge.

Hayek, F.A. (1948) *Individualism and Economic Order*. London: Routledge.

Henley, A. and Jones, R.E. (2005) *Earnings and Linguistic Proficiency in a Bilingual Economy*. Manchester School, University of Manchester, 73 (3), 300–320.

Hernandez i Marti, Gil-Manuel (2002) *La Modernitat Globalitzada: Analisi de l'entorn social*. Valencia, Tirant lo Blanch.

Hilgendorf, S.K. (2006) *English and the Global Market: The Impact in the German Business Domain*. Paper presented at the 16th Sociolinguistic Symposium, July 2006.

Hodgson, G.M. (1999) *Economics and Utopia*. London: Routledge.

Honig, B. (1996) Differences, dilemmas and the politics of home. In S. Benhabib (ed.) *Democracy and Difference: Contesting the Boundaries of the Political* (pp. 257–278). Princeton: Princeton University Press.

Honneth, Axel (ed.) (1986) *Kommunikatives Handeln. Beiträge zu Jürgen Habermas'*. Frankfurt: Suhrkamp.

Hood, N. and Truijens, T. (1993) European locational decisions of Japanese manufacturers: Survey evidence on the case of the UK. *International Business Review* 2, 39–63.

Jakobson, R. (1963) *Essais du linguistique générale*. Paris: Minuit.

James, A.R. (2000) English as a European Lingua Franca: Current realities and existing dichotomies. In J. Cenoz and U. Jessner (eds) *English in Europe: The Acquisition of a Third Language* (pp. 22–39). Clevedon: Multilingual Matters.

Jameson, F. (1993) *Postmodernism or the Cultural Logic of Late Capitalism*. Durham: Duke University Press.

Jeffrey, B., Craft, A. and Leibling, M. (eds) (2001) *Creativity in Education*. London: Continuum Books.

Jessop, B. (2002) *The Future of the Capitalist State*. Cambridge: Polity.

Jessop, B. (2004) Multi-level governance and multi-level metagovernance. In I. Bache and M. Flinders (eds) *Multi-level Governance* (pp. 49–75). Oxford: Oxford University Press.

Kant, I. (1963) *Critique of Pure Reason*. London: Macmillan.

Keeble, D. and Wilkinson, F. (eds) (2000) *High-Technology Clusters, Networking and Collective Learning in Europe*. Ashgate: Aldershot.

Kluckhohn, F.R. and Strodtbeck, F.L. (1962) Variations in value orientation. *American Anthropologist*, New Series, 64(4), 850–851.

Knapp, K. (1997) Cultural, organisational or linguistic causes of intercultural conflicts? A case study. In J. Benke (ed.) *Thriving on Diversity* (pp. 117–134). Bonn: Dummler.

Kurasawa, F. (2007) *The Work of Global Justice*. Cambridge, Cambridge University Press.

Lachenmaier, S. and Wossmann, L. (2005) *Does Innovation Cause Exports? Evidence from Exogenous Innovation Impulses and Obstacles, Using German Micro Data*. Oxford Economic Papers.

Laclau, E. and Mouffe, C. (1985) *Hegemony and Socialist Strategy*. London: Verso.

Laplantine, F. (2007) La question du subjet dans le social et dans les sciences sociales aujourd'hui. In M. Wieviorka (ed.) *Les Sciences Sociales en Mutation* (pp. 37–49). Paris: Éditions Sciences Humaines.

Lash, S. (1999) *Another Modernity, Another Rationality*. Oxford: Blackwell.

Levitas, R. (1998) *The Inclusive Society? Social Exclusion and New Labour*. London: Macmillan.

Lundvall, B-A. (ed.) (1992) *National Systems of Innovation: Towards a Theory of Innovation and Interactive Learning*. London: Pinter.

Lundvall, B.A. (2002) *Innovation, Growth and Social Cohesion: The Danish Model of a Learning Economy*. Cheltenham: Edward-Elgar.

Lyotard, J-F. (1984) *The Postmodern Condition*. Manchester: Manchester University Press.

Maillat, D. (1998) Vom 'Industrial District' zum innovativen Milieu: Ein Beitrag zur Analyse der lokalisierten Produktionssysteme. *Geographische Zeitschrift* 86, 1–15.

Maillat, D., Léchot, G., Lecoq, B. and Pfister, M. (1996) *Comparative Analysis of the Structural Development of Milieux: The Example of the Watch Industry in the Swiss and French Jura* Arc. Working Paper 96–07, Institut de recherches économiques et régionales, Université de Neuchatel, Neuchatel.

Mann, M. (1993) *The Sources of Social Power*. Cambridge: Cambridge University Press.

Marschan, R., Welch, D. and Welch, L. (1997) Language – The forgotten factor in multinational management. *European Journal of Management* 15 (5), 591–598.

Matushita, K. (1988) The secret is shared. *Manufacturing Engineering* 100 (2), 15.

Mauss, M. (1954) *The Gift*. New York: Free Press.

McInerney, C. (2002) Knowledge management and the dynamic nature of knowledge. *Journal of the American Society for Information Science and Technology* 53 (12), 1009–1018.

Milner, J-C. (1978) *L'amour de la langue*. Paris: Seuil.

Milner, J-C. (1992) De quelques aspects de la théorie d'Antoine Culioli projetés dans un espace non-énonciatif. In n.a. *La Théorie d'Antoine Culioli* (pp. 19–39). Paris: Ophrys.

MKW (2001) *Exploitation and Development of the Job Potential in the Cultural Sector in the Age of Digitalisation*. Report to DG Employment and Social Affairs. Brussels, EC.

Morgan, K. (1997) The learning region: Institutions, innovation and regional renewal. *Regional Studies* 31, 491–503.

Mouffe, C. (2000) Wittgenstein, political theory and democracy. *Polylog: Forum for Intercultural Philosophy* 2, http://them.polylog.org/2/emc-en.html.

Nahapiet, J. and Ghoshal, S. (1998) Social capital, intellectual capital, and the organizational advantage. *Academy of Management Review* 22 (2), 242–266.

NASSCOM-McKinsey (2006) *Report 2005 – Extending India's Leadership in the Global IT and BPO Industries.* Mumbai.

Nelson, R.R. (1993) *National Innovation Systems: A Comparative Analysis.* Oxford: Oxford University Press.

Nonaka, I. (1994) Dynamic theory of organizational knowledge creation. *Organization Science* 5 (1), 14–37.

Nonaka, I. and Konno, N. (1998) The Concept of 'Ba': Building a foundation for knowledge creation. *California Management Review* 40 (3) (Spring), 40–54.

Nonaka, I. and Tekuchi, H. (1995) *The Knowledge-Creating Company: How Japanese Companies Create the Dynamics of Innovation.* Oxford: Oxford University Press.

Ojala, T. (2001) *Intra-Organisational Use of Communication Tools in Value Nets: Cases from the ICT Industry.* Lappeenranta University of Technology, Dept. of Business.

Ong, A. (1999) *Flexible Citizenship: The Cultural Logic of Transnationality.* Durham: Duke University Press.

Ost, F. (1998) Le temps virtuel des lois postmodernes ou comment le droit se traite dans la société de l'information. In J. Clam and G. Martin (eds) *Les Transformations de la regulation juridique.* Paris: L.G.D.J.

Patrinos, H.A., Velez, E. and Psacharopoulos, G. (1994) Language, education and earnings in Asunción, Paraguay. *Journal of Developing Areas* 29 (1), 57–68.

Pecheux, M. (1982) *Language, Semantics and Ideology.* London: Macmillan.

Pekruhl, U. (2001) *Partizipatives Management. Konzepte und Kulturen.* München: Hampp.

Pianta, M. (2000) *The Impact of Technological Change on Growth in the 'New Economy'.* Paper presented at the Workshop on The New Economy of the Global Information Society. Brussels, April, 2000.

Piore, M. and Sabel, C. (1984) *The Second Industrial Divide.* New York: Basic Books.

Pleasants, N. (1999) *Wittgenstein and the Idea of a Critical Social Theory.* London: Routledge.

Portes, A. and Landolt, P. (1996) The downside of social capital. *The American Prospect* 26, 18–22.

Polyani, M. (1958) *Personal Knowledge: Towards a Post-Critical Philosophy.* London: Routledge and Kegan Paul.

Polyani, M. (1967) *The Tacit Dimension.* London: Routledge and Kegan Paul.

Porter, M. (1985) *Competitive Advantage: Creating and Sustaining Superior Performance.* New York: Free Press.

Porter, M.E. (1990) *The Competitive Advantage of Nations.* New York: Simon and Schuster.

Powell, W. (1996) Trust-based forms of governance. In R. Kramer and T. Tyler (eds) *Trust in Organizations: Frontiers of Theory and Research* (pp. 61–67). Thousand Oaks (CA): Sage.

Powell, W. and Snellman, K. (2004) The knowledge economy. *Annual Review of Sociology* 30, 199–220.

Przeworski, A. (1991) *Democracy and the Market: Political and Economic Reforms in Eastern Europe and Latin America.* Cambridge: Cambridge University Press.

Pudup, M.B. (1992) Industrialization after (de)industrialization: A review essay. *Urban Geography* 13 (2), 187–200.

Putnam, R.D. (1993) *Making Democracy Work: Civic Traditions in Modern Italy.* Princeton: Princeton University Press.

Putnam, H. (1988) *Representation and Reality.* Cambridge, MA: MIT Press.

Rasch, W. (2000) *Niklas Luhmann's Modernity: The Paradoxes of Differentiation*. Stanford: Stanford University Press.

Rawlings, R. (2003) *Delineating Wales: Constitutional, Legal and Administrative Aspects*. Cardiff: University of Wales Press.

Rawls, J. (1972) *A Theory of Justice*. Cambridge: Harvard University Press.

Rawls, J. (1996) *Political Liberalism*. New York: Columbia University Press.

Reich, R.B. (1991) *The Work of Nations*. New York: Knopf.

Reingold T. (2001) Arvonluonnin uusi aikakausi teoksessa. In J. Varis (ed.)(toim) *Kumppanuudella kasvuun* (pp. 18–28). Telecom Business Research Centre Lapeenranta: Lapeenranta University of Technology.

Ritzer, G. (1996) *The McDonaldisation of Society*. Thousand Oaks: Pine Forge.

Roemer J.E. (1994) *A Future for Socialism*. Cambridge: Harvard University Press.

Rosenau, P. (1990) Once again into the Fray: International relations confronts the humanities. *Millennium: Journal of International Studies* 1 (Spring), 83–110.

Ryle, G. (1945–46) Knowing how and knowing that. *Aristotelian Society Proceedings* 46, 1–16.

Sabel, C. (1989) Flexible specialization and the re-emergence of regional economies. In P. Hirst and J. Zeithin (eds) *Reversing Industrial Decline?* Oxford, UK: Berg.

Sabel, C. (1992) Studied trust: Building new forms of co-operation in a volatile economy. In F. Pyke und W. Sengenberger (eds) *Industrial Districts and Local Economic Regeneration* (pp. 215–250). Geneva: International Institute for Labour Studies.

Sandberg, A. and Augustsson, F. (2002) *Interactive Media in Sweden, 2001*. Stockholm: Arbeitslivsinstitutet.

Sandywell, B. (1996) *Reflexivity and the Crisis of Western Reason*. London: Routledge.

Sassen, S. (2006) *Territory, Authority, Rights: From Medieval to Global Assemblages*. Princeton: Princeton University Press.

Saxenian, A. (1994) *Regional Advantage: Cultural Competition in Silicon Valley and Route 128*. Cambridge: Harvard University Press.

Saxenian, A. (1999) *Silicon Valley's New Immigrant Entrepreneurs*. PPIC: San Francisco.

Schumpeter, P. (1949) *The Theory of Economic Development*. Cambridge: Harvard University Press.

Schumpeter, J.A. (1976) *Capitalism, Socialism and Democracy*. New York: Harper & Row.

Scott, D. (1996) The aftermaths of sovereignty. *Social Text* 48, 1–26.

Shapiro, D.M. and Stelcner, M. (1997) Language and earnings in Quebec: Trends over twenty years, 1970–1990. *Canadian Public Policy – Analyse de Politiques* 23 (2), 115–140.

Searle J.R. (1972) Noam Chomsky's revolution in linguistics. *New York Review* June 29, 16–24.

Seriot, P. (1997) Ethnos et Demos: La construction discursive de l'identité collective. *Langage et Société* 79, 39–53.

Smith, N. (1992) Geography, difference and the politics of scale. In J. Doherty, E. Graham and M. Malek (eds) *Postmodernism and the Social Sciences* (pp. 57–79). London: Macmillan.

Storper, M. (2002) Institutions of the learning economy. In M. Gertler and D. Wolfe (eds) *Innovation and Social Learning. Institutional Adaption in an Era of Technological Chance* (pp. 135–158). Basingstoke: Palgrave.

Tannen, D. (1989) *Talking Voices: Repetition, Dialogue and Imagery in Conversational Discourse*. Cambridge: Cambridge University Press.

Tapscott, D., Ticoll, D. and Lowy, A. (2000) *Digital Capital: Harnessing the Power of Business Webs*. Boston: Harvard Business School Press.

Thompson, J.B. (1984) *Studies in the Theory of Ideology*. Cambridge: Polity.

Tödtling, F. and Trippl, M. (2005) One size fits all? Towards a differentiated regional innovation policy approach, *Research Policy* 34, 1023–1209.

Toivonen, M. (2001) *Growth and Significance of Knowledge Intensive Business Systems (KIBS)*. Helsinki: Uudenmaan.

Touraine, A. (1992) *Critique de la Modernité*. Paris: Fayard.

Touraine, A. (1997) *Pourrons-nous vivre ensemble?* Paris: Fayard.

Touraine, A. (2007) La place du subjet. In M. Wiveiorka (ed.) *Les Sciences Sociale en Mutation* (pp. 25–36). Paris: Éditions Sciences Humaines.

Touraine, A. (2007) *Penser Autrement*. Paris: Fayard.

Trice, H.M. and Beyer, J.M. (1993) *The Cultures of Work Organization*. Englewood Cliifs, NJ: Prentice Hall.

Tricot, C. (2002) *Key Aspects of the Use of English in Europe*. EC, DGIV, Unpublished Report.

UNCTAD (2006) *Trade and Development Report, 2006*. New York: United Nations.

Vattimo, G. (1991) *The End of Modernity*. Cambridge: Polity.

Veblen, T.B. (1919) *The Place of Science in Modern Civilisation and Other Essays*. New York: Huebsch.

Vivarelli, M. and Pianta, M. (2000) *The Employment Impact of innovation: Evidence and Policy*. London: Routledge.

Wainwright, H. (1994) *Arguments for a New Left: Answering the Free-Market Right*. Oxford: Blackwell.

Wenger, E. (1998) *Communities of Practice: Learning, Meaning and Identity*. Cambridge: Cambridge University Press.

Wieviorka, M. (2008) *Neuf leçons de sociologie*. Paris: Laffont.

Williams, G. (1976) Differential risk strategies among farmers in the lower Chubut Valley, Argentina. *American Ethnologist* 3 (2), 65–84.

Williams, G. (1992) *Sociolinguistics: A Sociological Critique*. London: Routledge and Kegan Paul.

Williams, G. (1999) *French Discourse Analysis: The Method of Post-structuralism*. London: Routledge.

Williams, G. (2000) The digital value chain and economic transformation: Rethinking regional development in the new economy. *Contemporary Wales* 13, 94–116.

Williams, G. (2004) From media to multimedia: Workflows and language in the digital economy. *Noves*. Autumn.

Williams, G. (2005) *Sustaining Language Diversity in Europe*. London: Palgrave.

Williams, G. (2007) The changing nature of the media sector. In M. Cormak and N. Hourigan (eds) *Minority Language Media: Concepts, Critique and Case Studies* (pp. 88–107). Clevedon: Multilingual Matters.

Williams, G. (2008) Reversing language shift – A sociological visit. *Plurilingua* XXX, 161–179.

Williams G. and Britt-Kenz, M. (2003) Technology and economic development in the periphery. *Tripodos* 14, 101–123.

Williams, G., Roberts, E. and Isaac, R. (1978) Language and aspirations for upward social mobility. In G. Williams (ed.) *Social and Cultural Change in Contemporary Wales.* London: Routledge and Kegan Paul.

Williams, G., Strubell, M., Vilaro, S. and Williams, G.O. (2007) *Diversity in the Teaching of Languages in Europe, 1999–2004.* Report Presented to DG Education and Culture, Brussels.

Williams, R. (1980) *Problems in Materialism and Culture.* London: Verso.

Wittgenstein, L. (1958) *Philosophical Investigations* I (1st edn). Oxford: Blackwell.

Wittgenstein L. (1972) *Philosophical Investigations* (2nd edn). Oxford: Blackwell.

Wittgenstein, L. (1975) *On Certainty.* Oxford: Blackwell.

Wittgenstein, L. (1988) *Tractatus Logico-Philosophicus.* London: Routledge.

Withers, K. (2006) *Intellectual Property and the Knowledge Economy.* London: Institute for Public Policy Research.

Wolin, S.W. (1996) Fugitive democracy. In S. Benhabib (ed.) *Democracy and Differences: Contesting the Boundaries of the Political* (pp. 31–46). Princeton: Princeton University Press.

Young, I.M. (1996) Communication and the other: Beyond deliberative democracy. In S. Benhabib (ed.) *Democracy and Difference: Contesting the Boundaries of the Political* (pp. 120–136). Princeton: Princeton University Press.

Zolo, D. (1992) *Democracy and Complexity: A Realist Approach.* Cambridge: Cambridge University Press.

Index